CARING FOR NATURAL

RANGELANDS

CARING FOR NATURAL RANGELANDS

Ken Coetzee

UNIVERSITY OF KWAZULU-NATAL PRESS

Published in 2005 by University of KwaZulu-Natal Press
Private Bag X01
Scottsville 3209
South Africa
Email: books@ukzn.ac.za
Website: www.ukznpress.co.za

ISBN 1-86914-071-0

Editor: Michelle Paterson
Managing editor: Sally Hines
Layout: RockBottom Design
Cover design: Flying Ant Designs
All illustrations and diagrams by Ken Coetzee

Printed and bound by Interpak Books, Pietermaritzburg

Contents

Acknowledgements viii
Foreword ix

CHAPTER ONE
Introduction: Caring for natural rangelands 1
1.1 Introduction 2
1.2 The approach 2
1.3 Establishing a land ethic 3
1.4 What can be done? 4
1.5 Landscape restoration and rehabilitation in perspective . . . 5

CHAPTER TWO
Healing the land: Dealing with soil erosion 7
2.1 Introduction 8
      2.1.1 When is soil erosion unnatural? 10
2.2 Objectives of soil erosion control 12
2.3 Procedure for effective control 14
      2.3.1 Reasons why erosion control efforts are sometimes
             unsuccessful 14
      2.3.2 Scales for mapping 14
      2.3.3 A practical strategy for action 17
2.4 Control methods 18
      2.4.1 Treating gullies and rills 20
      2.4.2 The use of rubber vehicle tyres 27
      2.4.3 The use of geotextiles in soil erosion control 29
      2.4.4 Using hollows or puddles for rehabilitation 33
      2.4.5 Brush-packing, mulching and creating
             a microclimate 37
      2.4.6 The use of logs to combat soil erosion on slopes 39
      2.4.7 The radical reconstruction of eroded bad-lands 41

      2.4.8 Radical reconstruction: restoring natural drainages . . . 42
      2.4.9 Seeding and planting for rangeland rehabilitation 44
2.5 Monitoring the success of soil erosion control efforts 47
      2.5.1 Fixed-point photographic monitoring 49
      2.5.2 Gully profile measurement 50
      2.5.3 Soil erosion condition guide 50
      2.5.4 Stock and wildlife exclosures 52

CHAPTER THREE
Access to the land: The sensitive construction and
maintenance of field roads and tracks 55
3.   Introduction 56
      3.1.1 Roads and soil erosion 56
3.2 Principles of road design and use 59
      3.2.1 Types of field roads and tracks 59
      3.2.2 Specifications for road surfaces 60
3.3 Planning a road network 61
      3.3.1 Questions that should be asked before planning a
             new road in undisturbed wildlands 62
      3.3.2 The costs of a road compared to the long-term gains . . . 62
3.4 Construction methods 63
      3.4.1 A sensitive approach to road construction 63
      3.4.2 Gravel road construction 64
      3.4.3 Hard surfacing 65
      3.4.4 Water drainage off road surfaces 67
      3.4.5 Dissipating accumulated run-off water 69
      3.4.6 Drainage crossings and retaining walls 71
      3.4.7 Concrete fords 73
      3.4.8 Pipes and culverts 74
      3.4.9 Road cuttings 77
3.5 Maintenance 78
      3.5.1 Checklist of important maintenance inspection sites . . . 78
      3.5.2 Borrow pits 79

3.6   Road damage rehabilitation 80

     3.6.1   Closing and rehabilitating unneeded field roads 80

     3.6.2   The rehabilitation of road cutting slopes 83

     3.6.3   The use of brush-packing and stakes to stabilise
          steep roadside slopes 84

     3.6.4   Vertical cut-slope rehabilitation 86

     3.6.5   The rehabilitation of larger borrow pit sites 87

     3.6.6   The rehabilitation of small borrow pits 88

3.7   Responsible road use in rangelands 89

     3.7.1   Some guidelines for responsible road
          use in rangelands 89

     3.7.2   Driving off the road network is simply too costly 90

     3.7.3   Some thoughts on co-operative road management 90

CHAPTER FOUR

Clearing the land: Conrolling alien plant invasions 91

4.1   Introduction 92

     4.1.1   Why bother to control alien plant invasions in natural
          rangelands? 95

4.2   Objectives for control programmes 96

4.3   A strategy for control 97

     4.3.1   Planning 97

     4.3.2   Mapping 98

     4.3.3   Prioritising control areas and the stages for
          effective control 99

     4.3.4   Control programme schedules 100

4.4   Control methods 101

     4.4.1   Felling trees 102

     4.4.2   Ring-barking, debarking and frilling trees 104

     4.4.3   Controlling dense, bushy invasions 106

     4.4.4   The use of a rotary tractor-drawn brush-cutter 107

     4.4.5   Tree plugs 108

     4.4.6   The control of larger cactus plants with herbicide 110

     4.4.7   The control of dense stands of cactus with herbicide . . 111

     4.4.8   Pulling alien plants with a tractor 112

     4.4.9   The tree puller 113

     4.4.10   Biological control 114

     4.4.11   The use of fire to eradicate alien plants 116

     4.4.12   Follow-up control 117

4.5   Rehabilitation 118

     4.5.1   The rehabilitation of riverbanks 120

4.6   Monitoring 122

Appendix: List of scientific names of the animal
          species mentioned in the text 126

Bibliography 127

Index 128

Dedication

This book is dedicated to the memory of my father, Robert Henry Coetzee,
whose love of nature rubbed off on me at a very early age during our ramblings in
the mountains of the Cape Peninsula.

Acknowledgements

In this book, the many generations of dedicated and caring land management practitioners are acknowledged for the vast contribution that they have made towards a more sensitive approach to the management of our natural environment. These people are unsung environmental heroes who have unselfishly dedicated their lives to this cause and campaigned for better care of the land, in most cases without recognition or reward. Not least of this group are the game rangers, nature conservators, nature conservation scientists and game guards, a relatively small group who have pioneered and developed so many of the land-care methods that we use today and will continue to use in the future.

Many thanks are due to Professor Sue Milton for her encouragement and useful suggestions. I also wish to acknowledge all my friends and associates for their continuous encouragement which played no small part in getting the work on this book completed.

This book would not have been possible without the ongoing help and support I received from my loving wife, Madeline.

Foreword

Natural rangeland covers two-thirds of South Africa and is a source of forage for grazing animals, medicines, fuel and building materials to those who live on the land, as well as contributing to the national economy through the livestock, game and tourism industries, and through the capture and purification of water resources on which crops, industries and cities depend. South Africa's diverse flora and fauna, which are largely excluded from cities, cropland and plantations, survive in natural veld, most of which is outside formal conservation areas.

Despite their enormous value to the nation, rangelands show many scars as a result of careless or uninformed use and abuse. Poor grazing management, badly planned access roads, dams and borrow pits, and invasion by thickets of alien plants are literally eroding away the natural capital of the country. Rapid discharge of rainwater through erosion gullies dries out the landscape, reducing the productivity of the vegetation and the profitability and aesthetic appeal of the land. Problems of this type are large scale, persistent and expensive to repair. Restoration involves planning, dedication and possibly a change in philosophy.

Most farmers and conservators inherit environmental damage with the land they manage. Both repair of past damage and the development of new ranch and tourism facilities necessitate construction and maintenance of roads, collection of stones, soil and brushwood or clearing of vegetation. Care is needed because today's mistakes are tomorrow's problems. Although there is no single correct way to prevent or restore environmental damage, success may be achieved through long-term planning and an understanding of the ecological and physical principles that underlie the development of effective erosion controls, stable water-courses, durable roads and cost-effective alien vegetation control. Systems for monitoring results are also extremely important.

There are a number of books available on the management of vegetation, livestock and game in southern African rangelands, but this book is the first to deal with the principles of rangeland repair from the bottom up, and to give advice at the pick-and-shovel level at which most rangeland restoration takes place. It is based on the author's 30 years of experience as a manager and adviser to conservators and ranchers and on a sound understanding of the effects of structures and vegetation on soil and water movement. The advice is practical and the technical drawings illustrate a wide range of approaches to management planning, erosion control, road building and alien vegetation clearing. It is a valuable resource for conservators, ranchers, extension officers, environmental consultants, planners and all others to whom society entrusts the care of the land.

Professor Sue Milton
Part-time Professor of the Conservation
Ecology Department, University of Stellenbosch,
and Honorary Professor, Percy Fitzpatrick Institute,
University of Cape Town

CHAPTER ONE

INTRODUCTION

Caring for natural rangelands

1.1   Introduction

1.2   The approach

1.3   Establishing a land ethic

1.4   What can be done?

1.5   Landscape restoration and rehabilitation in perspective

1.1   INTRODUCTION

During my many years of association with natural rangelands, formerly as a rangeland manager and more recently in an advisory capacity, I have observed that very few natural areas are completely free of the destructive legacy of modern landscape development.

Most often, the consequences of these landscape modifications suggest that the general attitude of landscape users has been one of careless exploitation. There has been little regard for the future implications of unsustainable land uses and little or nothing is ever replaced or returned to the land.

Humans have been modifying their environment for thousands of years – this is what humans do. The earliest modifications had little impact, but as human numbers and ingenuity increased, this resulted in the gradual depletion of natural resources like the complete degradation of many primeval forests. In more recent times, modification has frequently resulted in the development and establishment of certain natural resources, such as monocultural tree plantations and food crops, which inevitably leads to a loss of biodiversity and most often results in gradual habitat deterioration.

The hand of modern man thus lies heavily on the landscape and the signs of landscape and ecosystem deterioration are to be seen everywhere. Economic activities such as mining, industry, fishing, natural forest exploitation, agriculture and even tourism have all had their typical impact. Legislation to help prevent further deterioration has been promulgated across the globe, but is often ineffective due to the difficulties of implementation and policing and the ever-increasing spiral of poverty, human population expansion, corruption and poor decision making.

Rangelands are one of the most extensive natural systems that have become degraded by the hand of modern man. The cumulative effects of over-utilisation of the natural grazing and consequent erosion of the critically valuable soil reserves have resulted in the advance of desert and semi-desert conditions all around the globe.

The ever-increasing demand for natural resources, most often harvested or used in an unsustainable way, manifests itself in an increasingly urgent need for restorative environmental management. Habitat restoration or rehabilitation, however, is prohibitively expensive and is often considered to be the exclusive field of expertise of a relatively small group of professional rehabilitation experts.

Landowners, range managers and tenant farmers who are confronted with rangeland management problems, usually a legacy from the past, may therefore be forgiven if restoration projects, however urgent, are not initiated. This cumulatively results in ever-worsening range conditions and an acceleration of the damaging symptoms.

In this account, I will not dwell on the causes of landscape degradation or comment on who is to blame for it, but I wish rather to concentrate on practical methods that can be used to heal the scars and by so doing, give nature the opportunity to heal itself. Thankfully nature is amazingly forgiving and will gratefully reward any kindness with astounding rejuvenation.

With this book I would like to inspire rangeland managers and farmers to rethink and reconsider the symptoms of rangeland degradation and to start again with a fresh approach that is unencumbered by the attitudes, prejudices, impractical norms and restrictions that are often a part of the problem with practical rangeland restoration.

> The hope of the future lies not in curbing the influence of human occupancy – it is already too late for that – but in creating a better understanding of the extent of that influence and a new ethic for its governance (Leopold, 1933).

1.2   THE APPROACH

In 1933, Aldo Leopold suggested that the wildlife of North America could be restored by using the same tools with which it was destroyed. Similarly, the axe, plough, herbivores, fire and mechanisation – the very tools used to degrade rangelands – can be used to restore them if used in a versatile and imaginative way.

Leopold went on to say that few environmental fields depend as heavily on commitment, ingenuity and resourcefulness as that of restoration management. Land care is an integral component of the almost forgotten art of woodcraft which is based on the skills derived from individual and collective experience of many generations.

This volume attempts to bridge the ever-widening gap of land-care experience by providing some ideas that may help with the restoration and rehabilitation of degraded rangeland. The techniques described need not be followed to the letter. They should provide examples of how to think, understand and experiment, rather than be implemented as prescriptions.

There is no single or correct way in which to approach a rangeland restoration project. There are in fact endless answers, or combinations of answers, to every landscape restoration problem. A solution for each problem must be worked out according to its own particular situational characteristics, taking into account variability in soil types, climate, vegetation, land use and land-use history.

The approach presented involves no elaborate or costly technology or highly specialised knowledge – it rather provides new insights and practical strategies for decision making and implementation.

The solutions to many of the land care problems that face land managers today are sometimes much simpler than is at first anticipated. A practical and straightforward approach is outlined in this book as a way to get to grips with land management problems, however small this start may be. The methods described are purposefully simple and most can be implemented by unskilled or semi-skilled workers with some guiding supervision or limited training, and the tools already familiar to them.

This book is therefore intended to be a useful reference for the following interest groups:

- Land management practitioners: farmers, game rangers, foresters, landowners, land managers, land management contractors and rehabilitation consultants. For this group, the book provides methods and practical ideas about planning and implementation.
- Environmental biologists: ecologists, botanists, zoologists, herpetologists, environmental scientists and environmental agencies. For this group, the book is designed to link their biological field of expertise with an improved understanding of the realities of practical field engineering.
- Environmental education practitioners: lecturers in environmental studies, teachers, extension educators and students of environmental studies. For this group, the book provides practical examples of a range of land rehabilitation options and the planning needed to implement them successfully.

In short, this volume attempts to link practical land restoration practice with the range of individuals who may implement, study, regulate, finance or have some other interest in land-care projects.

1.3   ESTABLISHING A LAND ETHIC

Fifty-four years ago, leading American conservationist Aldo Leopold wrote the following about land ethics in his book *A Sand County Almanac*:

> All ethics so far involved rest upon a single premise: that the individual is a member of a community of interdependent parts. His instincts prompt him to compete for his place in that community, but his ethics prompt him also to co-operate (perhaps in order that there may be a place to compete for). The land ethic simply enlarges the boundaries of the community to include soils, waters, plants, and animals, or collectively: the land. This sounds simple: do we not already sing our love for and obligation to the land of the free and the home of the brave? Yes, but just what and whom do we love? Certainly not the soil, which we are sending helter-skelter downriver. Certainly not the waters, which we assume have no function except to turn turbines, float barges, and carry off sewage. Certainly not the plants, of which we exterminate whole communities without batting an eyelid. Certainly not the animals, of which we have already extirpated many of the largest and most beautiful species. A land ethic of course cannot prevent the alteration, management, and use of these 'resources', but it does affirm their right to continued existence, and, at least in spots, their continued existence in a natural state. In short, a land ethic changes the role of *Homo sapiens* from conqueror of the land-community to plain member and citizen of it. It implies respect for his fellow-members, and also respect for the community as such.

Modern man has certainly moved away from a clear commitment to a responsible land ethic. Land is simply used as a medium for commercial utilisation, for economic gain and without any spiritual connection to it. As natural resources diminish, as a result of expanding human populations, the economics of survival play an increasingly important role. A small piece of land that could support an agricultural family 100 years ago will fall far short of bringing in a reasonable income today. Value systems and the modern cost of living have resulted in increased pressures on the land as people try to derive more profit from it to make ends meet.

Whatever the history behind landscape deterioration, modern man has clearly lost the memory of a land ethic. Unsustainable exploitation of natural resources is even evident where landowners survive comfortably and profit from their industry. This can surely only be the result of ignorance and greed.

The early Native Americans clearly understood that their survival depended on an intimate, careful and reverential relationship with the natural environments that supported them. They recognised that death was a gift of renewal to the living and that only a sustainable use of this gift of renewal would ensure their survival. The discerning nature of Indian identification with the animals and plants of their world was fundamental to their holistic view of life, and their sustainable use of the wildlife and plants that fed them.

This ancient land ethic was an essential and integral part of life and survival of all of the earth's early native peoples. Much the same land ethic was fundamental to the Australian Aborigines, African Khoi-San, Asian Eskimos and the Central Asian nomads.

With the expansion and integration of human populations, technology was born. Travel and colonisation, improved hunting skills and the use of fire and the plough to manage landscapes followed. Formerly nomadic herdsmen no longer had to move their stock to find water because perennial boreholes were provided, and long-standing rotational grazing practices were quickly forgotten. New values based on technology, rather than ancient land knowledge passed on from father to son, now prevail and the long-standing knowledge upon which the original land ethics were based has mostly been forgotten. With this forgetfulness comes the degradation of natural landscapes as a result of unsustainable land-use practices.

Modern range managers need to reverse the trend of landscape deterioration. A land ethic must be reborn and it must be instilled in every land management practitioner from owner to humble worker. This is much easier said than done. Environmental education programmes and training courses generally provide information about the building blocks of any environmental system, inter-dependence and the interrelationships that make any system function. But instilling a land ethic requires more than this basic but vital information. An emphasis on the appreciation of land as a basic but exhaustible resource is required. The teaching of a land ethic must therefore be an intellectual as well as an emotional process.

A suitable land ethic must be willingly and enthusiastically pursued by range managers as a way of life rather than as yet another new-age method for increasing production. In Leopold's words: 'It is inconceivable to me that an ethical relation to land can exist without love, respect, and admiration for land, and a high regard for its value. By value, I of course mean something far broader than mere economic value; I mean value in the philosophical sense.'

1.4   WHAT CAN BE DONE?

There are many land-care treatments ranging from the oldest and simplest to complex modern technical solutions. The land manager is often confronted with conflicting ideas, each prescription being promoted as the only correct solution to the problem. Technical experts, academics and consultants often disagree on exactly how to go about solving land-care problems. Sometimes models are designed and used to help make choices, all of which only makes the situation even more confusing for the land manager.

Land management problems are often complex and invariably involve a linked chain of different, connected aspects. The rehabilitation of a river, for example, may involve soil erosion control in the river catchment area and a change in land use from sheep and cattle grazing to wildlife and tourism. The task of the land manager is complicated and the solutions to the problems need to be carefully considered. To make a difference, the manager must be totally committed to land care. Establishing a land ethic is the first step in the right direction. A land ethic will help to restore a pioneering spirit and pride in every land management effort, however small.

With the necessary commitment to land care established, a useful approach is to take a fresh and unprejudiced look at the problem, to determine the cause and to work out what to do about the cause and the symptoms. This approach is dealt with in each of the following chapters of the book in more detail. Making the right decisions at this early stage of any land-care project is critical for the outcome to be successful as well as cost effective.

While taking this fresh look, one must not become daunted by the size of the problem and the scale of the rehabilitation task. Even one single committed individual can make a significant difference. By taking carefully considered action and dealing effectively with the very causes of land management problems, it is possible for a single individual to initiate a healing process that can change the face of a degraded landscape forever. Never easy or straightforward, landscape rehabilitation is nevertheless achievable and every success, however small, will contribute to the ultimate solution.

Initially, one must not be daunted by the apparent cost of rehabilitation management. Quick solutions to rehabilitation problems are sometimes effective, but are always expensive. There are usually much cheaper options to be found yielding the same results. The use of hand labour rather than mechanisation is certainly more appropriate in areas where unemployment is a problem. The use of natural organic products rather than chemical fertilisers is preferable and natural organic materials can be used rather than synthetic or manufactured materials. A self-help approach, driven by commitment to a sound land ethic, is often more effective than using rehabilitation contractors who come with a hefty price tag and do not always commit to the long-term maintenance of the rehabilitation work. Small but effective steps, as described in the following chapters, will be affordable.

One must try to imagine the project completed, then work backwards through all of the steps that must be taken to get there – without wondering what each step will cost. At each stage in the vision, ask yourself 'how can we achieve that?' but do not permit negative and limiting thoughts to block the process. It is all about commitment to a responsible land ethic.

1.5 LANDSCAPE RESTORATION AND REHABILITATION IN PERSPECTIVE

Ecological restoration is a relatively young discipline and restorationists today are active in ecosystems as divergent as coral reefs and tropical forests. The American Midwest prairies, however, have played the leading role in the development of the art of restoration since its beginnings, approximately half a century ago.

Today restoration is increasingly critical for the recovery and conservation of degraded habitats, rare plants, animals and natural communities. But what exactly is meant by restoration, rehabilitation and revegetation? These terms are frequently interchangeably used, although incorrectly, to describe the same process.

- Revegetation: This entails the establishment of only one or a few plant species with the objective to cover the ground with a protective and aesthetically pleasing vegetation cover. Results are achieved quickly and no attempt is made to achieve the pre-disturbance state.
- Rehabilitation: This emphasises the reparation of ecosystem processes, productivity and services. It therefore returns some of the functions of the original pre-disturbance ecosystem and the historical or pre-existing ecosystem is used as a reference. The desired results take longer to achieve than revegetation projects.
- Restoration: Restoration shares with rehabilitation the reparation of ecosystem processes, to as close to the original structure and function as possible, but differs in that it also includes the re-establishment of the pre-existing biotic species composition and community structure.

Restoration generally requires a great deal more post-rehabilitation after-care and it takes much longer to achieve the desired result. The end result, however, is much closer to the pre-disturbance state than that of rehabilitation.

Rehabilitation is probably a better description of the majority of work that is usually, but erroneously, described as restoration. Putting rehabilitation into perspective can be expedited by examining some of the lessons learned by the early restoration and rehabilitation practitioners:

1. We need to recognise the difference between reversible and irreversible changes that are brought about by the activities of humans. Efforts must then be invested in a direction in which it will be practical to reverse changes, rather than attempt the near impossible. In this volume I advocate a practical hands-on approach, which can be achieved at relatively low cost by small groups or individuals with a commitment to landscape restoration. These actions should be directed towards landscape improvement projects in which man-induced changes are reversible.

2. We must understand how humans impact on their environment. Similarly, we need to understand the ecosystem that needs to be rehabilitated. This combined understanding (human impact plus ecosystem functioning) will lead to well directed and ultimately successful rehabilitation projects. Failure to appreciate these important aspects, and how they interact, will certainly lead to disappointing results and wasted time and effort.

3. Nature is amazingly resilient and it is also very forgiving. With an investment of only time and effort, all but the most severely degraded situations are reversible or can at least be much improved.

4. Humans and nature cannot be viewed apart. The ecological restoration of man-induced changes to the natural environment should be viewed as the artificial recreation of the natural ecosystem and not ultimately as an artificial ecosystem. The local ecological integrity of the rehabilitation work done will contribute to the eventual naturalness of the rehabilitated landscape. Rehabilitation should, therefore, be seen as an essential nature conservation action.

5. Rehabilitation and restoration work of any kind is deeply rewarding and engaging. Although it will always be tiring and seemingly endless, the results (if the work is effectively performed) are always very satisfying. Getting involved in hands-on restoration projects is certainly physically

tiring, but it is a particularly rewarding tiredness that cannot be achieved by simply making a financial contribution towards nature conservation projects. This is reflected in the ever-increasing number of volunteer groups for restoration projects in many parts of the world.

6. The approach to restoration and rehabilitation work varies from innovative experimentation to objectively based and sophisticated scientific investigation. Whatever approach is followed, the methods used should always be based on the best information available. Natural landscapes must, however, not be permitted to deteriorate further while restoration and rehabilitation practitioners wait for scientifically generated guidelines. This is where innovative experimentation, based on previous experience, is the only practical course of action to take. It is, therefore, sometimes necessary to act with imperfect knowledge to prevent the imminent loss of biodiversity and abiotic resources. The practical knowledge that has been derived from unrelenting trial and error has a huge role to play in the success of landscape restoration activities.

7. The experience of restoration and rehabilitation practitioners must be communicated as widely as possible. This knowledge must be shared with those who need it most if landscape restoration is to become a new way of looking at our natural resources. Persons with this valuable experience should ensure that proven methods and guidelines be communicated through a variety of different media to a specific target audience. Uncommunicated practical experience is lost when the practitioner moves on, changes vocation or dies. We simply cannot afford to lose this kind of knowledge while forests decline, rangelands desiccate and alien plants advance on the remaining natural wildlands.

8. Landscape rehabilitation and restoration implies a long-term commitment, a dedication to the task that underpins an ethical relationship with the land as well as plenty of hard work. It is not for the faint-hearted, but rather for those who have the courage to take on and combat man's greatest folly – the destruction of his own home!

CHAPTER TWO

HEALING THE LAND

Dealing with soil erosion

2.1   Introduction

2.2   Objectives of soil erosion control

2.3   Procedure for effective control

2.4   Control methods

2.5   Monitoring the success of soil erosion control methods

2.1   INTRODUCTION

We are all aware of what soil erosion is and what causes it, but few appear to be seriously concerned about it. Soil erosion is a quiet crisis, irrepressibly at work, moving valuable soil away in such small amounts at a time that it is hardly noticed. This loss of topsoil is chronic and irreversible.

Every patch of bare exposed soil surface, or network of erosion gullies, represents lost productivity, in terms of both forage and habitat. The environmental inhospitality of the exposed earth prevents the establishment of the protective plants that are food, cover and shade for so many organisms, each representing an important piece of the landscape jigsaw puzzle.

With each rain or windstorm more unprotected grains of valuable topsoil are dislodged and carried away by water and wind. In this way the ever-increasing area of exposed soil is further removed from its productive potential. The compounded loss of unconsolidated sand grains provides run-off water with an unresisting channel for its relentless downhill and erosive flow. With each successive rainfall event more unprotected particles of soil are carried away, the flow becomes a rill, the rill becomes a gully and eventually the original bare patch becomes a wasteland of soil erosion, unproductive for the needs of both man and wildlife.

The capability of the soil to resist water erosion is dependent on soil particle size, chemistry and organic material content, as well as the nature and extent of the vegetation cover. Sandy soils have a relatively large pore space, which gives them a greater capacity for water infiltration than silty or clay soils. With their smaller pore spaces, silty and clay soils are prone to rapid run-off flow with lower rainfall infiltration. This rate of overland flow is likely to increase as the slope angle increases. Rainfall events in arid areas are often intense and usually exceed the infiltration rate. This results in overland run-off flows which attain much higher velocities than in non-arid areas.

Erodability of the soil by wind is determined by the speed, turbulence, frequency, duration and direction of the prevailing winds. Soil surface erodability by wind is also influenced by physical soil attributes like particle size, cohesiveness, moisture content, organic matter, the presence of stones and rocks and the nature and type of vegetation cover.

Wind generally removes the finer topsoil particles of silt, clay and organic material. The silt and clay particles are critical in soil structure because they bind the soil components and improve the capacity of the soil to retain moisture. The loss of these particles to the wind therefore impacts on the soil structure as well as its capacity to retain moisture. Fine silt and clay particles also have the highest concentrations of nutrients attached to them so the loss of these components also reduces soil fertility.

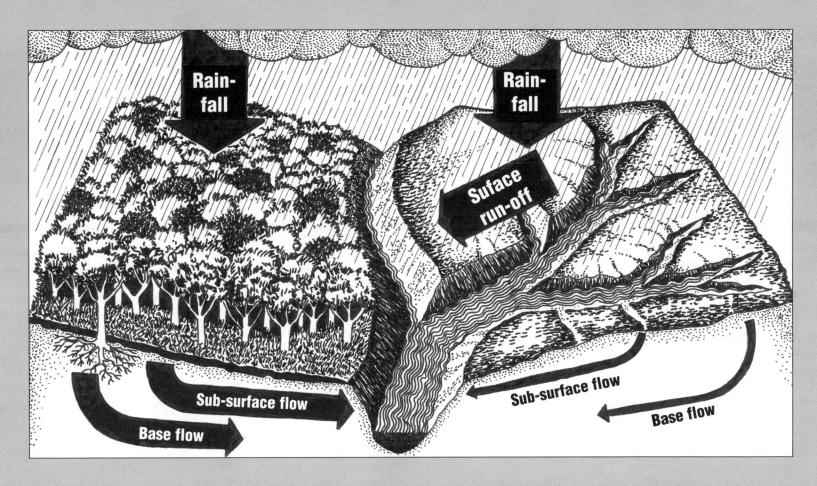

BOX 2.1

The relationship between rainfall, the rate of infiltration and erosive surface run-off

Under the natural conditions of undisturbed rangelands the vegetation cover plays a key role in the volume and rate of run-off water. The four factors that affect run-off volumes are:

1. Kind, amount, intensity and distribution of rainfall;

2. Size, shape, length and steepness of drainage basins;

3. Soil and its plant cover; and

4. Changes in the soil and its cover through land use.

As illustrated, land-use practices that drastically reduce the natural vegetation cover and leave the soil surface exposed to the elements will increase surface run-off dramatically with a consequent reduction of infiltration. The result is that a process of aridification begins where the vegetation cover is reduced, and the exposed soil surface becomes more vulnerable to the erosive force of the increased surface run-off. Not only is most of the rainfall carried away in drainages and streams but the water also carries the valuable topsoil away with it. Where the natural vegetation cover is retained, infiltration is greater and there is little or no surface run-off. The better vegetation cover protects the soil surface against the erosive effects of surface run-off.

2.1.1   When is soil erosion unnatural?

Soil removal by wind or water is part of a natural geomorphological process, the inevitable and universal process of landmass erosion. This erosion of the ancient parent rocks is slow and results in the formation of the soils that support and maintain the plants which protect it. Under natural conditions a fragile balance exists between the rate of this soil formation and the rate at which it is degraded or eroded.

In contrast to this natural erosive process, the rate of soil erosion can be enormously speeded up or accelerated through the activities of man. Under these conditions soil is removed much faster than it can be formed, most often resulting in the loss of valuable life-giving topsoil. Accelerated soil erosion is a rapid process, undoing in a period of just a few short years what took nature thousands, or perhaps even millions, of years to produce.

Accelerated soil erosion usually occurs when there is a change in plant cover, which changes the rate of rainfall infiltration and run-off. With a reduction of plant cover, interception of rainfall by plant foliage is reduced and a reduction of fallen leaves and stems leaves the mineral soil surface even more exposed to the elements.

This degradation is the result of man's historical and ongoing failure to understand and manage soil effectively and most often begins with deforestation, ploughing, burning and overgrazing.

There are numerous examples worldwide that illustrate that the use of soil for cultivation, or that the modification of the natural vegetation cover, invariably results in an increased rate of soil erosion. The devastating results of overgrazing in North Africa, extensive insensitive ploughing in North America and slash-and-burn agriculture in tropical forest regions are classic examples of the causes of vastly accelerated and unnatural soil erosion.

In 1936 Quincy Claude Ayres compared artificial, or unnatural, soil erosion to the natural erosion process as follows:

> Natural processes, including erosion, have brought about the formation of soil from the parent rocks; and the distribution and assortment of the soil by wind, water, and ice have been immensely encouraging, if not indispensable, to all forms of life.
>
> A basic distinction should be made, however, between the rate of change as it occurs in nature, whereby soil-building forces are substantially in balance with those of destruction, and the rate of change precipitated by man in the conquest of his environment. The one is inherently natural, and the other must be considered artificial. What takes Nature hundreds or even thousands of years to manufacture, man can and often does destroy almost overnight by haphazard land use and improvident husbandry.

The human activities that most commonly lead to wind erosion are those that change or remove the protective vegetation cover and those that destabilise the natural soil surfaces, such as earth moving, land clearing, ploughing, burning, overgrazing, mining, trampling by domestic stock and even off-road vehicle use.

The compaction, crusting and sealing of soil surfaces diminish water infiltration capacity and increase surface run-off, which often leads to soil erosion. Compaction, crusting and sealing also impede seedling growth and root penetration and retard oxygen and carbon dioxide interchange with plant roots. The sealing of surfaces can be caused by physical trampling, but is most commonly caused by the clogging of soil pores by fine-grained silt and clay particles dispersed by raindrop impact. Soils with low humus content, poorly sorted sand fractions and high silt content are particularly vulnerable and the effect is most prevalent in areas where the vegetation cover does not adequately protect the soil surface from the impact of raindrops.

Overgrazing of vegetation with livestock or wildlife is often accompanied by the effects of trampling and compaction. The most common consequence of overgrazing, however, is a dramatic decrease in vegetation cover which leads to accelerated erosion of the soil surface by wind and water. The degradation often occurs in areas close to livestock watering points or may be concentrated in certain selected parts of the landscape, such as along riverine channels, pediments and plateaus. Box 2.2 illustrates the different forms of soil erosion, each of which is shaped by topography, soil characteristics and climatic conditions.

Over-exploitation of natural vegetation for other domestic uses like fuel wood, fencing and construction exacerbates the impacts of overgrazing further, particularly in arid regions, contributing to soil exposure and accelerated soil erosion.

In 1864 George Perkins Marsh provided evidence that man was seriously damaging his natural environment through a chain of varying causes that most often resulted in soil erosion. He wrote as follows:

> When the forest is gone, the great reservoir of moisture stored up in its vegetable mould is evaporated, and returns only in deluges of rain to wash away the parched dust into which the mould has been converted. The well-wooded and humid hills are turned to ridges of dry rock, which encumbers the low grounds and chokes the water courses with its debris, and – except in countries favoured with an equable distribution of rain through the seasons, and a moderate and regular inclination of surface – the whole earth, until rescued by human art from physical degradation to which it tends, becomes an assemblage of bald mountains, of barren, turfless hills, and of swampy and malarious plains. These are parts of Asia Minor, of Northern Africa, of Greece, and even of Alpine Europe, where the operation of causes set in action by man has brought the face of the earth to a desolation almost as complete as that of the moon (Marsh in Stallings 1957).

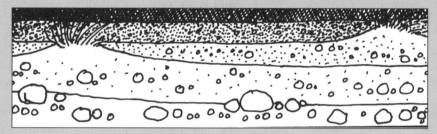

BOX 2.2
Forms of soil erosion

The five forms of soil erosion that are the most prevalent in areas with degraded soil conditions are as follows:

Rills and gullies are channels cut by flowing water. They may have been initiated by water flowing down stock paths or roads. Their presence is a sure sign that water flows rapidly off the landscape, carrying both litter and soil with it.

Terracettes are abrupt walls about 1–10 cm high, aligned with the local contour. Terracettes are progressively cut back up-slope by water flow, the eroded material being deposited in an alluvial fan down-slope of the feature.

Sheet erosion is the progressive removal of very thin layers of soil across extensive areas by wind and water. This is not always easy to detect with assurance and may need to be inferred from other soil surface features, such as eroded materials or surface nature. When at an advanced stage, many sheeted surfaces are covered by layers of gravel or stone left behind after erosion of finer material.

Hummocking is confined to soils with sandy-textured surface layers and is the result of re-sorting of sand by wind resulting in the sand accumulating around obstructions, often to depths of many centimetres or even metres. A consequence of hummocking is that fine-grained materials and litter are widely dispersed during windy phases and are lost to the system.

Pedestalling is the result of soil removal by erosion of an area to a depth of at least several centimetres, leaving the butts of surviving plants on a column of soil above the new general level of the landscape. Exposed roots are typical of this erosion form. This is a sign that the soil type itself is very erodable and that loss of vegetation in the landscape was preceded by erosion, and not the other way around.

2.2   OBJECTIVES OF SOIL EROSION CONTROL

Before launching oneself into an enthusiastic and energetic programme to combat accelerated soil erosion, it is necessary to consider whether intervention is essential (see Box 2.3). There is little sense in investing time, money and effort in an erosion system that has already become stabilised with a protective vegetation cover that results in reduced run-off and little or no soil erosion.

Before we start with descriptions of the range of options that are possible for the active rehabilitation of degraded areas, it is necessary to decide exactly what it is that we want to achieve. Objectives for soil erosion control treatments may differ from site to site but in essence these objectives can be broadly summarised as follows:

- To reduce the effects of raindrop splash erosion on exposed soil surfaces.
- To keep rainwater on the soil surface for as long as possible and thus increase the rate at which water infiltrates the soil.
- To reduce the speed of run-off water and so reduce the erosive force of water on unprotected soil surfaces.
- To provide the methods to hold back and retain soil, plant debris, animal faeces and seeds that may be carried away by run-off water.
- To provide protected and stable sites for pioneer vegetation re-establishment.
- To change mineral and organic imbalances in degraded soils and thereby improve them for pioneer vegetation establishment.
- To improve water retention of the soil.

In practice the rehabilitation requirements for a particular soil erosion control project may include combinations of the above goals.

In addition to these practical objectives, there are also the more general, or umbrella, objectives for soil erosion control. The rehabilitation of degraded rangeland is important in terms of aesthetics and tourism. No discerning eco-tourist wishes to be confronted with unsightly soil erosion systems when observing wildlife. Aesthetic appeal also impacts on other aspects of eco-tourism like photographic safaris and hunting expeditions for the same reason.

The most important general objective for landowners is that of economics. Degraded rangeland results in a loss of potential income due to the reduced productivity of the range. Eroded areas do not support good forage for livestock or wildlife due to the general aridification and reduced fertility of the soils. Productivity of rangeland can be improved, if not restored, if all of the degraded areas are stabilised and revegetated.

Another aspect of economics that should be considered is that of land value. Degraded rangeland is worth little and if it continues to deteriorate, the erosion of the original investment will also occur along with the erosion of the soil, and eventually the land will lose its marketability. The active rehabilitation of eroded land should therefore be viewed as a way in which to improve land value in the longer term.

Conservation of nature is a worthwhile objective for any region. All patches of natural rangeland should be viewed as refuge conservation areas, whatever the primary objective of land ownership may be. Healthy rangeland cover supports a vast diversity of birds, reptiles, amphibians, mammals and invertebrates, which will remain conserved for as long as the rangeland is protected and well managed. The conservation value of natural rangelands for plants is inestimable and the rehabilitation of degraded areas will therefore promote the long-term conservation of this biodiversity.

Finally, responsibility also plays a role and can be seen as an important objective for soil erosion control. We are all merely custodians of the rangelands that we own, hire, manage or use. Being a custodian implies the role of guardian and protector of the rangeland. This adequately describes our responsibility to the land, part of which is care of the soil and the vegetation cover that protects it. The rehabilitation of degraded rangeland is an ideal way in which to meet this responsibility.

When considering the objectives of soil erosion control actions, it is prudent to consider why it is that soil erosion control projects are often unsuccessful and consequently abandoned. The reasons are varied but can most often be traced to over-ambitious expectations, inappropriate location of control structures, ineffective or half-hearted application of the techniques and a lack of follow-up maintenance.

All too often, the intentions are good and the basic methods are known, but without careful planning and a realistic set of goals, erosion control projects are doomed to failure. For example, the construction of one big silt trap weir in a deep erosion gully may yield impressive results initially, but the costs of such an approach and the failure of the method used to halt accelerated erosion in the upper catchment of the erosion system usually results in disillusionment and discontinuation of the work. The application of small silt traps spread throughout the catchment fingers of the erosion system would have yielded a greater impact result, at much lower cost, and the results would certainly encourage further investment in soil erosion control.

The lack of follow-up maintenance contributes hugely to the discontinuation of many erosion control projects. Erosion works are often well constructed and appropriately located, but if even the slightest undercutting by run-off water is not timeously prevented, all of the time and money invested will have been wasted.

The following section provides a step-by-step strategy that will help to ensure that your erosion control actions are effective.

BOX 2.3

Is intervention necessary?

Many years ago when I was working as a nature reserve manager, I was particularly concerned about the effects of accelerated soil erosion on my reserve which had been overgrazed with small domestic stock.

A group of about six mature eland bulls had taken up residence in the dense bush of an eroded stream bed, and as eland bulls often do, caused considerable damage to the trees by breaking off branches, which littered the stream bed.

Some time later, after heavy rains, I noticed that these branches had matted together and snagged up against tree trunks and roots across the stream bed, and had trapped other debris, thus forming natural silt and debris traps. Behind each snag was a layer of topsoil, organic plant debris and animal droppings in which grass and reeds later took root and spread along the stream banks, stabilising them naturally.

Nature can heal herself in time, but a good policy to follow is to try to rehabilitate any accelerated soil erosion that has occurred as a result of injudicious land use. Back on my reserve, the eland certainly played their small part, but it took many years of additional effort to stabilise the effects of past overgrazing with small stock.

2.3   PROCEDURE FOR EFFECTIVE CONTROL

The following strategy and procedure can be used to help plan soil erosion control action on any land, no matter how extensive or severe the problem may be.

Firstly, we must take a long-range view of the soil erosion problem, and view the offending erosion through the eyes of a soaring bird. Accelerated soil erosion is usually a symptom of some misguided landscape management practice or disturbance; it has a cause and the visible scars on the landscape are the effects. The route to follow with soil erosion reclamation is firstly to eliminate the causes before any attempt is made to heal the effects. Refer to Figure 2.1 which illustrates this principle.

After dealing with the causes of the erosion, one is faced with the seemingly impossible task of rehabilitation of what is most often a vast network of sterile, crumbling gully fingers or bare, capped soil pavements where few plants are able to survive.

The best course of action is to start with unsophisticated mapping of the soil erosion system. Map each erosion system (drainage system) and allocate an identification number to each. An aerial photograph of the property is ideal for mapping, but standing on high ground and directly mapping what you can see onto a topographical map works just as well. Figure 2.2 illustrates what a typical soil erosion map may look like.

The mapping need not be precisely accurate, or to exact scale – the important requirement is simply to build up a picture of soil erosion distribution in the area of concern. With all the important areas mapped, one can then assess the extent of rehabilitation requirements and prioritise them according to their severity. The seemingly insurmountable soil erosion problem now becomes a collection of sites on a map – something visible at a glance and with priorities for action. Suddenly, because these first steps have been taken, one becomes inspired and the problem appears to shrink a bit, because a positive start has been made. Now that we have a picture of what was previously just a problem, it is possible to devise a practical strategy for dealing with soil erosion.

2.3.1   Reasons why erosion control efforts are sometimes unsuccessful

In the absence of careful and practical planning, the following are some of the reasons why many erosion projects are unsuccessful. Take care that you do not repeat these mistakes when drawing up a plan of action for your erosion problem.
- Failure to understand the processes involved.
- Impulsive actions with no overall planning.
- Insufficient attention to financial implications of control actions.
- The use of inappropriate methods.
- Trying to 'fill up' or fix advanced erosion systems, rather than preventing them from degenerating further.
- Incorrect application of methods and poor workmanship.
- Lack of maintenance after construction.
- Failure to eliminate the cause of the accelerated erosion.

The above list indicates that failure is more often related to a lack of careful planning than the inability of recognised erosion control methods to deal with the problem effectively.

2.3.2   Scales for mapping

A map or aerial photograph with a sufficiently detailed scale is needed for soil erosion system mapping. The most useful scale is in the region of 1:10 000 to 1:20 000 (a scale of 1:10 000 means that one cm on the map is equal to 10 000 cm or 100 m on the ground) (see Figure 2.2).

If maps of this scale are not available for your particular area, then use can be made of 1:50 000 topographical maps, but it will be necessary to photocopy the map and enlarge it by about 150%. If these options are equally unattainable, then the only alternative is to draw your own map of the area of concern. When doing so, remember to include landscape features like rivers, roads, rocky outcrops, dams and fences. These features will also help you to estimate the distances on your map as accurately as possible. You can then set up your own scale by simply pacing a set distance on the ground, say 100 m, and measuring the corresponding distance on your map.

When drawing your own map from scratch, start by drafting a 1 cm x 1 cm block grid on the entire sheet of paper. This grid will provide scale and comparative measurement to your map. To ensure that your sheet of paper is big enough for the map, use a sheet of about 150 cm x 90 cm. Draw a line along one side edge of the paper and mark off 1 cm intervals along it. Then draw a line along the top edge of the sheet at 90° to the side-line, using a set square or any other rectangular object such as a book or a large envelope. Mark off 1 cm intervals along this line and then do the same along the bottom (also at 90°) and other side edge of the sheet. Join the 1 cm marks across the page and down the page and your grid is complete.

Before drafting topographic or landscape details onto the map, you need to orientate the map to magnetic north. The vertical lines on the map can be directed north using a magnetic compass to indicate the northerly direction. Use high points in the landscape for a bird's eye view and map the important features in and around your soil erosion system.

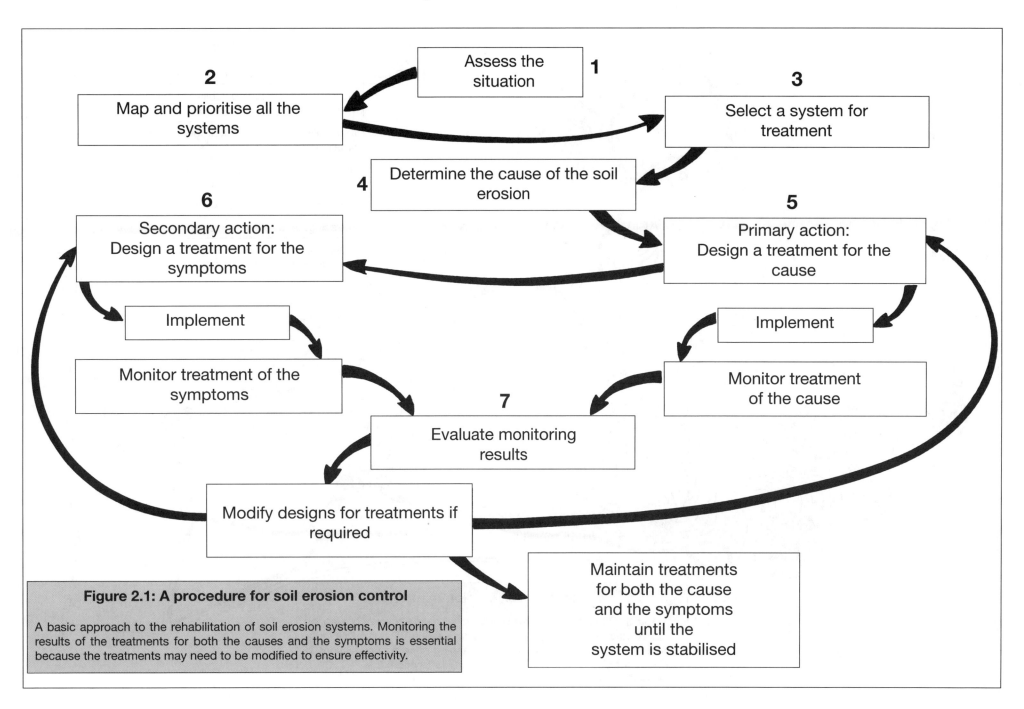

2
Map and prioritise all the systems

Assess the situation **1**

3
Select a system for treatment

4 Determine the cause of the soil erosion

6
Secondary action: Design a treatment for the symptoms

5
Primary action: Design a treatment for the cause

Implement

Implement

Monitor treatment of the symptoms

Monitor treatment of the cause

7
Evaluate monitoring results

Modify designs for treatments if required

Maintain treatments for both the cause and the symptoms until the system is stabilised

Figure 2.1: A procedure for soil erosion control

A basic approach to the rehabilitation of soil erosion systems. Monitoring the results of the treatments for both the causes and the symptoms is essential because the treatments may need to be modified to ensure effectivity.

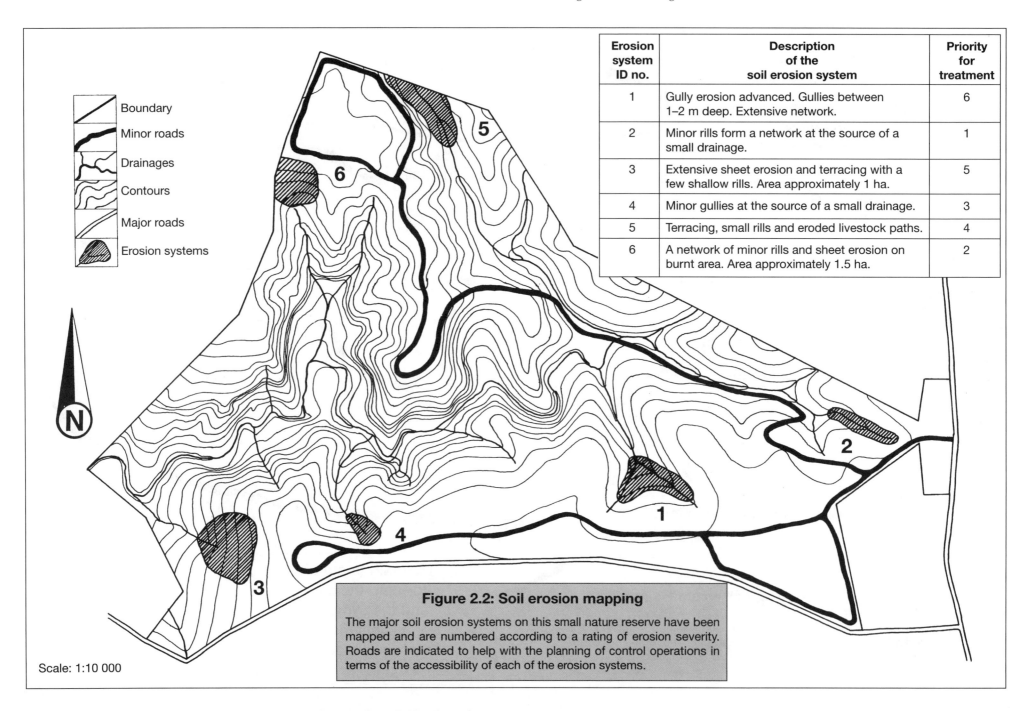

Erosion system ID no.	Description of the soil erosion system	Priority for treatment
1	Gully erosion advanced. Gullies between 1–2 m deep. Extensive network.	6
2	Minor rills form a network at the source of a small drainage.	1
3	Extensive sheet erosion and terracing with a few shallow rills. Area approximately 1 ha.	5
4	Minor gullies at the source of a small drainage.	3
5	Terracing, small rills and eroded livestock paths.	4
6	A network of minor rills and sheet erosion on burnt area. Area approximately 1.5 ha.	2

Boundary

Minor roads

Drainages

Contours

Major roads

Erosion systems

N

Scale: 1:10 000

Figure 2.2: Soil erosion mapping

The major soil erosion systems on this small nature reserve have been mapped and are numbered according to a rating of erosion severity. Roads are indicated to help with the planning of control operations in terms of the accessibility of each of the erosion systems.

2.3.3   A practical strategy for action

Step 1: Planning

Once a particular soil erosion system has been selected for treatment, the scope of the task must be evaluated in terms of the following:

1. How much input is required? This can be determined by evaluating the condition of the system and thus the number and type of control structures needed.

2. Establish which resources are available. Are natural resources like branches, brush, manure, mulch and stones readily available or within easy transport distance, or must manufactured materials be purchased?

3. Can you do the work yourself, using local workers for the construction work or will people have to be specially employed and brought in to do the work?

4. Are suitable vehicles available to transport workers and for materials and are implements and heavy earth-moving machinery available or will they have to be hired where necessary?

5. How much funding is available? And how much can be done with the available funding?

The above aspects all relate to cost and financial resources. As already established, we must not be deterred from our important objective by the projected costs, but must rather strive to find practical, cheaper and effective alternatives where necessary.

Step 2: Decide on the methods to use and mark out the job

When the above evaluation has been done, it will be possible to decide finally on the method or combination of methods to be used. Select a priority area for treatment and then mark the position of each structure or treatment in the erosion system. The best marking method is simply to drive in an old fence iron standard or sharpened wooden stake on both sides of the treatment area. Marking out the sites will guide the workers, but will also help to complete the overall 'picture' of the work before you begin. Priority sites for treatment will be discussed in the next section about methods.

Step 3: Do the work and finish it

Proceed with the construction work starting at the top end of the erosion system and working downstream towards the most severely eroded parts. It is good management practice to complete each structure before moving on to the next. Take care to leave each construction site in an environmentally acceptable condition. This means removing all excess wire, excess building materials and other refuse from each site.

Step 4: Build in follow-up maintenance

Each control structure should be inspected after every rainfall event. These structures seldom do the job completely the first time. Weaknesses in design or application, or even workmanship, may result in undercutting, wash-aways and holes around barriers, which must be repaired as quickly as possible to ensure that time and money are not wasted. Follow-up maintenance is critical and failure to do this is often the reason for poor results. Follow-up maintenance should be carried out at least after every period of rainfall.

Step 5: Implement a monitoring system

Establish a fixed-point photographic monitoring system. Mark the fixed-point site with a permanent peg and fully describe the monitoring method to be used. It is extremely important that the consecutive photographs are taken of exactly the same locality. A fixed-point photographic monitoring method is more fully described in section 2.5. Photographs of a number of rehabilitation sites spread throughout the erosion system, with repeat photographs on an annual basis, will clearly show the changes that indicate progress or the need to adapt the methods used.

Step 6: Evaluation and adaptation

Monitoring without evaluation and modification of the erosion control methods where necessary will simply be a waste of time. After each round of monitoring, progress should be evaluated and methods suitably adapted or reinforced to ensure maximum effectiveness.

Evaluation should not, however, be restricted to monitoring sites. Constant checking of the erosion control work at all localities in the field will help to gauge the effectiveness of the control efforts. This will help to ensure that the available financial resources are invested in the most effective manner possible and that the treated systems recover in the shortest time possible.

2.4 CONTROL METHODS

Different kinds of erosion often occur at a particular site, which makes it difficult to prescribe a specific control method per erosion system. A practical approach is to use a combination of suitable methods in each system and to plan a control programme for each system individually.

Various methods have been used in the past in an attempt to re-establish vegetation on capped, bare patches. The soil on these bare patches and other sparsely vegetated sites develops a hard surface crust due to long exposure to sun, wind, raindrop impact and a high magnesium or sodium content. This is known as capping and results in sites that are not suitable for seed germination because of the changed microclimate and microhabitat conditions.

At the same time penetration of water into the soil is almost totally inhibited by this sealed crust and steps must be taken to increase water infiltration through the crust as much as possible. For other kinds of erosion, control must be aimed at slowing concentrated run-off water flow and spreading the flow as widely as possible to reduce its velocity. Box 2.4 illustrates the relationship between run-off and range condition.

When choosing methods for soil erosion control one should adopt the principle that vegetation cover is the key to the problem. Re-establishing the protective plant cover should thus be the primary objective, whatever method is used.

Inexpensive, simple techniques are needed to slow water run-off and ensure water infiltration on bare, sparsely vegetated and gully-eroded areas. Every effort employed in the control of soil erosion should be aimed at slowing run-off water after rain, increasing the water infiltration rate and retaining maximum moisture in the soil for as long as possible. These objectives and the implementation of the following methods, and modifications of these methods, should serve to improve localised soil surface conditions for the germination of pioneer plants. The re-establishment of a vegetation cover will pave the way for general soil stabilisation, range improvement and eventually greater productivity.

A frequent error with erosion control is the heavy emphasis that so many landowners and managers put on mechanical control methods, rather than using preventative methods and improved range management practices. It makes little sense to start with a programme of mechanical control structures when the accelerated run-off from the area of over-utilised vegetation remains unchanged. As recommended in Figure 2.1, the primary action must be to design a treatment for the cause of the problem first. Once this is achieved with the desired effect, it is time to consider mechanical control methods.

Many of the methods described are traditional and have been in use for longer than anybody can remember, handed down from generation to generation, each applying its own degree of modification and improvements.

The objective with these methods is to present practical and affordable options for soil erosion control for owners and managers of natural rangelands. The employment of more technical alternatives such as engineering constructions are not considered in this guideline, which rather provides methods that can be applied by anybody who can work with a pick and shovel and do the most elementary field construction work.

The methods describe ideas that need not be applied as a prescription but should rather be adapted for local conditions and the availability of natural resources. Each method should be carefully considered and modified to fit the particular requirement. Very often, a combination of methods may provide the best solution. The methods described will provide a foundation for further innovative thinking, which is an important requirement for effective erosion control and landscape management.

Whatever method, modification or combination of methods is used, it is extremely important that careful and detailed records of the designs, locality of the structures and effectiveness of the methods be kept.

In our efforts to care for and rehabilitate our natural landscapes we cannot afford to repeat the mistakes made in the past. Valuable resources and time must rather be invested in further improving methods known to be effective. Successes with erosion control and rehabilitation efforts should be shared with other landscape management practitioners in the region and also more widely for the benefit of the more distant land managers.

Use can be made of popular farming, nature conservation and environmental journals, magazines and newsletters to publish details about successful methods. Soil, climatic and land-use factors vary significantly from region to region, and what proves to be a quick wonder cure in one area may yield disappointing results in another. We must therefore constantly adapt and improve, make fine adjustments and actively seek out the best methods for local applications. This is part of the long-term commitment that must be made in order to achieve the results that will ultimately lead to landscape rehabilitation.

BOX 2.4

The relationship between range condition, run-off and range improvement

When rangeland is degraded, it has long and relatively straight run-off flows, allowing water to run out of the local ecosystem unchecked, with very little infiltration of soil. This run-off results in soil erosion through the eventual formation of rills and gullies, terracettes and sheet erosion. The soil surface also becomes capped and impervious to water and valuable topsoil is lost. Important organic material such as leaves, seeds and animal droppings are carried away by the water flow because there is little plant cover to hold it in place on the soil surface.

Rangeland with more vegetation cover causes water flow to meander, with plant hummocks blocking, redirecting and absorbing water in transit and trapping silt and organic material. Little topsoil is lost and the trapped organic material forms a protective mulch, which provides favourable sites for seed germination. The run-off water flow is considerably slower and much of it is absorbed into the soil and less is lost to the local ecosystem.

Rangeland in good condition has a dense protective plant cover and a natural plant species diversity consisting of shrubs, grasses and ephemeral plants. Run-off water is slowed, spread, broken up and absorbed into the soil and little is lost. The build-up of organic material is not lost to the system and productivity of the range is high due to the retention of humus and the continuous improvement of the topsoil through nutrient recycling. Water retention is improved due to the protective organic layer and a high infiltration rate. Germination sites are numerous and protected.

2.4.1 Treating gullies and rills

It is much simpler, and cheaper, to treat this type of erosion in the early stages of formation than to try to repair the damage once a deep gully has formed. Small ruts that are just starting to open up can be easily controlled by filling them with brush, straw, manure or even stones. Prevention, rather than cure, yields the best results.

The following aspects must be taken into consideration when planning the control of gully erosion:

- Priority should be given to erosion in the initial stages rather than to gullies in an advanced stage of erosion.
- Run-off into gullies should be minimised by range conservation and soil erosion control measures in the catchment area of the gully, especially those measures that retard run-off and promote rainwater infiltration.
- The stabilisation of gullies (preventing further degradation) must be given priority over attempts to reclaim the gullies completely (complete obliteration).
- Control should be concentrated where gullies have only advanced for short distances into the catchment, rather than where gullies have advanced far into the catchment and can go no further.
- Treatments should be concentrated in areas of clearly active soil erosion, rather than relatively stable (vegetated) gullies.

An extremely important principle with any soil erosion control method is that when natural materials are gathered for use in control structures, care must be taken to ensure that the removal (for example, of stones) does not become the cause of a new erosion problem at the source of the material. Stones, for example, should only be collected along roads where they are displaced during road-making, or from piles of stones cleared off irrigation lands. Similarly, natural vegetation should not be destroyed by vehicles collecting or delivering materials for gully control.

Where stones are in short supply, consideration should rather be given to the use of alternative materials that will result in lower environmental impact.

Figures 2.3a, 2.3b, 2.3c and 2.5 illustrate some of the frequently used methods of gully erosion control. Figure 2.4 illustrates the most effective approach for the control of a network of gullies. This sequence should guide all erosion control actions.

Gully checks, or gabion structures, often fail if the treatment does not include the establishment of a vegetation cover. Seeding, or planting, should therefore immediately follow the check dam construction for the most effective results.

The type of gabion, or barrier, that is used should be determined by the availability of material close to the erosion system to be treated. It makes little sense to transport stones over great distances, at great expense, when alternative materials are available closer to the work site. A certain degree of imaginative innovation is therefore required when determining which type of barrier to construct.

The indiscriminate removal of stones from natural rangeland is not a good idea because each stone may shelter a microhabitat, shade the soil, reduce excessively high soil temperatures and preserve soil moisture. Removing stones will thus destabilise the site they are removed from, thereby risking a new source of erosion.

Consider stones as animal habitat. Turn a number of stones over in any natural rangeland and you will probably find an amazing variety of invertebrates including ants, termites, beetles, woodlice, centipedes, slugs, spiders and scorpions. These creatures, together with the microscopic soil organisms on which they are dependent, are the architects, miners and builders of soil. To build and enrich the soil they need moisture, protection from the sun and protection against the host of larger predators that feed on them.

Loading and removing all the handy-sized loose stones from an area of rangeland for the construction of an erosion control gabion may therefore disrupt a great number of microhabitats, food chains and possibly the productive potential of the soil at the site.

Surface stones in stable rangeland also play an important part in soil erosion prevention. They divert and reduce the speed and force of run-off water and they trap water-carried soil particles and organic matter. They help to trap valuable plant litter and keep it in place over the soil, protecting and enriching the soil and the important detritivores that live in it.

Stones have an important function in rangeland ecology and soil protection and their removal, for whatever purpose, must therefore be very carefully considered.

The range of alternative gully control methods should thus be explored rather than simply using traditional stone gabions. Brush, for example, is a renewable resource, if sensitively harvested, but the removal of a stone cover will modify the structure of a site forever.

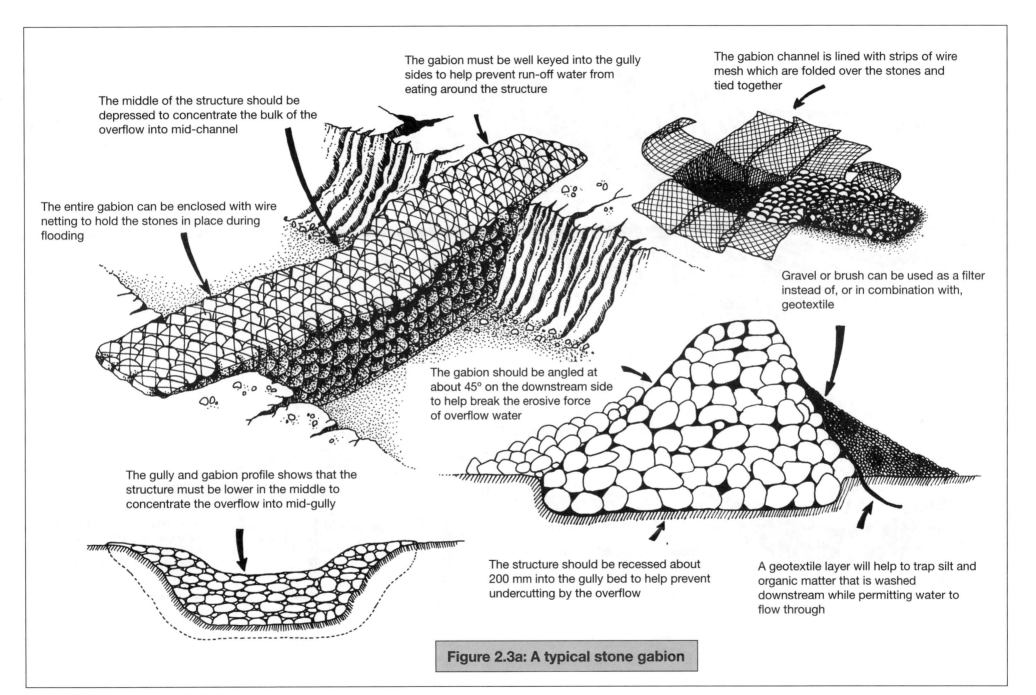

The gabion must be well keyed into the gully sides to help prevent run-off water from eating around the structure

The gabion channel is lined with strips of wire mesh which are folded over the stones and tied together

The middle of the structure should be depressed to concentrate the bulk of the overflow into mid-channel

The entire gabion can be enclosed with wire netting to hold the stones in place during flooding

Gravel or brush can be used as a filter instead of, or in combination with, geotextile

The gabion should be angled at about 45° on the downstream side to help break the erosive force of overflow water

The gully and gabion profile shows that the structure must be lower in the middle to concentrate the overflow into mid-gully

The structure should be recessed about 200 mm into the gully bed to help prevent undercutting by the overflow

A geotextile layer will help to trap silt and organic matter that is washed downstream while permitting water to flow through

Figure 2.3a: A typical stone gabion

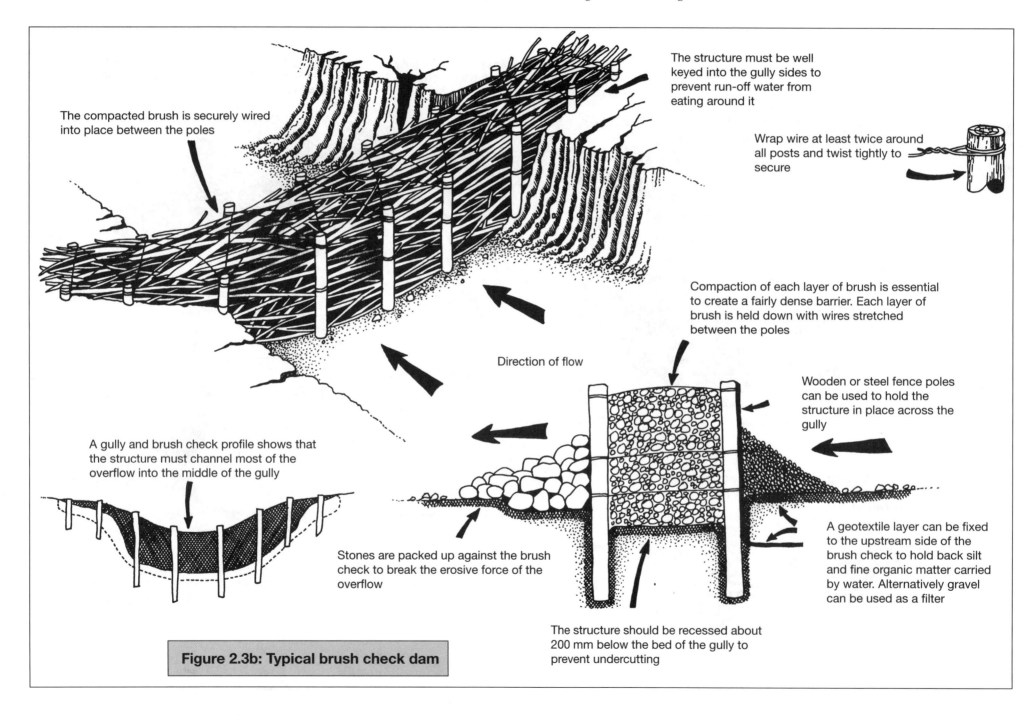

The compacted brush is securely wired into place between the poles

The structure must be well keyed into the gully sides to prevent run-off water from eating around it

Wrap wire at least twice around all posts and twist tightly to secure

Compaction of each layer of brush is essential to create a fairly dense barrier. Each layer of brush is held down with wires stretched between the poles

Direction of flow

Wooden or steel fence poles can be used to hold the structure in place across the gully

A gully and brush check profile shows that the structure must channel most of the overflow into the middle of the gully

Stones are packed up against the brush check to break the erosive force of the overflow

A geotextile layer can be fixed to the upstream side of the brush check to hold back silt and fine organic matter carried by water. Alternatively gravel can be used as a filter

The structure should be recessed about 200 mm below the bed of the gully to prevent undercutting

Figure 2.3b: Typical brush check dam

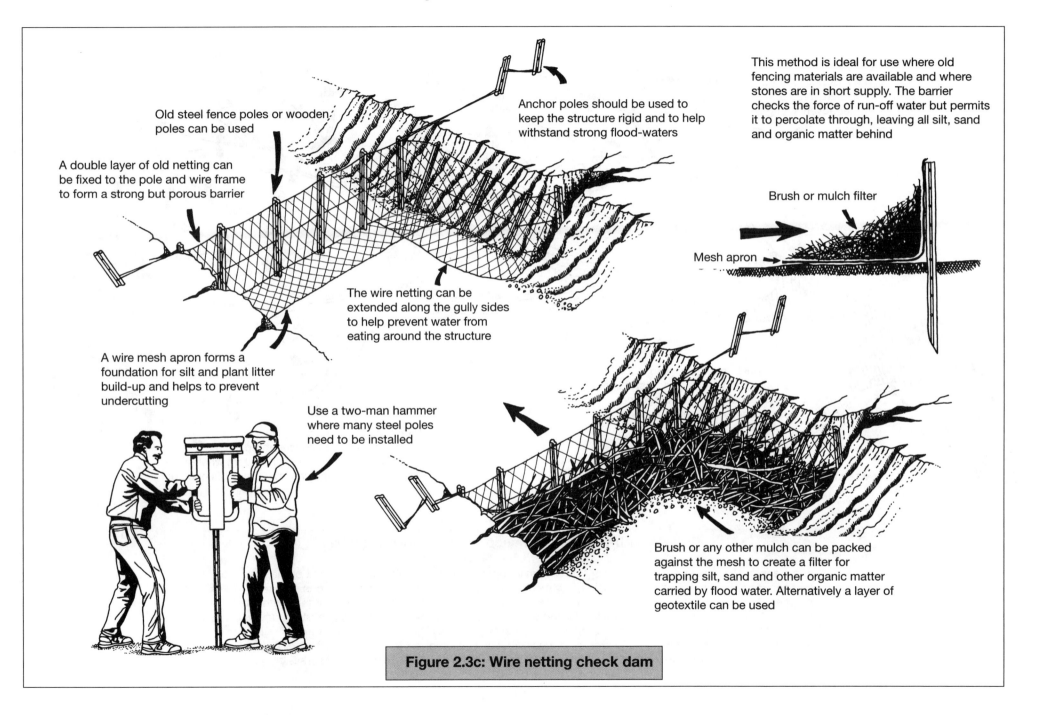

Old steel fence poles or wooden poles can be used

Anchor poles should be used to keep the structure rigid and to help withstand strong flood-waters

This method is ideal for use where old fencing materials are available and where stones are in short supply. The barrier checks the force of run-off water but permits it to percolate through, leaving all silt, sand and organic matter behind

A double layer of old netting can be fixed to the pole and wire frame to form a strong but porous barrier

Brush or mulch filter

Mesh apron

The wire netting can be extended along the gully sides to help prevent water from eating around the structure

A wire mesh apron forms a foundation for silt and plant litter build-up and helps to prevent undercutting

Use a two-man hammer where many steel poles need to be installed

Brush or any other mulch can be packed against the mesh to create a filter for trapping silt, sand and other organic matter carried by flood water. Alternatively a layer of geotextile can be used

Figure 2.3c: Wire netting check dam

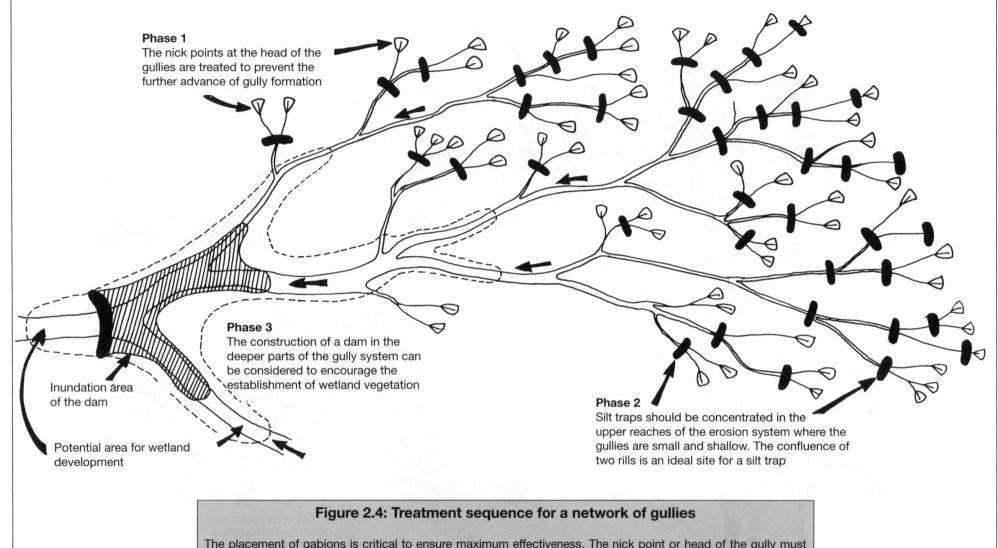

Phase 1
The nick points at the head of the gullies are treated to prevent the further advance of gully formation

Phase 3
The construction of a dam in the deeper parts of the gully system can be considered to encourage the establishment of wetland vegetation

Inundation area of the dam

Potential area for wetland development

Phase 2
Silt traps should be concentrated in the upper reaches of the erosion system where the gullies are small and shallow. The confluence of two rills is an ideal site for a silt trap

Figure 2.4: Treatment sequence for a network of gullies

The placement of gabions is critical to ensure maximum effectiveness. The nick point or head of the gully must be treated first, rather than the gully itself, using modified combinations of the various methods illustrated in this chapter. Once the nick points are treated, the confluences of gullies in the upper reaches of the system can be treated. Attempting to control the erosion further down, in the deeper parts of the gully system, will result in wasted effort and money. Unchecked run-off water will destroy treatment structures and nick points will continue to advance. Once the system is fully stabilised, consideration can be given to the construction of a dam in the lower reaches to encourage wetland development as a treatment for the more deeply eroded areas.

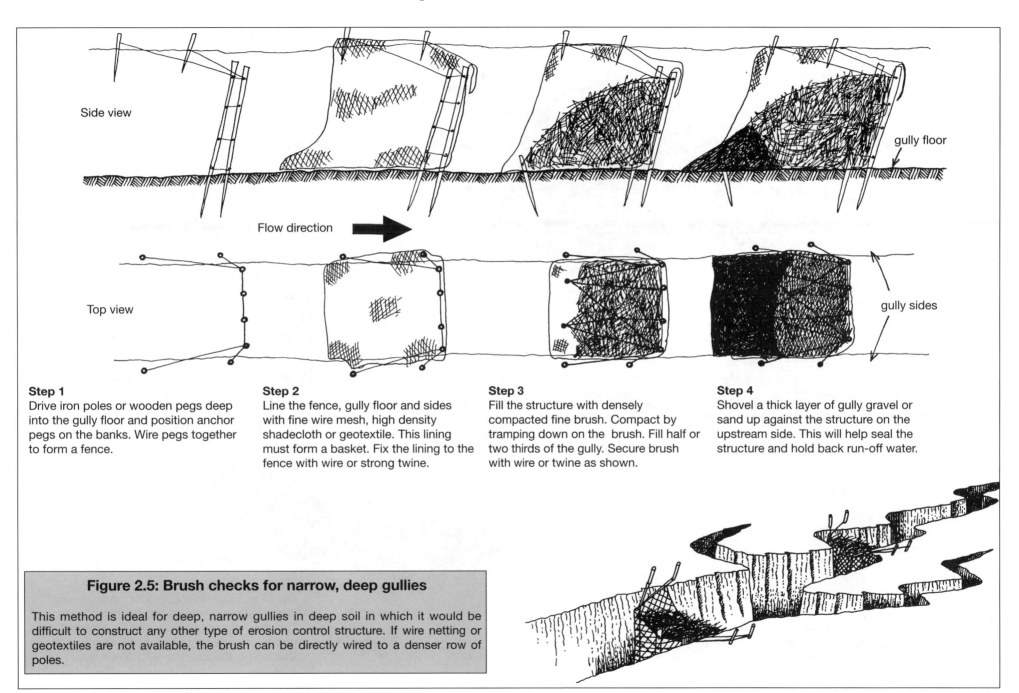

Side view

gully floor

Flow direction

Top view

gully sides

Step 1
Drive iron poles or wooden pegs deep into the gully floor and position anchor pegs on the banks. Wire pegs together to form a fence.

Step 2
Line the fence, gully floor and sides with fine wire mesh, high density shadecloth or geotextile. This lining must form a basket. Fix the lining to the fence with wire or strong twine.

Step 3
Fill the structure with densely compacted fine brush. Compact by tramping down on the brush. Fill half or two thirds of the gully. Secure brush with wire or twine as shown.

Step 4
Shovel a thick layer of gully gravel or sand up against the structure on the upstream side. This will help seal the structure and hold back run-off water.

Figure 2.5: Brush checks for narrow, deep gullies

This method is ideal for deep, narrow gullies in deep soil in which it would be difficult to construct any other type of erosion control structure. If wire netting or geotextiles are not available, the brush can be directly wired to a denser row of poles.

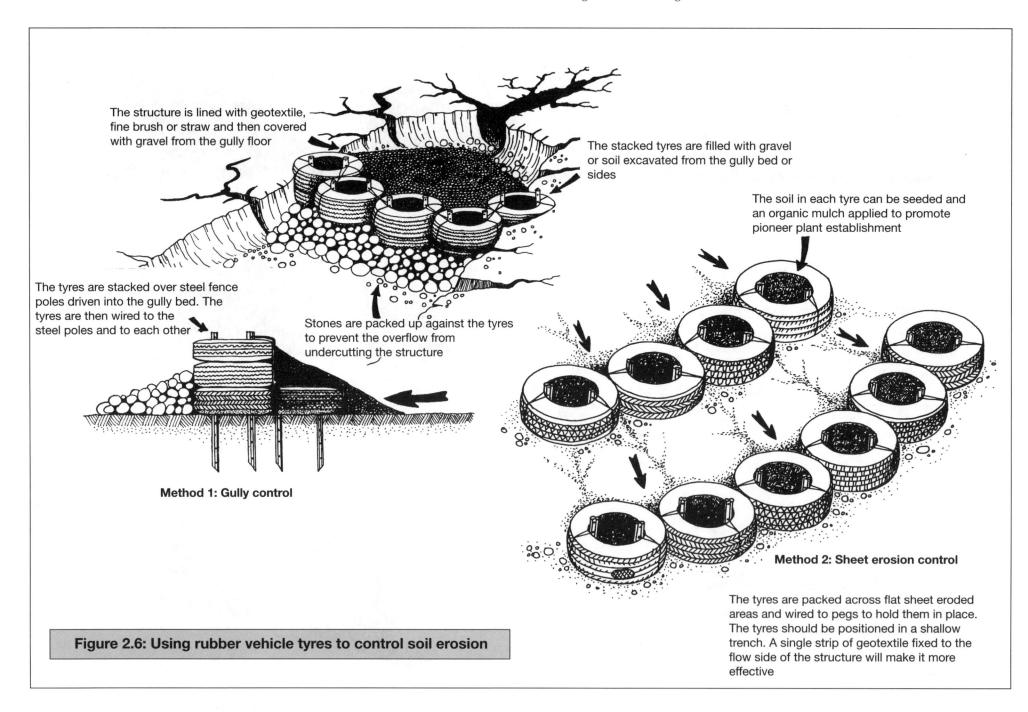

The structure is lined with geotextile, fine brush or straw and then covered with gravel from the gully floor

The stacked tyres are filled with gravel or soil excavated from the gully bed or sides

The soil in each tyre can be seeded and an organic mulch applied to promote pioneer plant establishment

The tyres are stacked over steel fence poles driven into the gully bed. The tyres are then wired to the steel poles and to each other

Stones are packed up against the tyres to prevent the overflow from undercutting the structure

Method 1: Gully control

Method 2: Sheet erosion control

The tyres are packed across flat sheet eroded areas and wired to pegs to hold them in place. The tyres should be positioned in a shallow trench. A single strip of geotextile fixed to the flow side of the structure will make it more effective

Figure 2.6: Using rubber vehicle tyres to control soil erosion

2.4.2 The use of rubber vehicle tyres

Using worn out vehicle tyres for erosion control in rangeland may, at first, seem aesthetically abhorrent, but rubber tyres can be very useful, are freely available, are cheap, and are easy to work with. The tyres can be used to build barriers in erosion gullies and are particularly useful where gullies have become very wide and where water flow can be expected to be fast and destructive. The secret to success in the use of tyres is that the construction must be robust enough to prevent the tyres from being washed down the gully during the first rainstorm after construction.

The tyres are stacked over iron fencing standards which must be driven deeply into the gully floor, as illustrated in Figure 2.6. Each tyre must then be firmly wired in place to the iron standards. As more tyres are stacked on top of each other, each must be wired to the one under it and to the pole. Very secure construction is essential. Care must be taken to key the construction into the gully sides (at least a full tyre depth). Once the desired height is reached, the tyres can be filled with loose soil and gravel from the gully walls or floor. The top tyres in the mid-gully part of the structure should be at least 200 mm lower than the sides at the gully walls. This will concentrate run-off in the middle of the gully.

The structure should then be lined with geotextile, fine brush or even straw on the flow side and then covered with an angled layer of gravel. Packing stones up against the tyres will prevent overflow from eating into the gully floor and thus undermining the barrier. If stones are unavailable, use well-secured brush to break the force of water overflow.

Tyres are particularly useful in areas where natural materials such as stones and brush are not plentiful enough to be used for soil erosion control structures. The rubber does not degrade and will not contaminate the environment. The only problem with using tyres is that they are considered to be unsightly. This can be overcome, to some extent, with a well secured, light covering of camouflaging brush if it is available. Alternatively, the construction can be covered with jute geotextile if jute is used to 'seal' the structure.

Rubber tyres can also be very useful in the control of water flow across sheet-eroded areas. The tyres are simply placed flat, in lines, across the site and securely wired in place to a line of iron standards driven into the ground (see Figure 2.6).

The tyre barrier will slow the water flow enough to ensure increased infiltration. Sand and organic material will also be held in place behind the tyres, helping to improve soil conditions. Wind-blown sand will also be checked by the barrier, as will wind-blown plant debris and seeds. Each tyre can be filled with a fine mulch to create protected sites for seed germination. The soil inside the tyres can be lightly loosened and seeded before the layer of mulch is applied.

Tyres can also be used to stabilise the cut-back at the nick point of erosion gullies. The nick point can be widened to accommodate a single tyre, which must be wired to steel or wooden pegs driven into the earth. The tyre can be filled with compacted gravel or earth into which pioneer vegetation must be established. Mulch can be used to protect germinating seeds. Compacted mulch, fine brush or even gravel can be used to fill any cracks between the outer tyre wall and the soil surface.

Tyres are well suited to the construction of large check dams in wide gullies and if well constructed, can also be used in deep gullies. Tyres can be used effectively to combat severe soil erosion by creating a stepped barrier consisting of layers of filled tyres, starting with the widest layer at the bottom and working up to a single tyre layer at the top.

The key to success, however, with the use of tyres for soil erosion control lies in the manner in which they are retained in position in the gully. The tyres must be firmly secured to anchors driven deeply into the sides and floor of the gully and they must also be wired to each other both horizontally and vertically. This will ensure that the barrier is a rigid and tightly united structure that will not easily be damaged or lost to flooding water.

Further success with the use of tyres can be ensured by filling and compacting each individual tyre in the construction, lining the structure with a pervious geotextile that will hold back water-borne silt and organic material, and quickly establishing the vegetation that will ultimately hold the soil together both on and upstream of the structure.

Tyres are widely used for permaculture gardening as they hold mulched and composted soil in place, keep the moisture in the soil and provide some protection from the elements. The use of discarded rubber tyres also has a recycling function. Discarded tyres are not used for much else and massive stockpiles of tyres are a common site in dumping areas. Burning the vast resource of used tyres will contribute to air pollution. The effective use of used tyres for soil erosion control is thus a largely unexplored option that has tremendous potential in the rehabilitation of degraded landscapes.

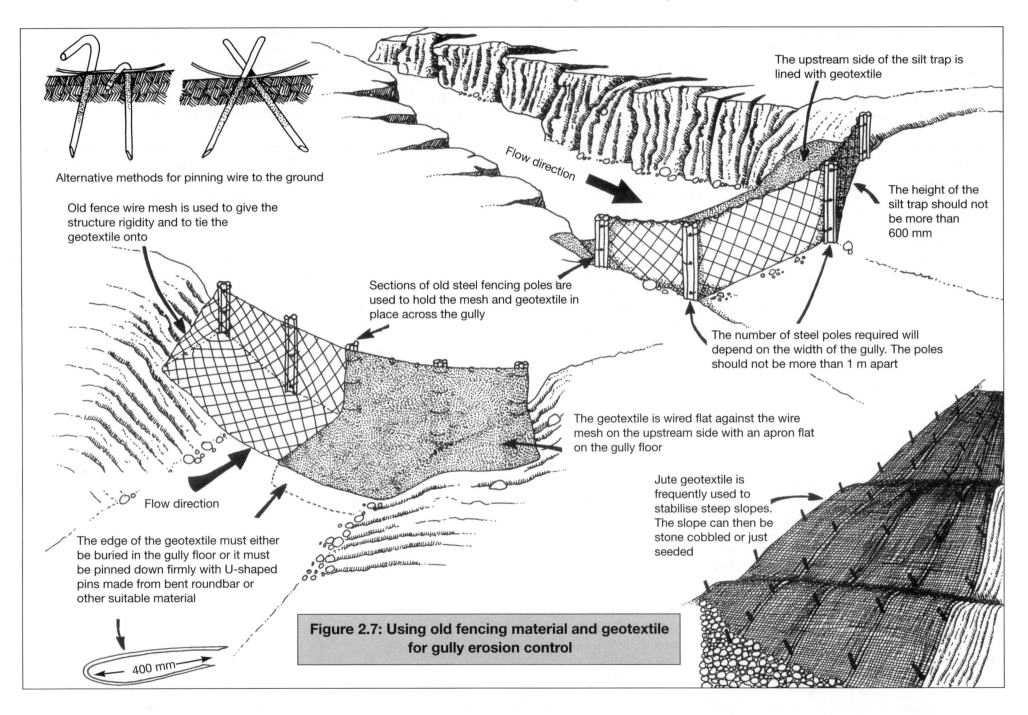

Alternative methods for pinning wire to the ground

Old fence wire mesh is used to give the structure rigidity and to tie the geotextile onto

Sections of old steel fencing poles are used to hold the mesh and geotextile in place across the gully

The edge of the geotextile must either be buried in the gully floor or it must be pinned down firmly with U-shaped pins made from bent roundbar or other suitable material

Flow direction

400 mm

The upstream side of the silt trap is lined with geotextile

The height of the silt trap should not be more than 600 mm

Flow direction

The number of steel poles required will depend on the width of the gully. The poles should not be more than 1 m apart

The geotextile is wired flat against the wire mesh on the upstream side with an apron flat on the gully floor

Jute geotextile is frequently used to stabilise steep slopes. The slope can then be stone cobbled or just seeded

Figure 2.7: Using old fencing material and geotextile for gully erosion control

2.4.3 The use of geotextiles in soil erosion control

Geotextiles, irrespective of the material that they are made from, are an excellent way in which to hold back water-transported silt and organic material, while still permitting water to flow through the barrier.

Geotextiles are either made out of inorganic, woven polypropylene plastic strands or from the organic, natural fibres of the jute plant, coconut coir or sisal. Both products are available in the form of woven netting or cloth of varying aperture size and density. A distinct advantage in the use of the organic products is that they are a completely natural plant fibre which decomposes in time and contributes to the humus content of the soil. Jute can also absorb up to five times its dry weight in water. This can help with the retention of moisture needed for seed germination in rehabilitation projects.

The geotextiles can be used as filters in conjunction with most kinds of erosion control structures. Lining the control structure on the upstream flow side with a layer of geotextile will ensure that all water-transported material is deposited behind the control structure, while allowing water to slowly percolate through. Brush dams can thus be replaced by geotextiles in areas where a suitable bush or tree cover is not available for use in erosion control. Similarly, in areas where handy-sized stones and rocks are in short supply, geotextiles can be used instead, as illustrated in Figure 2.7. Figure 2.8 illustrates the use of shadecloth for gully erosion control. The shadecloth can be replaced by a fine-weave jute or sisal geotextile, if preferred.

Geotextiles, particularly the jute and sisal variety, can also be used as a flat ground cover on exposed, degraded soil surfaces. The material is simply spread over the ground after soil surface loosening and seeding treatments. The geotextile must then be secured in place, either with rows of stones, wooden pegs or bent staples of thick wire.

The geotextile is ideal to use as a ground cover in areas in which brush, reeds or other suitable mulch cover is not available. The jute layer will help to reduce the raindrop splash impact, hold soil particles in place, keep the soil surface temperature down and retain soil moisture. It is, in fact, a wonder treatment and should be more widely used for soil erosion control, particularly in areas where other materials are unavailable. Organic geotextile mats can also be used under stone-packed structures (Figure 2.3), under tyre structures (Figure 2.6), in place of brush-packing (Figure 2.10), to hold back loose soil (Figure 2.11) and to cover newly disturbed contour bunds and earth dam walls (Figures 2.12 and 2.14).

Organic woven geotextile can also be used for a great variety of soil erosion prevention structures associated with road building (refer to Chapter Three).

Jute or sisal geotextile can be effectively used as a silt trap 'bag' as illustrated in Figure 2.8. A weave with a fine mesh size will work best. Once a gully treated in this way is stabilised with vegetation, the geofabric material will slowly decompose, leaving no foreign plastic behind, as is the case with plastic shadecloth or plastic geotextile. A good practical tip is that one should line all rock gabions, brush checks and other gully erosion control structures with geotextiles.

Steep, unstable slopes are often stabilised with layers of jute geotextiles which will keep the soil surface in place, improve the moisture regime of the slope and reduce raindrop splash erosion, as illustrated in Figure 2.7.

Organic geotextiles can be used very effectively to restore sheet-eroded areas or other areas that are devoid of a vegetation cover. The first step is to loosen the soil lightly in strips across the area by hand or with a tractor-drawn implement to break the surface-sealing crust. The loosened strips are then seeded with a suitable fast-growing pioneer such as grass.

The strips are then covered with a 100–200 mm layer of mulch. This can be any organic material such as crop residue, hay, cut grass, wood chips, leaf litter or chopped reeds. Once the mulching is complete, a strip of geotextile is laid over the treated area and pinned down with steel wire hooked pins or wooden pegs. The textile will prevent the loss of the mulch during windy conditions and will also help to create a protective organic soil blanket which will improve the soil surface microclimate for the germinating grass seeds.

This method has wide application potential and is suitable for restoring a vegetation cover on disturbed slopes, borrow pit sites, behind gabions and other gully checks and any other unnaturally exposed soil surfaces.

Although geotextiles (both the organic and the inorganic) are relatively expensive, they do provide an excellent alternative where organic mulching materials are in short supply and where extreme weather conditions may damage efforts to re-establish a protective vegetation cover. Geotextiles are much quicker to install than other organic mulch cover options and they are often more robust than most natural mulches, needing little maintenance. There is therefore usually a cost saving to be made in terms of installation time and maintenance when using geotextiles.

The use of geotextile is a practical and robust option for most erosion control applications and should be seriously considered in any soil erosion control planning exercise.

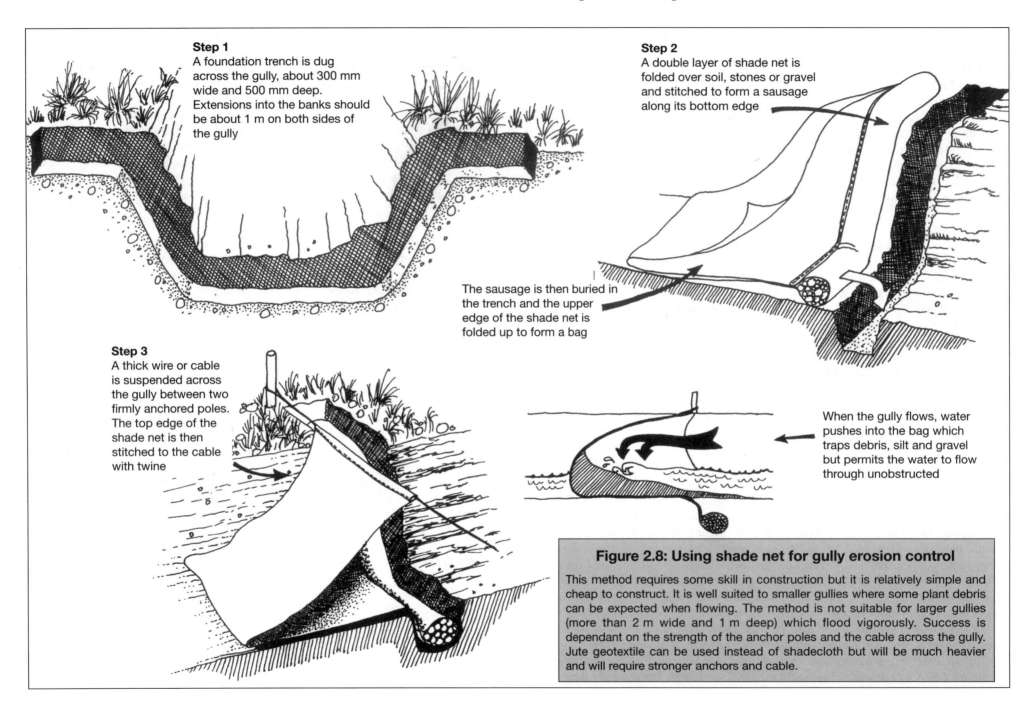

Step 1
A foundation trench is dug across the gully, about 300 mm wide and 500 mm deep. Extensions into the banks should be about 1 m on both sides of the gully

Step 2
A double layer of shade net is folded over soil, stones or gravel and stitched to form a sausage along its bottom edge

The sausage is then buried in the trench and the upper edge of the shade net is folded up to form a bag

Step 3
A thick wire or cable is suspended across the gully between two firmly anchored poles. The top edge of the shade net is then stitched to the cable with twine

When the gully flows, water pushes into the bag which traps debris, silt and gravel but permits the water to flow through unobstructed

Figure 2.8: Using shade net for gully erosion control

This method requires some skill in construction but it is relatively simple and cheap to construct. It is well suited to smaller gullies where some plant debris can be expected when flowing. The method is not suitable for larger gullies (more than 2 m wide and 1 m deep) which flood vigorously. Success is dependant on the strength of the anchor poles and the cable across the gully. Jute geotextile can be used instead of shadecloth but will be much heavier and will require stronger anchors and cable.

BOX 2.5

Animal impact and rangeland rehabilitation

Using its powerful claws the shy aardvark digs extensive burrow systems in which to sleep by day. When unoccupied these burrows collapse, forming large hollows in which wind-blown organic material and plant seeds collect and in which water collects when it rains. In this way, a perfect site for plant establishment is created, even in areas of hard compacted earth formerly devoid of any vegetation cover.

When foraging the aardvark digs into underground termite nests and then licks up the angry swarming termites with its sticky tongue. A foraging aardvark may dig into many nests in one night, leaving behind it a string of holes in which plant material, seeds and water can collect, forming new sites for seed germination. These holes are broken through the hard, crusted soil surfaces, thereby enabling the infiltration of rainwater that would otherwise have run-off into the nearest drainage channel.

Many other animals also dig while foraging. Diggers like porcupines, foxes, mongooses, badgers and baboons assist with the cycle of natural rangeland rehabilitation when they dig for food. Similarly, burrows of animals like whistling rats, gerbils, moles, ground squirrels and some mongooses contribute to increased rainwater infiltration.

Much smaller burrowing animals like the vast numbers of scorpions, dung beetles, wasps and spiders that we seldom see, also make their considerable contribution to improved rainwater infiltration.

Some non-diggers that also participate in rangeland rejuvenation are large heavy herbivores like eland, buffalo, rhinoceros, hippopotamus and elephant which leave deep footprints in soft or wet soil. These hoof prints trap plant debris, wind-blown seeds and rainwater, all of which results in improved seed germination opportunities.

Simulating the 'diggers', by making artificial hollows in degraded areas where soil surfaces have become capped and are impervious to rainwater infiltration, promotes rehabilitation. The rehabilitation process can even be somewhat accelerated by treating these hollows with manure, a protective vegetation cover and by seeding each hollow shortly before rains. This simple but effective method of rangeland rehabilitation, which we have learned by observing the aardvark and other animals, is illustrated in detail in Figure 2.9.

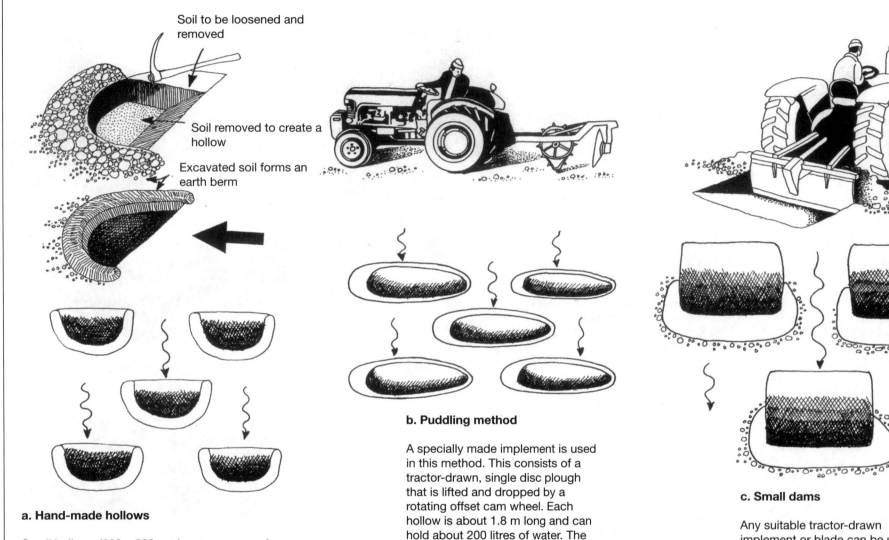

Soil to be loosened and removed

Soil removed to create a hollow

Excavated soil forms an earth berm

a. Hand-made hollows

Small hollows (600 x 500 mm) can be cut by hand using a pick and shovel. This method is suitable for smaller capped areas. The excavated soil is piled to form a low berm on the down-slope. Hollows can be approximately 2 m apart in rows 1 m apart.

b. Puddling method

A specially made implement is used in this method. This consists of a tractor-drawn, single disc plough that is lifted and dropped by a rotating offset cam wheel. Each hollow is about 1.8 m long and can hold about 200 litres of water. The rows of hollows can be approximately 1 to 2 m apart.

c. Small dams

Any suitable tractor-drawn implement or blade can be used. The size of the hollow thus depends on the size of the implement used. Depending on the soil, hollows can be cut to a depth of between 200 and 800 mm. The hollows can be made 2 m apart in rows that are 2 m apart.

Figure 2.9: The use of hollows to control soil erosion

2.4.4   Using hollows or puddles for rehabilitation

The method involves making hollows for water collection across the soil surface, resulting in the following:

- Hollows, or small dams, which break through impervious soil capping and in which run-off water collects during rainstorms, resulting in infiltration rather than run-off.
- The cumulative and erosive run-off on degraded rangeland can be slowed down, and much of it held back, by means of an extensive network of hollows.
- Silt and organic material transported by run-off water collects in the hollows and is permanently retained in them and not lost to the area.
- Wind-blown seeds, humus, animal droppings and dry plant material also collect in the hollows. After rains seeds germinate in the moist soil of the hollows and are protected as they grow, by the accumulated plant debris.
- A network of hollows covering a degraded area results in numerous protected plant establishment sites helping to transform and improve the soil moisture and microclimate of the area. Effective rehabilitation becomes possible under the more favourable microclimatic conditions in the hollows.
- Hollows also provide some protection from the effects of wind erosion.

It must, however, be appreciated that a total vegetation cover is dependent on the long-term rainfall and position of a particular site in the landscape. It would be unreasonable to expect a total cover of perennial plants in an area with a rainfall of below 250 mm per year. The expectation should rather be to help the site attain a former, more natural condition, albeit a sparse cover of pioneer vegetation. Reactivating natural processes on a formerly degraded site is thus the practical objective. Figure 2.9a illustrates the construction of hand-made hollows suitable for treating capped bare areas on uneven terrain. The curved section lies in the downstream direction of water flow and helps to dam run-off water. The hard soil capping is loosened with a pick to a depth of the pick tine. The loosened soil is then shovelled onto the curved edge to form a low earth retaining wall. These hollows can be made 2 m apart, in rows that are 1.5 m apart. A large number can be made inexpensively by one person in a day.

If, for example, only 50 hollows are made by hand in one day, and each one holds 50 litres of water, approximately 2 500 litres of rainwater will be held back and will infiltrate the soil through the hollows. Formerly, all of the 2 500 litres of water would have been lost into the nearest drainage system with little or no contribution to soil moisture and the local water table.

The puddling plough, illustrated in Figure 2.9b, can be specially made for treating extensive, capped and exposed areas. This simple implement is drawn by a tractor and makes a line of small dams which are approximately 1.8 m long, 300 mm wide and 250 mm deep, with the water-holding capacity of each being about 136 litres. Rows of hollows are made 2 m apart and must lie across the direction of water flow. In this way an entire patch can be worked into a series of hollows that trap run-off water after every rainstorm.

It is extremely important that implements such as the puddling plough are used with great care in areas that do still have some vegetation cover. It would make very little sense to rip out the roots, or whole plants, of already established vegetation in an effort to restore a protective vegetation cover. In areas with widely spaced or sparse cover, it would be more practical to cut hollows by hand in between the plants so that the existing plants are not disturbed. It is important to remember that every individual rooted plant within any restoration area is valuable. They provide shade for seedlings, intercept raindrops, protect the soil, produce seeds and organic mulch and harbour a range of micro-fauna. These are exactly the services that are required for restoration of the landscape.

With such an implement and the will to improve vast patches of degraded rangeland, large volumes of run-off water can be harvested and used for plant establishment. Only 100 hollows will ensure the infiltration of approximately 13 600 litres of precious moisture.

Another method, using a machine with ordinary grader, bulldozer or loader blades and buckets for constructing small dams, is illustrated in Figure 2.9c. The principle is exactly the same as for the previous two methods, except that a larger water storage hollow is made. Rectangular hollows are made with an earth wall on the 'downstream side'. These small dams can be approximately 3–4 m long, 1.5–2 m wide and 50–100 cm deep.

These larger hollows must be further treated with the application of a 100–200 mm layer of organic mulch or fine brush-packing. The reason for this is that the soil of the larger hollow may again seal after the first few rains. The mulch will keep it moist and encourage new topsoil formation and the germination of seedlings. Rangeland restoration using hollows can be greatly advanced by seeding and mulching each hollow. Commercially available seed can be used or seed can be harvested directly from the range. Grass seed is most effective, but pioneer annual and perennial shrubs can also be sown. Care must, however, be taken to try to establish plants that are suitably adapted to the harsh environmental conditions in the degraded rehabilitation area.

A little animal manure added to each hollow will help to improve soil quality, and mulching with any available organic plant material or finely chopped brush will help to protect germinating seedlings and keep the soil moist.

Hollows, or zaï, have been traditionally used in northern Africa since ancient times for improving degraded farming land as crop planting pits in arid areas. Usually about 10 cm deep, the zaï are dug out with a traditional hoe. The pits are made in lines across the field and a small amount of manure is added to each pit before the first rains.

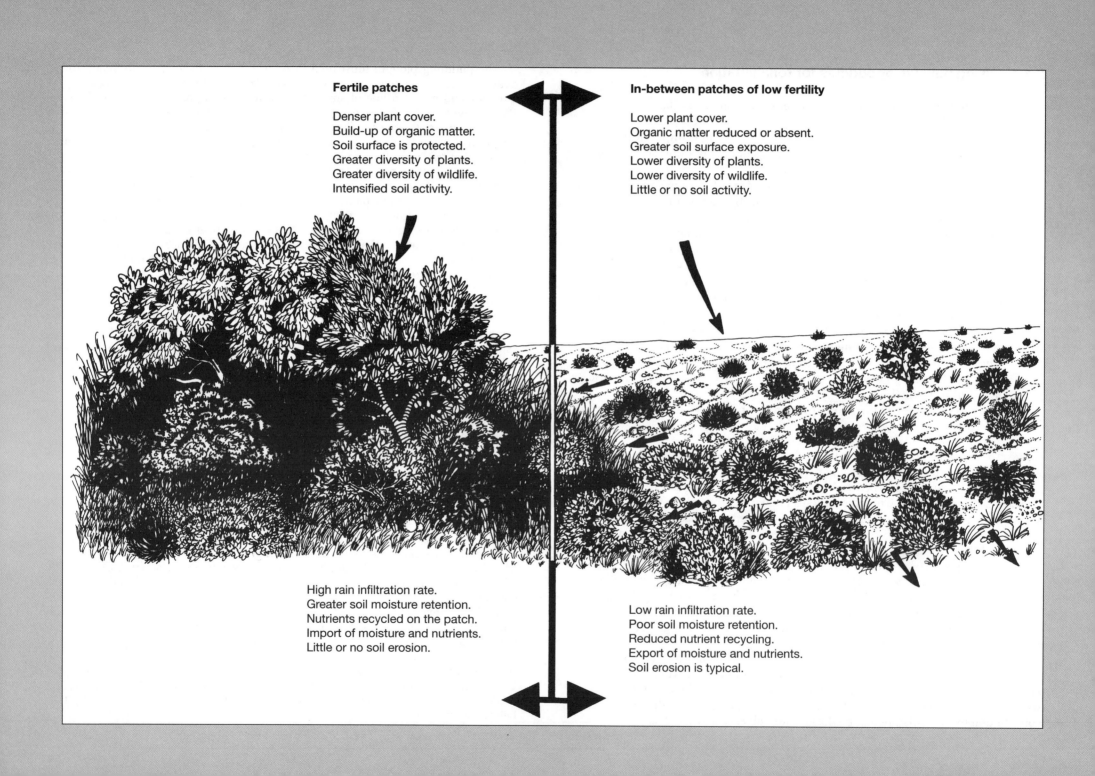

Fertile patches

Denser plant cover.
Build-up of organic matter.
Soil surface is protected.
Greater diversity of plants.
Greater diversity of wildlife.
Intensified soil activity.

In-between patches of low fertility

Lower plant cover.
Organic matter reduced or absent.
Greater soil surface exposure.
Lower diversity of plants.
Lower diversity of wildlife.
Little or no soil activity.

High rain infiltration rate.
Greater soil moisture retention.
Nutrients recycled on the patch.
Import of moisture and nutrients.
Little or no soil erosion.

Low rain infiltration rate.
Poor soil moisture retention.
Reduced nutrient recycling.
Export of moisture and nutrients.
Soil erosion is typical.

BOX 2.6

Fertile patches in rangeland

A very interesting characteristic of natural rangelands is the seemingly random occurrence of fertile patches. These patches are sites within a landscape where nutrients and soil water accumulate, making the fertility much higher than in the 'between-patch' areas. Soil stability is high and soil erosion is therefore rarely found in these patches. Because of the higher fertility the patches contribute significantly to overall range production. They are a kind of habitat oasis, providing quality forage and cover for a great variety of animals that cannot be sustainably supported in the between-patch areas. Termites and ants, spiders and scorpions, lizards and snakes, rodents, small carnivores and a variety of birdlife all focus their life activities on these fertile patches and thereby contribute to the fertility of the patch. Larger herbivores are attracted by better quality grazing and also help to fertilise the patches with their dung and urine. The burrowing activities of many of these animals ensure a mixing of soil nutrients and the aeration of the soil that helps to improve rainfall infiltration rates.

There is also a constant recycling of nutrients within the patch with little of the nutrients being lost from the patch as is the case with the between-patch areas. Run-off water from the between-patch areas continually brings additional nutrients and moisture to the patch and this is enhanced by the accelerated run-off from the more impervious soils of the between-patch areas. The replenishment of fertile patches also occurs through wind deposition, with the denser vegetation of the patch functioning as an effective trap for wind-carried silt, organic material and new seeds.

The capacity of a patch to accumulate and retain resources is often largely due to physical landscape features such as shallow depressions, lower pediments, flat areas within broken landscapes and drainage lines.

By encouraging the formation of fertile patches on degraded rangeland it is possible to rehabilitate these areas. Methods of erosion control that trap water and nutrients, preserve soil moisture, provide protected sites for plant germination and also eventually provide some cover for animals, are illustrated in Figures 2.6, 2.9 and 2.10. The use of these methods will not only control soil erosion but can also be the beginning of the restoration of former fertile patches.

When planning restoration action it is wise to take cognisance of typical fertile patch sites in the landscape and to initiate restoration work within these sites of former or future fertility. Examples of typical fertile patch sites include eroded drainages, low-lying former marshy sites, degraded floodplain sites, eroded and overgrazed valley floors and hollows. Initiating restoration actions within these areas in which water collects, or used to collect, will yield the desired results quicker than in the drier sites between them.

In some deserts and semi-desert rangelands fertile patches are the direct result of animal activity. These patches (or mima mounds) appear in the landscape as evenly-spaced circular mounds that usually support a visibly different vegetation to the general area, both in terms of species and plant form.

The reason why these patches are different is because they are more fertile than the adjacent areas due to the activities of harvester termites that live in them. The termites process the soil, making it finer, more alkaline and considerably more fertile. This process occurs when the termites bring organic material into their nests, use it for food and compost and eventually convert it into faeces which they deposit on the surface of the patch. This activity, over long periods, also improves the capacity of the soil in the patch to retain water. The combination of higher soil fertility and higher soil moisture content therefore makes these patches ideal sites in which the plants of wetter habitats can thrive within more arid surroundings.

Vegetation develops and flourishes and these patches provide excellent opportunities for a range of indigenous grazing and browsing herbivores but are, unfortunately, also targeted by domestic stock which thrive on the quality patch grazing. Overstocking and the subsequent continuous over-utilisation of these fertile patches results in a change in the vegetation, reducing it from a high diversity of palatable perennial plants to a low diversity of pioneer plants. Continuous over-utilisation of the patches, as well as the intervening areas, may eventually lead to the 'death' of the patch which then becomes bare soil that is vulnerable to wind and water erosion.

In areas where mima mounds have become severely degraded it would make good sense to restore them, or at least help them to restore themselves. As a first step, severely disturbed mounds should be fenced off to keep grazing and browsing herbivores from feeding on the struggling pioneer vegetation on them. The mounds can then be treated with a protective layer of organic mulch into which a variety of local pioneer plant seeds can be sown. Once a protective cover is established a greater diversity of plants typical of the mounds can be established within the fenced area. The fence should be retained until the site is fully recovered, a process that may take many years.

It is clear that the natural processes that involve the soil, the animals that live in it and the vegetation that grows on it, must be treasured and nurtured if rangeland productivity is to be maintained.

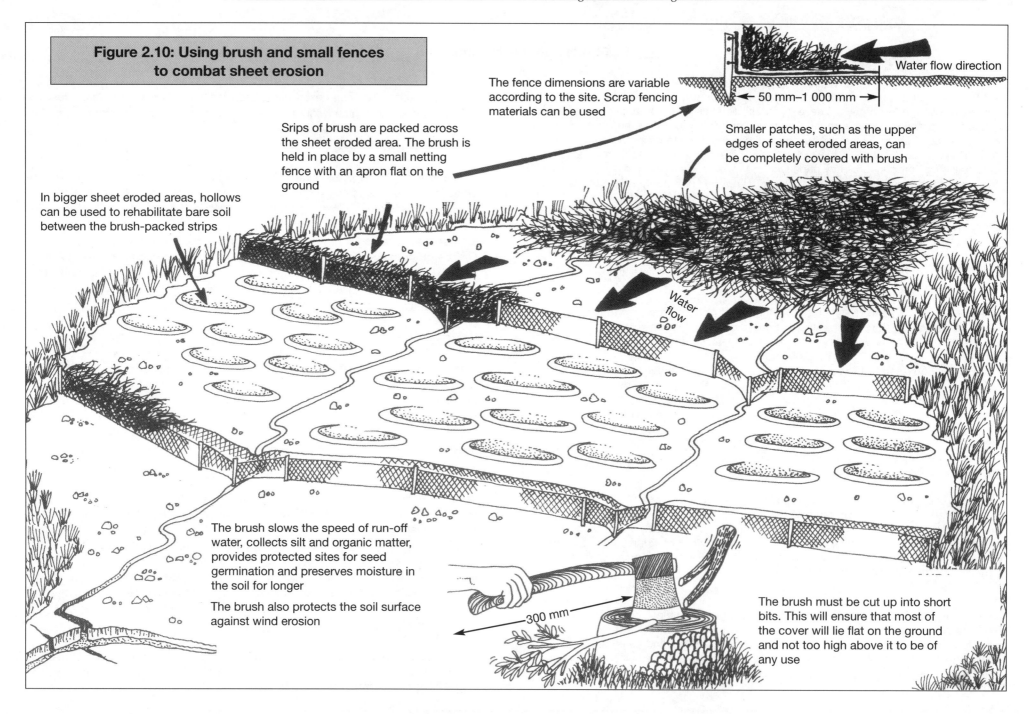

Figure 2.10: Using brush and small fences to combat sheet erosion

The fence dimensions are variable according to the site. Scrap fencing materials can be used

Water flow direction

← 50 mm–1 000 mm →

Srips of brush are packed across the sheet eroded area. The brush is held in place by a small netting fence with an apron flat on the ground

Smaller patches, such as the upper edges of sheet eroded areas, can be completely covered with brush

In bigger sheet eroded areas, hollows can be used to rehabilitate bare soil between the brush-packed strips

Water flow

The brush slows the speed of run-off water, collects silt and organic matter, provides protected sites for seed germination and preserves moisture in the soil for longer

The brush also protects the soil surface against wind erosion

←— 300 mm —→

The brush must be cut up into short bits. This will ensure that most of the cover will lie flat on the ground and not too high above it to be of any use

2.4.5   Brush-packing, mulching and creating a microclimate

Brush-packing, or mulching, is done by covering the soil surface with organic plant material such as branches, plant cuttings, leafy material, crop residues, straw and reeds. This treatment on exposed soil simulates the protective effect of a plant cover. The brush-packing or mulching is a valuable soil erosion control method due to the following:

- It functions as a protection against rain splash erosion.
- It assists with the retention of moisture in the soil.
- It decreases soil temperature and thereby improves the microclimate for soil organisms and germinating plants.
- It restricts soil and humus movement in run-off by collecting soil and organic material particles against the network of branches or mulch material lying on the soil surface.
- It protects the exposed soil against the effects of wind erosion and also serves to trap wind-blown sand grains.
- A mulch of chopped branches will protect germinating plants from grazing animals that seek out new succulent growth.
- It eventually decays and contributes to the organic content of the topsoil.
- It traps wind-blown plant seeds.
- It creates cover habitat for soil-living animals that burrow and help to aerate the soil.

Brush and mulch are spread evenly over the soil and should cover at least 70–75% of the soil surface to prevent soil erosion effectively. The correct quantity to put down depends on the type of brush or mulch used – too little will not protect the soil adequately and too much will suppress plant growth. A good rule of thumb is that the material used must not form a sealed cover. Sunlight, water and air must be able to infiltrate the layer freely to ensure successful plant germination and growth.

When using branches take care to cut the material up so that most of it lies relatively flat on the soil surface, giving it maximum protection. Branches can be packed in a 200 mm thick layer. When using reeds cut them up into short lengths and pack no thicker than about 100 mm as they can form a dense seal when they decompose, with the material being finer than brush. When using finer organic material it is a good idea to spread the material together with some coarser branch material so that a sealed surface does not form.

Brush-packing can be used in conjunction with almost any other soil control method or as a method on its own. In Figure 2.10 it is used together with small retaining 'fences' and hollows. The low fences are constructed across sloping sites to hold the brush-packing in place in strips across the site. In Figure 2.5 compacted brush-packing is used to block up deep narrow gullies and is held in place with anchored wire netting. In many cases brush-packing alone may be all that is required. In windy areas finer material may have to be held down with wire netting, geotextile or wire strands pegged over the brush-packed surface. Sometimes a few stones or bigger branches scattered over the mulch layer will be sufficient to prevent removal by strong wind.

Brush-packing or mulching is an ideal method for controlling water and wind erosion on exposed degraded soil surfaces in areas where a plentiful source of harvestable material is available. In areas where brush or mulch is limited, use should rather be made of the puddling method, or hollows as illustrated in Figure 2.9, or of organic geotextiles which can be used as a ground cover, as illustrated in Figure 2.7.

When harvesting brush for erosion control work, take care to harvest in such a way that no area is completely cleared of cover, especially the area adjacent to the system to be treated. Cut out every third bush some distance above the ground, or remove only 20% of the lower branches of each alternative bush or tree. Most woody plants used in this way will simply resprout and suffer no ill effects at all.

Brush material cleared away from roadways, fence-lines or construction sites is ideal for use in soil erosion control projects. Low grade agricultural by-products like oats or wheat hay, maize hay or any other organic chaff can also be used for mulching but will have to be held in place with wire netting, shadecloth or geofabric to prevent its removal by wind. These lighter types of mulch will, however, not last as long as chipped or chopped woody brush.

An excellent way to produce good quality mulch is to feed branches and other plant material through a chipper/shredder machine. Portable shredders are available in a range of capacity sizes. Bigger ones are capable of shredding branches of about 50 mm in diameter. A trailer-mounted chipper would be a very useful tool for bigger restoration projects, as it can be positioned and used at the site to be mulched. Chippers are particularly useful in areas where alien vegetation control programmes produce voluminous amounts of waste in the form of woody and leafy branch material.

Chipper machines, however, are very expensive and only really big restoration projects in which large amounts of chipped mulch will be used would warrant the purchase of one. They are powered by either diesel or petrol motors and the cost and availability of fuel is a further expense that must be carefully considered during the planning phase of the restoration project.

For smaller projects woody brush can simply be cut up by hand using either a slasher (mattox) or hand axe, on a log or tree stump base.

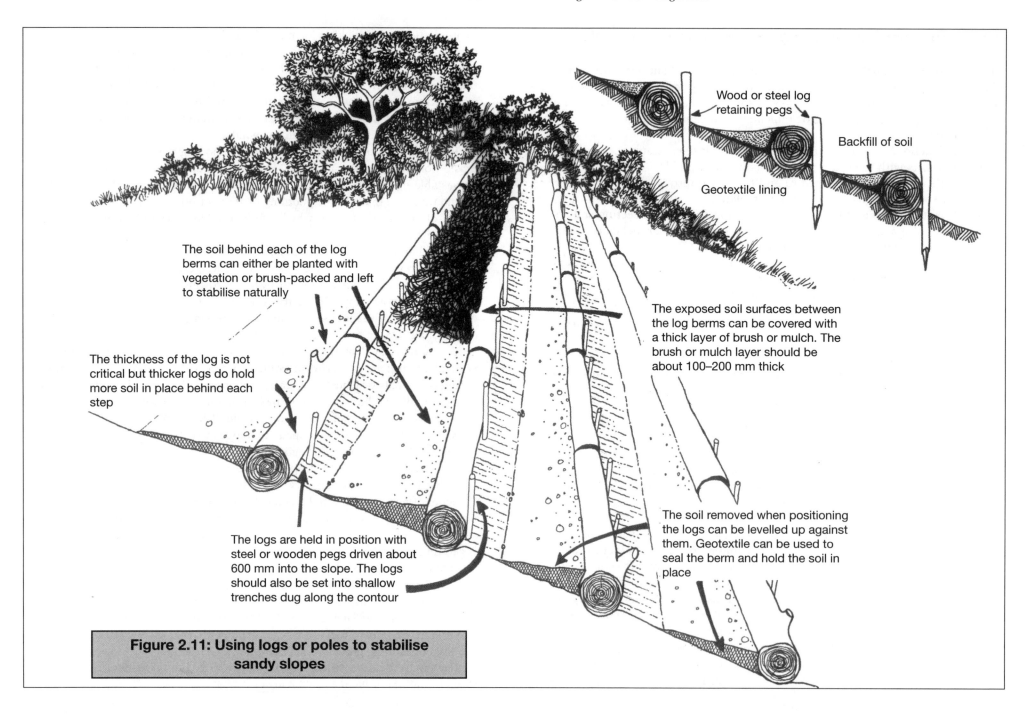

Wood or steel log retaining pegs

Backfill of soil

Geotextile lining

The soil behind each of the log berms can either be planted with vegetation or brush-packed and left to stabilise naturally

The thickness of the log is not critical but thicker logs do hold more soil in place behind each step

The logs are held in position with steel or wooden pegs driven about 600 mm into the slope. The logs should also be set into shallow trenches dug along the contour

The exposed soil surfaces between the log berms can be covered with a thick layer of brush or mulch. The brush or mulch layer should be about 100–200 mm thick

The soil removed when positioning the logs can be levelled up against them. Geotextile can be used to seal the berm and hold the soil in place

Figure 2.11: Using logs or poles to stabilise sandy slopes

2.4.6 The use of logs to combat soil erosion on slopes

As illustrated in Figure 2.11, logs or poles can be used as contour berms to create terraces that inhibit accelerated run-off on sandy slopes or slopes with loose, disturbed soil surfaces.

This method is only practical if logs are freely available or affordable in the area. It is often possible to combine the eradication of invasive alien trees, such as Eucalyptus species, with soil erosion control as illustrated. Thick wooden fencing poles can also be used and if it is more practical the logs can be replaced with large stones or rocks.

This method can also be used to stabilise severely eroded slopes but it will be necessary to fill the erosion gullies behind the logs with stone or dense brush with a geotextile lining to inhibit concentrated water flow. Before the brush-packing can take place, the gullies need to be blocked off to prevent storm-water from simply undercutting the log barriers.

This method is well suited to the establishment of vegetation behind the log barriers. The loose soil can be 'reshaped' up against the logs and a furrow made, in which run-off water will collect and in which plants can be established.

Use of this method, or variations of it, will ensure that topsoil is not lost down-slope, resulting in the exposure of infertile sub-surfaces. Where erosion has already taken place, use of this method will help to stabilise the slope and recreate fertile topsoil conditions.

Logs are relatively cheap, when available, and are particularly well suited for the rehabilitation of construction sites, after earth-moving or the clearing away of vegetation cover, before soil erosion can occur on the site.

The brush-packed strip behind the log barriers should be seeded with locally compatible fast-growing plants like grasses and annual pioneer plants. Once a vegetation cover is established, trees and shrubs can be planted behind the berms to help the rehabilitation process further.

The distance between the log berms will vary with slope steepness. On slopes as steep as 45°, the log berms will need to be closer together to ensure a sufficient depth and width of topsoil infill to cover the bare slope for vegetation establishment. On less steep slopes of between 40° and 15°, the topsoil infill can be spread up over the bare slope surface in between the log berms. The gentler angle of these slopes will ensure that most of the topsoil infill will stay in place, and even in extreme climates the log berms will keep most of the topsoil infill in place.

The finely chopped vegetation mulch that should be spread over the topsoil infill will also help to prevent soil losses during extreme weather conditions.

BOX 2.7

Attracting wildlife that can assist with rehabilitation

Useful animals can be attracted to degraded sites where rehabilitation projects are implemented in the following ways:

- Brush-packing: Provides cover for a large number of animals including reptiles, rodents, hares, small carnivores and a host of invertebrates. These creatures all leave their droppings and remnants of their meals, which decompose and help to build up the organic component of the topsoil. Many of them burrow into the soil, which helps with infiltration of rainwater.

- Perches for birds: Can be provided to attract seed- and fruit-eating birds. These birds then leave their droppings in the area. The droppings may contain viable plant seeds that can germinate and help to re-establish a protective plant cover.

- Seeding: By re-establishing a vegetation cover such as pioneer grasses and shrubs, forage is made available for herbivores such as tortoises, hares and rabbits, rodents and small antelope. These animals leave their droppings behind and this attracts a host of detritivores including dung beetles. Dung beetles bury balls of dung to feed themselves and their larvae and also tunnel into the soil which helps increase rainwater infiltration.

- Manuring and topsoiling: Both actions help to build up the organic content of the soil that is usually lost when soil erosion occurs. Nutrients, as well as soil organisms are introduced. Sods of healthy topsoil from nearby sites can be put in under areas of brush-packing. This will also help to restore soil fungi on which so many organisms are dependent. Improvement of the topsoil will recreate habitat and encourage soil organisms on which so many other smaller predators like lizards, snakes, birds and insectivores are dependent.

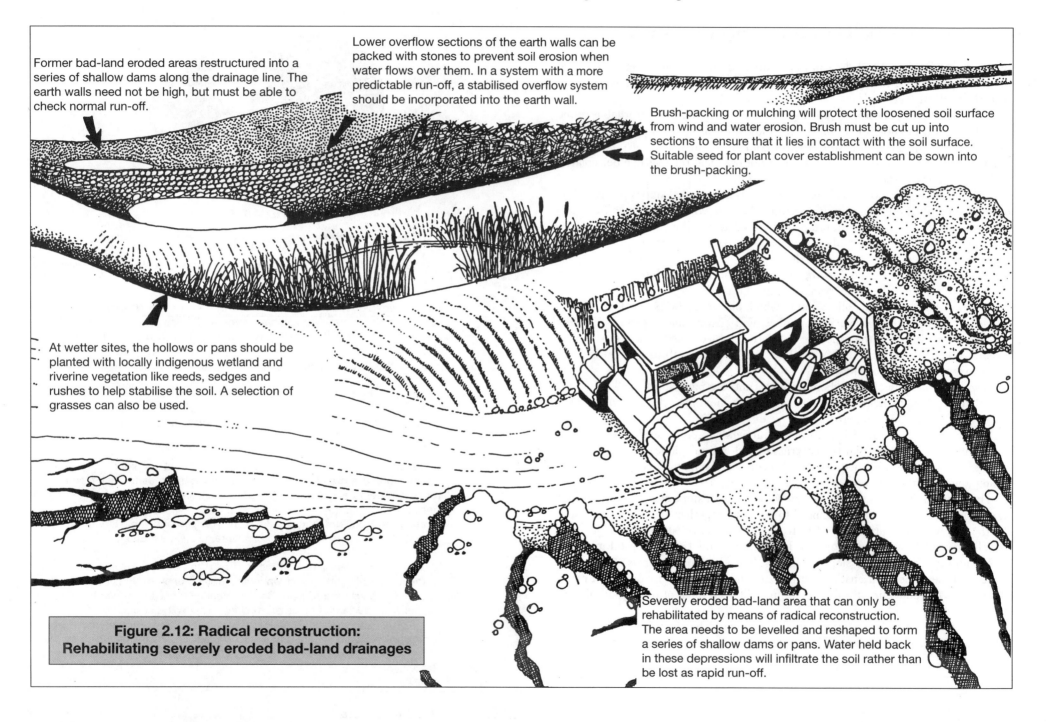

Former bad-land eroded areas restructured into a series of shallow dams along the drainage line. The earth walls need not be high, but must be able to check normal run-off.

Lower overflow sections of the earth walls can be packed with stones to prevent soil erosion when water flows over them. In a system with a more predictable run-off, a stabilised overflow system should be incorporated into the earth wall.

Brush-packing or mulching will protect the loosened soil surface from wind and water erosion. Brush must be cut up into sections to ensure that it lies in contact with the soil surface. Suitable seed for plant cover establishment can be sown into the brush-packing.

At wetter sites, the hollows or pans should be planted with locally indigenous wetland and riverine vegetation like reeds, sedges and rushes to help stabilise the soil. A selection of grasses can also be used.

Severely eroded bad-land area that can only be rehabilitated by means of radical reconstruction. The area needs to be levelled and reshaped to form a series of shallow dams or pans. Water held back in these depressions will infiltrate the soil rather than be lost as rapid run-off.

**Figure 2.12: Radical reconstruction:
Rehabilitating severely eroded bad-land drainages**

2.4.7   The radical reconstruction of eroded bad-lands

This method should only be used for areas where severe, unchecked soil erosion has resulted in irrecoverable and desiccated bad-lands with extensive networks of deep gullies. These areas are characterised by near vertical-sided gullies with crumbling surfaces that cut across the catchment area, often with less than a metre of the original soil surface between the gullies. Only small remnants of the original vegetation occur on these desiccated narrow islands between the gullies.

The approach to radical reconstruction is illustrated in Figure 2.12. It basically consists of the complete reconstruction of the eroded site by flattening the gully-eroded area and establishing a stepped series of shallow pans, or small shallow dams. These small dams check and hold back run-off water, but more importantly, they provide protected sites for plant cover establishment. The technique must include aspects of the previously described methods as illustrated in Figures 2.3, 2.6, 2.7, 2.10 and 2.11.

Care must be taken to provide adequately for the natural drainage off the site. Water will flow, especially after heavy thunderstorms, so adequate provision must be made to accommodate storm-water overflow. The dissipation of the erosive force of run-off water is discussed fully in Chapter Three and will not be repeated here. It is essential that overflow be channelled into drainages in such a way that run-off water does not simply replace the original bad-lands with a new soil erosion system.

One of the major errors most frequently made with treatments of this kind is that the volume and force of run-off water is underestimated. The result of this is that the berms or walls are either washed away during flash floods or are breached by erosion gullies and the process of erosion and aridification continues despite the efforts made.

The guiding principle with this type of control is that the erosion control walls should not be made too high. The goal is not to store water, but rather to repeatedly retard the speed of the run-off and hold back as much as possible for long enough to ensure maximum infiltration into the soil. The earth walls should therefore be constructed to permit excess water flow to pass over the wall during flooding rather than be an obstruction to the force of the flow.

The shape of the wall will also help to protect it during flash flood events. A gradually angled upstream slope of approximately 40° will ensure deflection of most of the force of the run-off water. In regions where destructive flooding can be expected, it will be necessary to stabilise the surfaces of the wall with a protective stone-paving surface.

The objective of this method is to concentrate and slow down the flow of run-off water, increase infiltration, trap organic nutrients and silt, preserve moisture in the soil and provide a sheltered environment for the re-establishment of a protective plant cover, rather than the construction of a series of water storage dams. In wetter areas the small dams can develop into a series of wetland ponds with a dense and protective cover of reeds, bulrushes, sedges and grasses, which will protect the soil surface during flooding.

It is very important to appreciate that the soil structure of these eroded bad-lands is usually severely altered and desiccated. When disturbed these soils become highly erodable and great care must be taken to ensure that radical reconstruction does not merely escalate the problem. Treatment must start at the upper end of the erosion system and each section, or dam, must be brush-packed, the overflow consolidated and seeded before the next section is treated. In this way it can be assured that no new erosion of the reconstructed area can take place before the newly repaired surface is adequately stabilised with vegetation. One must rather be content with slow but effective progress than run the risk of aggravating the soil erosion problem as a result of attempting to do too much at a time.

The implementation of this method requires sensitive supervision to ensure the best result and minimal irreversible damage to the area. Tractor and bulldozer operators cannot be expected to be sensitive to a minimal environmental disturbance approach, which is why close supervision is necessary.

It is further suggested that a limited experimental trial be done to test this method at a selected site before the method is applied more extensively.

Before any radical reconstruction is done it is essential that the area to be treated is carefully inspected to locate any special or feature plants that can be transplanted. Sites that can only be treated with radical reconstruction seldom still contain rare or special plants, but occasionally they still do occur on remnants of the original vegetation within the eroded area.

Sites that contain stable or viable populations of rare or special plants should not be treated by means of radical reconstruction unless the plants can be retained without disturbance. A general guideline is that a severely eroded site should only be treated with radical reconstruction if it is completely degraded in every way.

In Figure 2.14 the radical reconstruction of eroded bad-lands results in a dam. The objective is to flood the eroded area and eventually create a wetland habitat.

Erosion continues to eat into stable soil along the drainage

Crumbling and desiccated gully sides are too steep for normal control methods

Figure 2.13: Radical reconstruction: Restoring the drainage channel

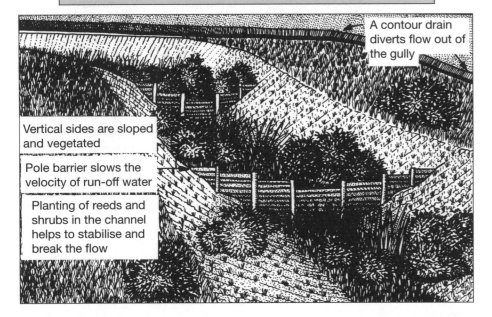

A contour drain diverts flow out of the gully

Vertical sides are sloped and vegetated

Pole barrier slows the velocity of run-off water

Planting of reeds and shrubs in the channel helps to stabilise and break the flow

2.4.8 Radical reconstruction: restoring natural drainages

Another method that can be used to rehabilitate a hopelessly degraded gully system by means of radical reconstruction is illustrated in Figure 2.13. Where the gully-eroded bad-lands have become deeply incised with crumbling sheer sides there is little point in attempting to stabilise only the gully floor. What is needed is treatment that will also rehabilitate the desiccated vertical surfaces and this can only be done by reshaping them.

The first step is to divert water out of the gully system at the head of the system. This is done by constructing a simple contour berm and dissipating the water via controlled outflow channels so that it does not start a new erosion system.

The system is then treated by shaping the gully walls all along the eroded drainage line, creating a more gentle and evenly sloped channel. Sloping by hand is possible but will require a huge effort, which will make it very costly. An advantage of using earth-moving equipment is that the shaped sides are, to some extent, compacted into place by the machine used. The reconstructed slope should not be too steep as this will make plant establishment more difficult. A slope of somewhere between 40° and 20° yields the best results.

Once the reconstruction has been completed, gabions or any other suitable gully control structures must be built at intervals along the channel to help check the force of the run-off water. The checks illustrated in Figure 2.13 are constructed out of wooden poles lined on the upstream side with geotextile and brush-packing. With the help of effective run-off diversion channels at the head of the system, concentrated run-off within the channel will be reduced, obviating the need for a major investment in the construction of erosion control structures. Whatever design is used, ensure that the structure is robust enough to guarantee the protection of the reshaped gully. Until a protective vegetation cover is well established the erosion control structure will be the sole protection for the reshaped bad-land system.

Once completely stabilised, the reshaped gully system must be vegetated with a suitable plant cover. In many areas grasses are a practical option with a sowing mix of fast-growing indigenous perennial species for longer-term cover.

Elements of some of the other methods already described like brush-packing, stone surfacing, contour fences and brush wattles can be used where practical along the slopes. Consideration can be given to establishing fast-growing trees and shrubs along the water course to help bind the soil in the channel with a dense network of finely interlocking roots.

Reeds and bulrushes are also an excellent option for wetter areas. The choice of species to plant must be carefully considered and great care must be taken to avoid alien species with a high invasive potential. The best option is to use locally indigenous plant species.

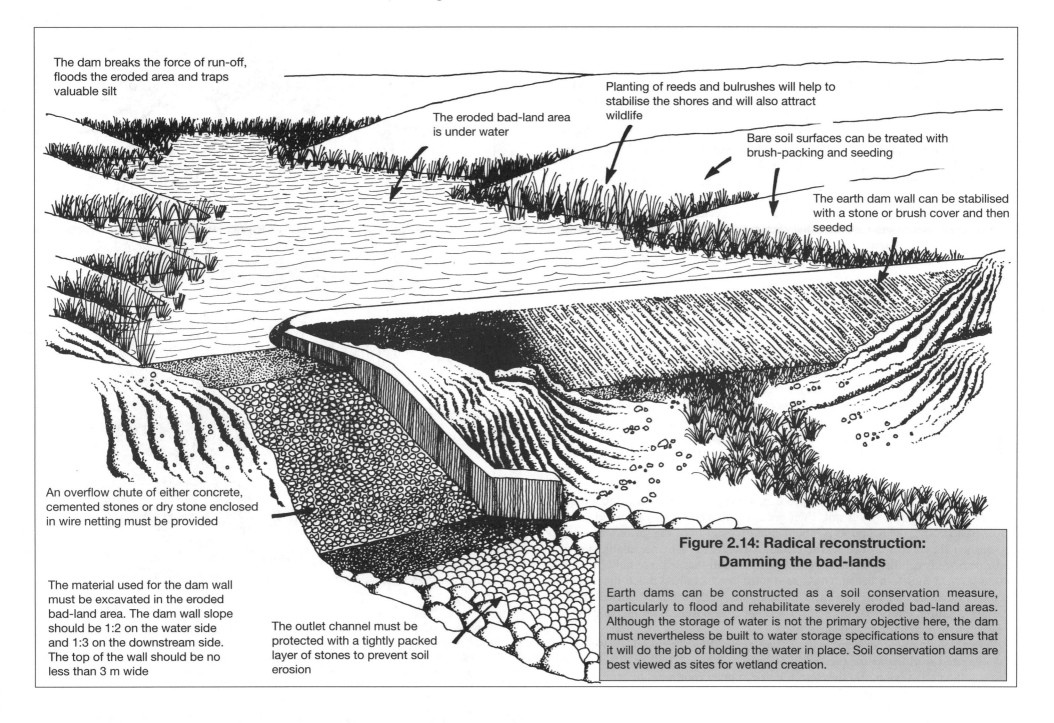

The dam breaks the force of run-off, floods the eroded area and traps valuable silt

Planting of reeds and bulrushes will help to stabilise the shores and will also attract wildlife

The eroded bad-land area is under water

Bare soil surfaces can be treated with brush-packing and seeding

The earth dam wall can be stabilised with a stone or brush cover and then seeded

An overflow chute of either concrete, cemented stones or dry stone enclosed in wire netting must be provided

The material used for the dam wall must be excavated in the eroded bad-land area. The dam wall slope should be 1:2 on the water side and 1:3 on the downstream side. The top of the wall should be no less than 3 m wide

The outlet channel must be protected with a tightly packed layer of stones to prevent soil erosion

Figure 2.14: Radical reconstruction: Damming the bad-lands

Earth dams can be constructed as a soil conservation measure, particularly to flood and rehabilitate severely eroded bad-land areas. Although the storage of water is not the primary objective here, the dam must nevertheless be built to water storage specifications to ensure that it will do the job of holding the water in place. Soil conservation dams are best viewed as sites for wetland creation.

2.4.9   Seeding and planting for rangeland rehabilitation

Once an erosion system has been stabilised it is necessary to establish a protective vegetation cover. Most often the erosion system is very different to its pre-eroded state and one can only aim to rehabilitate it to as close to its former condition as possible.

The choice of species to seed or plant is critical. The best option is to establish pioneer vegetation species that are most likely to survive in the stabilised area. Grass is always a good option because it is fast growing, relatively easy to establish and it binds the soil very well (see Box 2.8). The primary objective should be to establish a protective vegetation cover; thereafter other objectives like aesthetics and restoration of the original plant species mix can be attempted.

It is very important to recognise that each grass species has its own particular habitat preference. Some grasses thrive under cultivation but are actually adapted to arid conditions and will therefore be valuable for rehabilitative establishment in erosion control areas.

Similarly, the soil preferences of grasses will affect their usefulness for rehabilitation. Soil pH is important – grasses that do particularly well in alkaline soils (high in lime content) may struggle in acidic soils. Soil structure also plays its part. Grasses that thrive in loamy topsoil conditions will be a poor choice for sandy sites that have become aridified as a result of soil erosion.

It is a good general policy to establish local indigenous plant species, simply because it is already known that they thrive in the general area. There can be exceptions to this rule but one must be very cautious of alien plants because of the potential they have to become invasive in the absence of their natural control mechanisms. If use is to be made of alien species, make absolutely sure that their performance in the area is known and that they are considered to be suitable for the task by the formal agricultural and nature conservation authorities and experts.

Obtaining suitable seed is often a problem. Grass seed is usually available for pasture establishment, but if not, then grass plants can be transplanted from stable pasture sites. This option is labour intensive but once the grasses become established they will self-seed in the rehabilitation area. When available, grass and shrub seeds can be sown into lightly loosened soil that is preferably covered with a layer of mulch or brush. Grass seed must not be buried much more than its own thickness, and when sown in mulched areas, need not be buried at all. The only requirement is that the soil surface must be loosened, as the plants will not germinate on a hard, sealed surface.

Something of a wonder plant is the Indian grass *Vetivera zizanioides* (vetiver), which is used world-wide for the stabilisation of soil. It is a tall, erect perennial with a sod-forming habit and develops a dense spongy root mass up to two 2 m

BOX 2.8

A comparison of grass and small shrub roots

Grasses and shrubs with roughly the same canopy size are compared in terms of their soil binding capability. Grasses tend to have shallow roots that are more effective for soil surface stabilisation. Grass plants also produce a much denser basal cover which is more effective for slowing the speed of run-off water and increasing the rate of infiltration.

deep. Although it is a tropical grass, it has a wide range of tolerance and has been used effectively in monsoon tropical conditions, semi-desert conditions and within frost zones with extremely low soil temperatures. It can survive, and remain effective, under rainfall conditions ranging from 3 000 mm to below 300 mm per annum.

The grass is most often used as a barrier to soil erosion on bare areas and eroded slopes, but it is also used in strips between crops on unstable slopes. The dense growth retards water flow and effectively traps silt and organic material. Even a single line of plants across a sheet-eroded site has been shown to be very effective. Vetiver is water-tolerant, so it can also be used to stabilise and rehabilitate degraded and eroded former wetlands.

Vetiver is resistant to fire and can tolerate heavy utilisation by grazers as its crown is situated below the soil surface. It is able to tolerate almost any soil type, regardless of fertility, acidity, alkalinity or salinity, which means that it is particularly well suited to the degraded soil conditions typical of erosion systems. It is even able to thrive in loose sand, gravel or shale soils and also in the problematic and infertile sub-surface conditions that can be expected in soil erosion systems.

Vetiver is considered to be benign. Seeds are mostly infertile and the plant does not spread by means of stolons or rhizomes. It therefore remains where it is planted and where it is needed. This grass is a very useful option for the rehabilitation of degraded rangeland. It can either be used to stabilise soil behind control structures or it can be planted to serve as a barrier itself (see Figure 2.15). It can even be harvested for mulch material as it is capable of growing up to 2 m in only three weeks under ideal conditions. Cutting results in denser growth.

Vetiver is propagated by root division or slips, which are planted like seedlings. To quickly establish a thick hedge the slips can be planted approximately 10 cm apart, early in the wet season, as the establishing plants require some moisture initially. In drier areas slips should be planted in shallow trenches or hollows to optimise moisture conditions. A little mulch on the soil will help to preserve moisture.

Indigenous shrubs are easily established from seed collected from the rangeland and planted into nursery plastic bags or any other suitable container. Once the plants are growing well they can be planted out after rain, when adequate moisture is available. The planting time is important and seedlings should be planted out at the start of the active growing season of the area.

Many shrubs can be established from cuttings. Although the technique of making cuttings varies for different plant types, the following general guideline can be tested.

Trim a straight section of the stem of the parent plant to approximately 20–30 cm long, cutting it off just below a bud or joint at the base and just above a

Figure 2.15: The use of vetiver grass hedges as silt and organic debris traps

In Gundalpet, India, vetiver grass hedges are part of traditional farming practice. Even on fairly level land, they accumulate impressive amounts of soil behind them.

Figure 2.16a: A method and procedure for restoration planting

Plant the cuttings half their length into the soil

Step 1

Mix soil from the rehabilitation area with a little compost. Sow three to four seeds into each container and thin out when the plants are about 50 mm tall. Stem cuttings take about three to six weeks to root.

Use plastic soft drink bottles or household cleaner containers. Simply cut the top off and clean well. Cut a few drainage holes in the bottom and put a layer of gravel or geotextile in the bottom.

Create a small basin (about 300 mm wide) which can retain rainwater

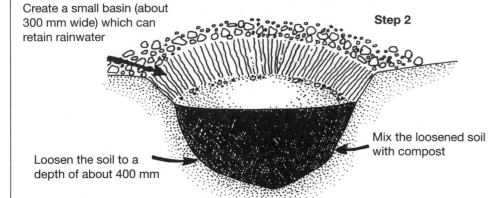

Step 2

Loosen the soil to a depth of about 400 mm

Mix the loosened soil with compost

Preparation of the planting site

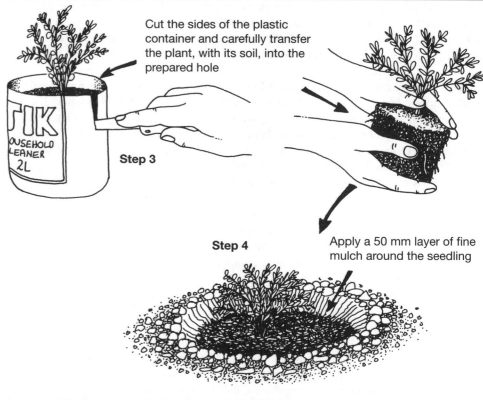

Cut the sides of the plastic container and carefully transfer the plant, with its soil, into the prepared hole

Step 3

Step 4

Apply a 50 mm layer of fine mulch around the seedling

Figure 2.16b: Shrubs with rooting tillers are very effective for restoration planting

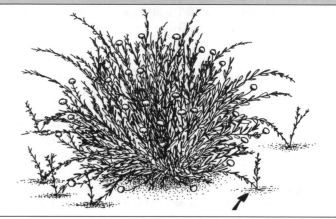

bud at the top. Strip all the leaves from the cutting. Remove a thin sliver of bark (2–4 cm long) at the base to increase the length of the area from which roots can develop (see Figure 2.16a).

The cuttings can then be planted to at least half their length into the soil in nursery bags, or directly into the rehabilitation area. Cuttings will need to be kept moist until they develop roots, so it is a practical option to first plant them into nursery bags and to care for them until they develop new roots and leaves, after which they can be transferred into the rehabilitation area.

Local shrubs that produce rooting tillers are excellent for rehabilitation establishment (see Figure 2.16b). They tend to spread quickly and create a dense protective plant cover over the soil, while binding the soil with a dense root network.

2.5 MONITORING THE SUCCESS OF SOIL EROSION CONTROL EFFORTS

It is absolutely essential that the progress and effectiveness of the soil erosion control methods employed be evaluated and recorded at regular intervals. Keeping such records will help to avoid making the same mistakes again and will, therefore, also help to ensure the best use of the available funding.

It is important that the same method of evaluation be used each time that monitoring is done, as this will ensure comparable results. Monitoring need not involve collecting vast amounts of data or useless information, nor does it need to be too complicated or technical. It should be goal-oriented, quick and easy to do and, most importantly, it must tell you what you want to know, which is simply: Is it working? Is it cost-effective? What needs to be modified or adapted to improve the effectiveness of the methods used?

There are various options for monitoring and the methods used depend on the objectives of the monitoring programme. Photography offers the best way in which to record progress at fixed points within a rehabilitation area. Vegetation condition transects will provide useful information about subtle vegetation changes like species composition and cover density, but will require a good knowledge of the plant species of the area as well as a knowledge of the important plant indicator species.

Remember that it is more important to evaluate the overall results of the control methods used (i.e. range improvement) than to measure the amount of silt that accumulates behind the control structures.

The very minimum monitoring requirement is to inspect each treated erosion system after every rainstorm and to establish which structures need to be repaired or improved. This is absolutely critical because undercutting that is not

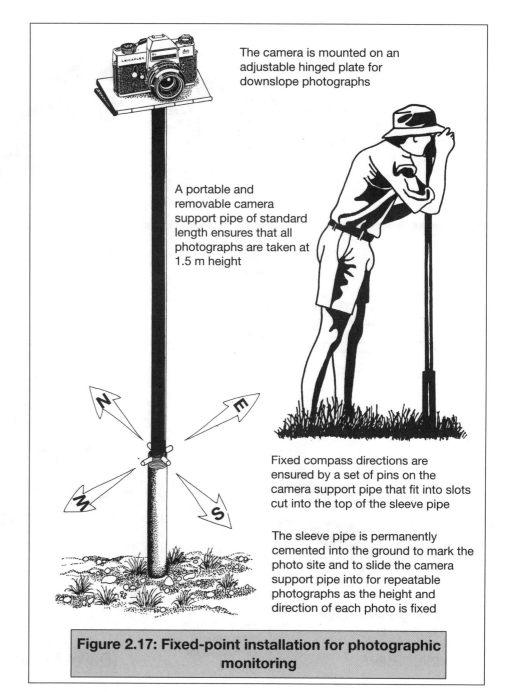

The camera is mounted on an adjustable hinged plate for downslope photographs

A portable and removable camera support pipe of standard length ensures that all photographs are taken at 1.5 m height

Fixed compass directions are ensured by a set of pins on the camera support pipe that fit into slots cut into the top of the sleeve pipe

The sleeve pipe is permanently cemented into the ground to mark the photo site and to slide the camera support pipe into for repeatable photographs as the height and direction of each photo is fixed

Figure 2.17: Fixed-point installation for photographic monitoring

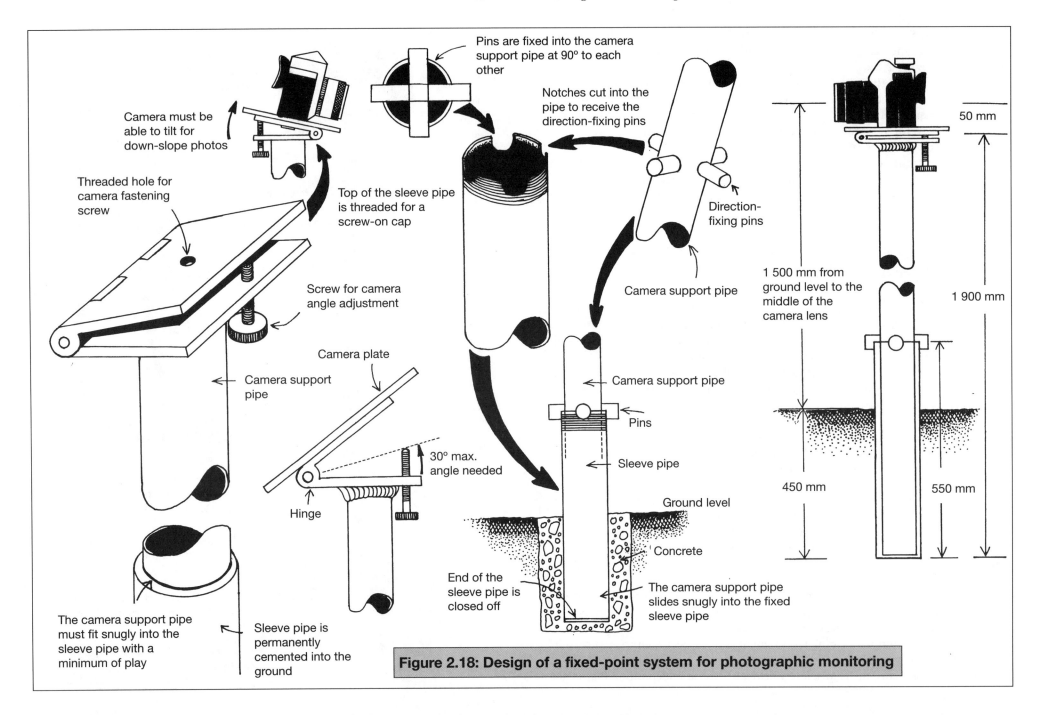

Camera must be able to tilt for down-slope photos

Threaded hole for camera fastening screw

Top of the sleeve pipe is threaded for a screw-on cap

Pins are fixed into the camera support pipe at 90° to each other

Notches cut into the pipe to receive the direction-fixing pins

Direction-fixing pins

Camera support pipe

Screw for camera angle adjustment

Camera plate

Camera support pipe

30° max. angle needed

Hinge

Camera support pipe

Pins

Sleeve pipe

Ground level

Concrete

End of the sleeve pipe is closed off

The camera support pipe slides snugly into the fixed sleeve pipe

The camera support pipe must fit snugly into the sleeve pipe with a minimum of play

Sleeve pipe is permanently cemented into the ground

50 mm

1 900 mm

1 500 mm from ground level to the middle of the camera lens

450 mm

550 mm

Figure 2.18: Design of a fixed-point system for photographic monitoring

Figure 2.19: Fixed-point photograph record sheet

PLOT NO:	DATE:	SURVEYOR:
GPS CO-ORDINATE:		
GRID REF NO:		

POINT DESCRIPTION: (How to find the plot marker)

HABITAT DESCRIPTION: (Use back of form, if necessary)

VEGETATION TYPE:

TREE & SHRUB SPECIES:

DWARF SCRUB SPECIES:

HERBACEOUS PLANT SPECIES:

COVER DESCRIPTION:

COVER TYPE	HEIGHT	% OF PLOT	DOMINANT SPECIES
CANOPY COVER			
GROUND COVER			

UTILISATION:

BROWSING INTENSITY:	PLANTS BROWSED	BROWSING HERBIVORES
HEAVY		
MODERATE		
LIGHT		

GRAZING INTENSITY:	PLANTS GRAZED	GRAZING HERBIVORES
HEAVY		
MODERATE		
LIGHT		

OTHER NOTES:

attended to will eventually result in wasted money and effort and possibly a bigger erosion problem.

It is particularly important to monitor the success of vegetation re-establishment efforts. To do this it is critical to record not only the plant species used, the density of the planting and the original dates of establishment initially, but also which species germinate well and which species survive. Recording a negative result is also extremely important so that alternative species can be tested or planting methods and planting times can be modified as required.

Where restoration projects are undertaken in areas where domestic or wild herbivores may impact on the vegetation re-establishment projects, it may be necessary to establish animal exclusion plots. The exclosures will help to determine what the overall impact of the herbivores actually is on the restoration planting projects.

It is important that all restoration monitoring be treated as a long-term project that should be run concurrently with the various restoration projects. Although the wisdom of monitoring may not initially be clear, the true value of any monitoring system lies in the immense value of the long-term results.

2.5.1   Fixed-point photographic monitoring

This monitoring technique is simple to implement and inexpensive to establish. A number of widely spaced fixed-point photographic sites need to be established throughout the rehabilitation area. Use of this technique results in a set of four photographs taken from a single point in each of the compass directions (see Figure 2.17). The photographs are taken from a fixed point, at a fixed height and in a fixed direction every time, which means that different sets of photographs, taken on different dates (however long the intervening period) are completely comparable. Figure 2.18 illustrates the design that ensures these fixed measurements.

The photographs will show changes in ground cover, vegetation density, plant canopy height and to some extent, species composition. At each photo point details of plant species composition, cover description and utilisation by animals can be recorded on a fixed-point photograph record sheet (Figure 2.19), which is then filed together with the photographs for future reference.

The location of each of the fixed-point monitoring sites should be marked on a map of the property and map co-ordinates or the grid reference of each site should be written on the record sheet. Each of the photographs must also be clearly marked with the photo site number and the date that the photograph was taken. This procedure is critical and will ensure that photographs do not get mixed up, which would make them useless for comparative assessment purposes.

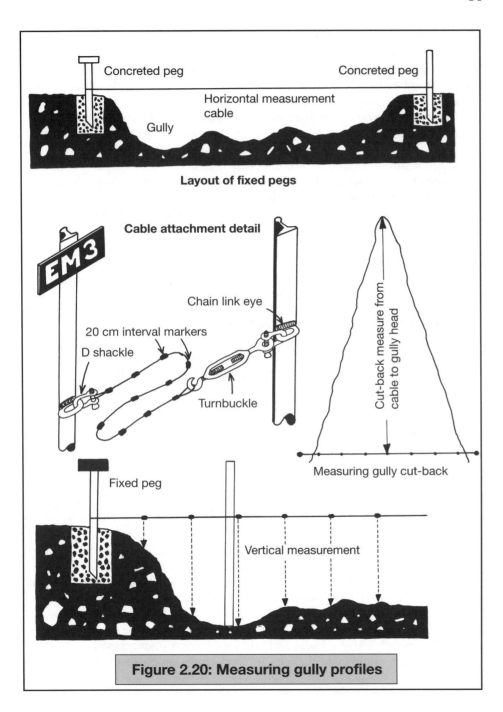

Figure 2.20: Measuring gully profiles

2.5.2 Gully profile measurement

The aim of this method is to measure the cross-sectional profile of gully erosion in an accurate and repeatable manner. Use of this method will provide precise information about gully erosion dynamics. Measurements are taken vertically from a cable that is suspended across the gully. Gully head cut-back is also measured perpendicular to the cable. The data collected can be plotted on graph paper for later comparative reference.

Care must be taken when installing the fixed pegs to ensure that the pegs will not be undermined by erosion of the gully in the short to medium term. The pegs need to be concreted in place to enable the tensioning of the measurement cable, as illustrated in Figure 2.20. A light turnbuckle is used to tension the cable and gully profile measurements can be made with a steel 1 m ruler or steel tape measure held vertically between the cable and the gully floor.

While gully profile measurement will provide a very precise indication of the soil erosion tempo, there are also other less objective but, nevertheless, useful methods that can be used to assess soil surface conditions. These subjective assessment methods are incorporated in the soil erosion condition guide illustrated in Figure 2.21. By using the objective gully profile measurement, together with the subjective soil erosion guide, a reasonably accurate evaluation of the rate of soil erosion can be made for any degraded or restored area.

2.5.3 Soil erosion condition guide

The occurrence and severity of soil erosion can be subjectively evaluated at different sites within any rangeland using the guide illustrated in Figure 2.21. Although not strictly defined as monitoring, this method can be used in conjunction with the described monitoring methods as a record of ongoing erosion severity or rehabilitation as a result of restoration efforts.

The guide is better suited as a general range condition assessment method and should be used together with vegetation condition assessment methods, including the fixed-point photographic method already described.

This guide can be most effectively used as a proactive aid for soil erosion control operation planning. Sites at which the guide is used should be indicated on a map of the property so that subsequent evaluations can be done at more or less the same locality for comparative purposes. The completed forms should then be filed together with a copy of the locality map to ensure that the sites can be located again when necessary.

It takes some time, however, to get used to using the soil erosion condition guide because decisions have to be made about the severity of the erosion in each class of erosion. The descriptions for each of the four classes of erosion severity

Figure 2.21: Soil erosion condition guide (adapted from Savory, 1990)							
Class	**1**		**2**		**3**		**4**
Soil movement	Little evidence of movement of soil particles.		Moderate movement is visible and recent. Slight terracing evident.		Soil movement with each event deposited against obstacles.		Sub-soil exposed over much of the area.
Surface litter	Litter accumulating and incorporated into soil. Rapid breakdown.		Little movement by wind and water evident. Slow breakdown.		Extreme movement, large deposits against obstacles.		Litter removed by animals, wind and water.
Pedestals	No evidence of pedestals.		Small plant and rock pedestals in flow patterns.		Most plants and rocks on pedestals. Some root exposure.		Plant roots exposed. Problem widespread.
Flow patterns	Little evidence of particle movement.		Well-defined; small and intermittent.		Flow patterns evident with deposition of soil, litter and fans.		Patterns numerous and noticeable. Large barren fan deposits.
Rills	Small rills absent or at infrequent intervals. Vegetation present in depression.		Rills 2.5 – 20 cm wide occuring in exposed areas, at frequent intervals, greater than 3 m apart.		Rills occur frequently and quickly, cutting sides; often exposing roots.		Rills joining at short intervals and denuding large areas.
Gullies	May be present in stable condition. Slopes and channel generally stable and vegetated.		Gullies present but with slumping sides from animal impact; vegetation becoming established.		Gullies numerous and well-developed. Active erosion evident along 25–50% of their length.		Sharply inclined gullies with little vegetation over large areas; gullies actively eroding over 50% of their length.
Score	**6**		**12**		**18**		**24**
Explanation of rating scores	Soil surface conditions are stable. No action required.		Conditions indicate some active erosion. Reconsider stocking rate and adjust accordingly.		Conditions deteriorating. Reduce stock and implement erosion control programme.		Situation is critical. Animal removal essential. Intensive erosion control required.

are very clear and the occasional indecision, doubt or inaccuracy will not really affect the outcome significantly.

One needs to practise using the form to get used to grading soil erosion severity and observing the small soil surface indicators that guide the grading. If there is persistent uncertainty regarding any particular aspect, it will be easy enough to photograph the indicator or physical feature and later seek guidance from a better informed or more experienced person.

2.5.4 Stock and wildlife exclosures

Excluding grazing and browsing animals is a simple way in which the impact of herbivory can be assessed. This may be particularly important in areas that need to be rehabilitated and which are farmed, or in which natural free-ranging wildlife still occur. It is not always possible to completely and semi-permanently fence off an area in which restoration work is done, although the complete exclusion of larger herbivores will significantly benefit the restoration process. Complete exclusion may be practical on farmed rangeland which has been fenced off into individual grazing units or camps.

In open and unfenced rangeland, smaller restoration project sites can be temporarily fenced off to exclude herbivores. This, however, may become too expensive, particularly for larger restoration areas which often include an entire drainage catchment area, frequently resulting in an impractically convoluted fence-line.

When it is impossible to exclude herbivores, an effort should at least be made to evaluate the impact that the herbivores have on the restoration area. Many larger herbivores will be attracted to the fresh, new growth of restoration planting projects and some will even prefer to forage and rest on degraded sites, a preference that will definitely have an impact on restoration efforts.

It is sometimes difficult to assess the degree of herbivore impact. The changes due to continuous utilisation are often too subtle to detect during occasional visits because the impact is generally gradual, the changes being small but continuous.

Exclusion plots are an ideal tool with which the rangeland manager can detect how much impact herbivores are having on the site. Exclosures can be constructed in restored areas so that the unutilised vegetation inside can be compared to the utilised vegetation outside the exclosure. In this way it will be possible to assess the degree of impact over time, both on a short-term and long-term basis.

Figure 2.22 illustrates a typical exclosure design, the actual specifications of which will depend on the animals that need to be excluded, fence height being critical. Where jumping wildlife such as most deer species, eland, kudu and impala occur, the exclosure must be at least 2 m high. For the exclusion of non-jumping or small wildlife such as wildebeest, zebra, gemsbok, rhinoceros, buffalo and steenbok, the exclosure need be no higher than 1.4 m.

The entire exclosure should be covered with wire netting or diamond mesh with an aperture size of no more than 75 mm. The impact of smaller wildlife such as hares, porcupines and hyraxes must not be overlooked and the mesh aperture size must exclude all herbivores except the smallest rodents and invertebrates.

Construction should be robust, particularly where larger wild herbivores like eland, buffalo, rhinoceros and hippopotamus may take to using the exclosure as a scratching post. Frequent damage may necessitate the installation of solar-powered electric wires around the outside of the exclosure. Regular maintenance is all-important, particularly where animals push against the poles or damage the netting. Although it may seem odd, animals love to destroy what the range manager painstakingly installs and this behaviour is not always related to finding food.

In fire-prone areas the use of steel fencing poles or pipes should be considered, rather than wooden poles.

Once erected, the exclosure must be clearly marked with a plate on which the date of erection and identification number of the exclosure is permanently engraved or hammered with a letter punch. Any other kind of marking will eventually deteriorate or burn off, thereby reducing the long-term significance of the exclosure.

A record of plant species within the exclosure should be kept as well as a series of photographs covering the interior of the exclosure. An evaluation of plant density inside and outside the exclosure should also be recorded for future reference. The valuable information gained by using exclosures (i.e. evaluation of grazing and browsing impact) will help to guide further management input.

Heavy impact on restoration planting can perhaps be reduced by closing nearby water points for wildlife, incorporating largely unpalatable plants into the revegetation programme or by temporarily fencing off smaller restoration units. Solar-powered electric wires can be a very effective deterrent and is a relatively affordable option for short-term exclusion of larger wildlife from restoration areas.

In summary, exclosures are useful and the cost of erecting them is more than justified by the results. They should, therefore, be included in the monitoring programme of any serious restoration project.

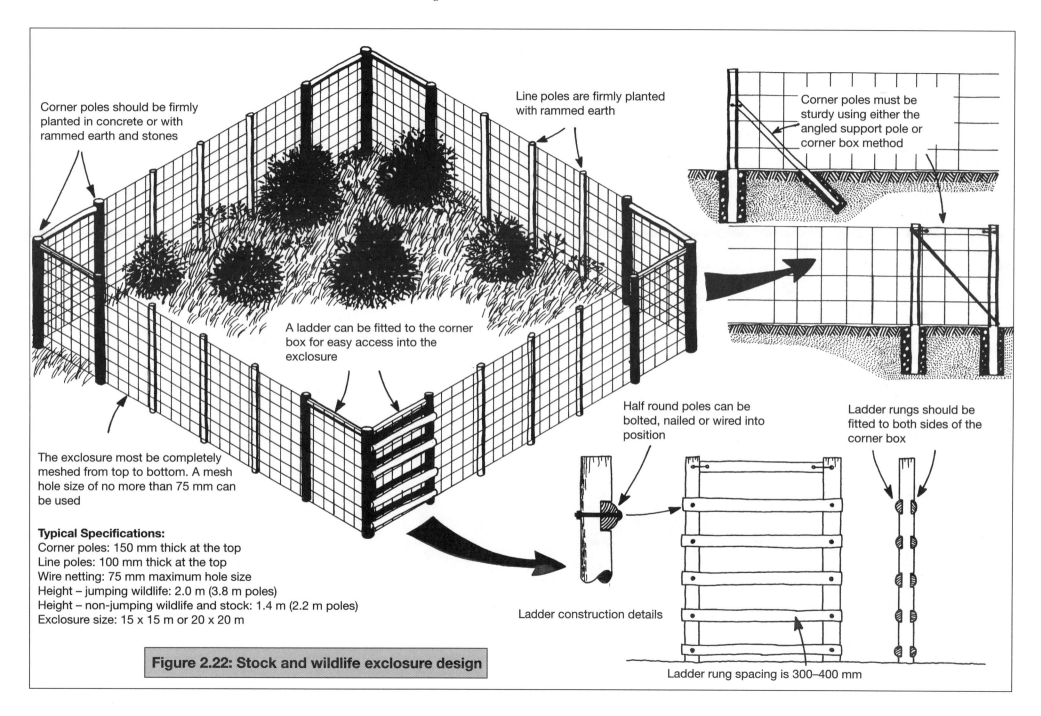

Corner poles should be firmly planted in concrete or with rammed earth and stones

Line poles are firmly planted with rammed earth

Corner poles must be sturdy using either the angled support pole or corner box method

A ladder can be fitted to the corner box for easy access into the exclosure

The exclosure most be completely meshed from top to bottom. A mesh hole size of no more than 75 mm can be used

Typical Specifications:
Corner poles: 150 mm thick at the top
Line poles: 100 mm thick at the top
Wire netting: 75 mm maximum hole size
Height – jumping wildlife: 2.0 m (3.8 m poles)
Height – non-jumping wildlife and stock: 1.4 m (2.2 m poles)
Exclosure size: 15 x 15 m or 20 x 20 m

Half round poles can be bolted, nailed or wired into position

Ladder rungs should be fitted to both sides of the corner box

Ladder construction details

Ladder rung spacing is 300–400 mm

Figure 2.22: Stock and wildlife exclosure design

CHAPTER THREE

ACCESS TO THE LAND

The sensitive construction and maintenance
of field roads and tracks

3.1   Introduction

3.2   Principles of road design and use

3.3   Planning a road network

3.4   Construction methods

3.5   Maintenance

3.6   Road damage rehabilitation

3.7   Responsible road use in rangelands

3.1   INTRODUCTION

Roads in natural regions are intrusive and destructive; they cause a disturbance and are often an eyesore. Unfortunately, access is sometimes a very necessary evil for a variety of reasons that have to do with the intensive management and economic feasibility of wildlands and farms.

Consider access into remote areas to fight undesirable wild fires, the transport of captured excess wildlife, hot pursuit anti-poaching efforts, the eradication of invasive alien vegetation, the transport of materials for rehabilitation projects and the general maintenance and monitoring that is an essential part of all intensive field management.

In many regions, roads or tracks into remote and attractive areas for scenic drives and game viewing are an essential requirement for modern eco-tourism. The income generated by the paying tourists, who are there to experience nature and to see the wild animals, can be used for the maintenance of the roads and conservation orientated management activities like the control of soil erosion and the eradication of invasive alien vegetation.

Whatever the objective, the construction of a road into undisturbed wildlands places a great responsibility on the landowner to undertake this in the most environmentally sensitive manner possible. In addition, the landowner must accept a long-term commitment to the maintenance of the road so that it does not have any cumulative long-term negative impact on the natural assets of the landscape through which it passes.

Not least of the environmental considerations is the visual impact that the road may have on the aesthetic character of the landscape. This aspect is all too often ignored or misunderstood, resulting in unsightly landscape scars.

Roads in natural rangelands need not degrade the habitats through which they pass. With appropriate planning and a sensitive approach to road construction, negative environmental impact can be sufficiently mitigated. When planned and constructed in this manner, the roads that have become so necessary for effective landscape management can become an acceptable intrusion into natural environments.

In this chapter we look at the impact of roads on the environment, the principles of environmentally sensitive road design, planning a road network, construction methods, maintenance and rehabilitation methods.

3.1.1   Roads and soil erosion

Figure 3.1 illustrates some of the typical problems that are associated with roads and tracks in the field. In almost every case poor construction design, inappropriately routed roads and insufficient attention to the drainage of run-off water are the cause of the problem and invariably result in the erosion of the roadway and the landscape through which the road passes.

All too often, field roads and tracks used for logging, construction, fence building and even tourism are simply neglected until abandoned, when they can no longer comfortably be used for access. They then persist as erosion gullies. The problem is particularly acute in landscapes with steep slopes and in areas which experience heavy downpours and flash flooding.

Even the shallowest of wheel ruts can become a channel for water, accelerating the flow downhill and taking the finer road surface material with it, eventually undermining the surface and converting the wheel ruts into small gullies. Unchecked, the wheel ruts can eventually grow into accelerated erosion gullies which carry away all that was formerly the road surface, after which the road becomes impassable. This situation not only results in the loss of an initial investment in road access and closure of the route, but also results in a new soil erosion problem area, requiring expensive and innovative attention.

Similarly, the inappropriate routing of a new road can accelerate the rate of soil erosion as a result of the channelling of run-off water over soil surfaces not sufficiently vegetated to withstand the erosive force of concentrated run-off water. The disturbances of road cuttings, borrow pits and rubble screes on slopes below roads are all sites for potential accelerated soil erosion in need of stabilisation and run-off water dissipation.

Roads routed through sensitive marshland and wetland seeps generally result in deep mud ruts. The exposed wetland surfaces, vulnerable without the protective plant cover, dry out and become susceptible to erosion by run-off water.

Other sensitive sites such as sparsely vegetated sand and gravel surfaces in arid areas, can also become degraded by the presence of roads and tracks. The frequent use of unimproved tracks alters the structure of the road surface, turning it into fine powder which easily blows away with the wind. Eventually the track becomes a set of water channels which develop into erosion gullies at an alarming rate.

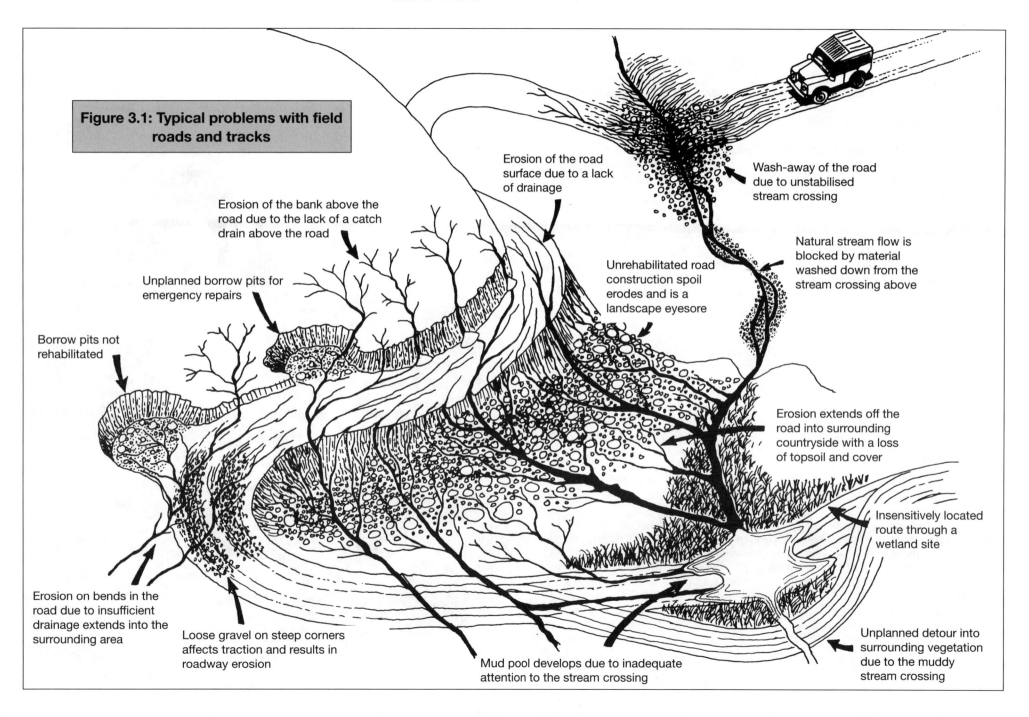

Figure 3.1: Typical problems with field roads and tracks

Erosion of the road surface due to a lack of drainage

Wash-away of the road due to unstabilised stream crossing

Erosion of the bank above the road due to the lack of a catch drain above the road

Natural stream flow is blocked by material washed down from the stream crossing above

Unplanned borrow pits for emergency repairs

Unrehabilitated road construction spoil erodes and is a landscape eyesore

Borrow pits not rehabilitated

Erosion extends off the road into surrounding countryside with a loss of topsoil and cover

Insensitively located route through a wetland site

Erosion on bends in the road due to insufficient drainage extends into the surrounding area

Loose gravel on steep corners affects traction and results in roadway erosion

Mud pool develops due to inadequate attention to the stream crossing

Unplanned detour into surrounding vegetation due to the muddy stream crossing

BOX 3.1

The impacts of roads on animals and plants

The impacts that roads may have on animals and plants are generally unobserved. Although some of these impacts may be positive, most are negative and these potential impacts must be considered when planning a new road.

The negative impacts of roads are disastrous and permanent. Roads and the various constructions needed on them create barriers for small animals, cutting off dispersal routes and fragmenting habitats. The loss of vegetation cover along the roadway modifies the habitat of small sedentary animals. Animals crossing or moving along roads become easier targets for predators. Compacted road surfaces and concrete constructions impact on subterranean and burrowing animals like blind snakes and moles.

Dust kicked up by vehicles on field roads coats roadside plants which are then not available to the animals that are dependent on them. Roads often become sources of soil erosion which modifies the landscape and desiccates the soil of the area, impacting on a wide range of animals and plants.

Sometimes roads limit the dispersal of seeds which collect on or against roadway structures and do not reach suitable germination sites, thereby impacting on the value of flowering and seeding 'events' in arid areas.

Low-water bridges and drifts may cut off the movement of fish and other aquatic animals and thereby limit the breeding success of these organisms.

The positive impacts of roads are few by comparison and do not really improve overall conditions for the habitat or landscape or even the species that benefit.

Rock hyraxes and mongooses often make use of rock-piles or retaining walls, used in road construction, for temporary refuge or even permanent dens.

To discover that many animals use roads as easy walkways, one has only to examine the variety of tracks on them early in the morning, from rhinoceros to porcupine and mongoose. Predators use roads to locate potential prey, sometimes catching their prey on the open roadway. Many birds select powdery road surfaces for sand-bathing and sunning themselves. Numerous antelope select road surfaces for creating their dung middens. Aquatic animals like frogs and insect larvae may be found in muddy vehicle wheel ruts and pools at drainage humps in wet areas. Animals crossing roads at night are often killed because they become blinded and disorientated by vehicle lights.

It is extremely important to be aware of the negative impacts of roads in natural rangelands and to try to mitigate these impacts wherever possible.

3.2   PRINCIPLES OF ROAD DESIGN AND USE

The following general principles can help to ensure the most sensitive routing, construction and use of roads in rangelands. Most of these principles will be discussed in more detail in the balance of this chapter.

Principle 1

Use the landscape as a guide to routing: Road routing must take advantage of the topography and must not work against it. By being sensitive to the topography, potential drainage, incline, surface and aesthetics, the usual problems can be reduced.

Principle 2

Avoid sensitive areas in the landscape: Sensitive sites such as wetlands and sand dunes are often problem areas for roads. Negative environmental impact must be avoided and there can be no justification for roads that endanger plant or animal well-being and survival.

Principle 3

The means must be available for maintenance: Before a road is built, it is important to ascertain whether the necessary finance, materials and sources of materials are available for ongoing maintenance.

Principle 4

Aesthetics is important – visual impact must be mitigated: This principle ties in with aspects of topography, avoiding sensitive areas like very steep slopes and forests and the implementation of effective maintenance and restoration efforts.

Principle 5

Off-road drainage is critical: This aspect cannot be neglected because inadequate drainage will ultimately result in the loss of the road due to the erosion of the surface. Unchecked run-off will also cause accelerated soil erosion in the natural rangeland through which the road passes.

Principle 6

Build and maintain to the required standard: Road routing design, drainage and surfacing must all be guided by the use that the road is built for. Heavy duty vehicle use and accessibility with sedan motor cars will require higher standards of construction than a simple management track for off-road vehicles.

Principle 7

A code of road-use ethics must be adhered to by all road users: Deviation from the road network, for example, must not be permitted and all road users must be aware of the regulatory code of ethics.

3.2.1   Types of field roads and tracks

A **Tourist class:** This road must conform to the high standard of both surface quality and maintenance required for tourism. These roads must have an all-weather surface that is suitable for the average two-wheel drive motor car in the worst weather conditions. Roads of this standard are essential for access to all major tourist infrastructure from the nearest urban centres or public road network.

The main features of this class of road are:
- Raised, cambered and smooth gravel surface or hard surface.
- Adequate cross-road and under-road drainage.
- Hard surfaced, low-water fords.
- Hard surfacing of steep and stony sections.

This standard of road is also suitable for access with heavy vehicles to management infrastructure such as storage and animal holding pens.

B **Improved management road:** This class of road should be accessible to two-wheel drive pick-up trucks in most weather conditions. The surface need not be as good as that of the tourist class of road, but road surface drainage and drainage crossings must be good enough to prevent the road from being repeatedly washed away during periods of heavy rainfall.

These roads should permit relatively comfortable access to all parts of the area for management and recreation purposes. They should be regularly maintained and surfaced where necessary.

Unguided access for the general public (tourists) to areas on roads of this class should be restricted to four-wheel drive vehicles or persons who are familiar with the hazards of the area. Use of this class of road during extremely wet conditions should be discouraged due to the damage caused to the road surface by wheel ruts in soft mud.

C **Unimproved management track:** These tracks are the type required to provide access to landowners or managers into natural and relatively undisturbed and undeveloped areas. The tracks are generally unsurfaced and usually consist of a route cleared of major obstacles to vehicular travel. Attention to off-road drainage, however, remains important and accelerated soil erosion must not occur as a result of the road or its use.

Although generally unimproved, these tracks should nevertheless provide relatively easy access to remote areas and infrastructure. Tracks with extremely stony surfaces and very uneven surfaces are hard on vehicles and very heavy on vehicles' tyres. The track route should therefore be carefully selected to provide a relatively comfortable ride and minimum damage to the vehicles used on it.

These tracks are often used as four-by-four recreational vehicle trails and off-road motorcycle and mountain bicycle trails.

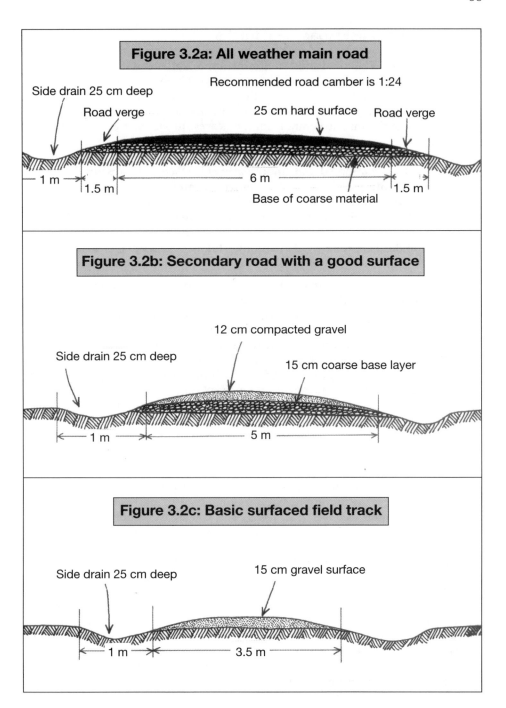

Figure 3.2a: All weather main road

Side drain 25 cm deep

Recommended road camber is 1:24

Road verge

25 cm hard surface   Road verge

1 m   1.5 m   6 m   1.5 m

Base of coarse material

Figure 3.2b: Secondary road with a good surface

12 cm compacted gravel

Side drain 25 cm deep

15 cm coarse base layer

1 m   5 m

Figure 3.2c: Basic surfaced field track

Side drain 25 cm deep   15 cm gravel surface

1 m   3.5 m

3.2.2 Specifications for road surfaces

A All weather surface main road: This road surface conforms to tourist class and heavy vehicle access class standards and is usually restricted to the major access roads in an area. Road construction of this quality is highly desirable but very expensive.

The road is 6 m wide to accommodate heavy vehicles as well as two lanes of traffic. The main feature of this class of road is the hard surface of the road, either concrete interlocking blocks or asphalt, which should be no less than 25 cm thick. The base, or sub-surface, must be carefully prepared with compacted layers of sub-grade put down before the hard surface is laid down. The primary advantage of this surface is that it is relatively maintenance-free for extended periods if correctly constructed.

The side drains collect water off the cambered road surface and channel the run-off to culverts that cross under the road. The road surface should be shaped to a camber of 1:24.

B Secondary road with a good surface: This type and the following road construction are more likely to be used in rangelands. A good surface is built up out of layers of gravel. The base layer should consist of at least 15 cm of coarse, stony gravel, particularly in areas with a clay sub-surface. For light road use 15 cm is considered to be a minimum thickness. The thicker this layer of the road, the greater the load-bearing capacity in wet conditions. This layer should be compacted as illustrated in Figure 3.3.

A layer of finer gravel, 12 cm thick, forms the road surface and this layer should be cut to give the road a camber of 1:24 to ensure that water does not collect on the road surface.

Side drains of between 50 cm and 100 cm wide should be constructed where efficient drainage is required and wherever possible. Cross-road drainage can be used to divert the run-off out of side drains.

C Basic surfaced field track: This is the type of road most frequently encountered in rangelands. The road route is cleared of obstructions and a mixed aggregate road surface is put down. A minimum surface thickness of 15 cm is generally required on a sandy sub-surface, but on roads with a clay substrate, an additional 10 cm layer of coarser material will be needed as a base layer. The quality of this base layer is dependent on what the road will be used for. If it is to be used for light utility vehicles and tourist vehicles, the specification required is much less than if the road is to be used for heavy transport vehicles. As with all roads, side drains and cross-road drainage is critical where effective drainage is required.

3.3 PLANNING A ROAD NETWORK

Once it has been concluded that a road or road network is necessary, a start can be made with planning the route. Initial planning should be done on a map or aerial photograph of the area and all existing roads and tracks should be marked on the map.

An option that results in the least impact is to link existing roads, rather than construct new routes. Once all the existing routes and possible linkages are exhausted, the sections of necessary new road can be identified on the map. If at all possible, inspection of the potential route can be done from the air – the elevation provides a clearer perspective than is possible on the ground.

The proposed route should then be evaluated using all the available background information about soils, drainage, vegetation, site sensitivity and potential visual impact. The proposed route should also be evaluated in terms of the initial costs of construction and the subsequent long-term costs of maintenance. It is important at this stage to consider all possible alternative routes in terms of comparable bio-physical impacts and costs.

This part of the planning process should result in an environmental sensitivity analysis, which may be required in some areas, in report form, by the environmental authorities who are required to approve all new road construction plans.

An important consideration when deciding on a suitable route is the type of access that the road will be used for. There is little sense in bulldozing a strip of road at great cost, both economically and to the environment, if the road is only to be used occasionally for hunting, where a rough hand-made track would be adequate.

The following is a rough guide to route layout that will help to reduce potential environmental damage:

- Avoid areas with a high potential for soil erosion. In many cases, only slight changes to the route can help to avoid soil erosion problems.
- Vary road steepness grades where possible to reduce concentrated water run-off on the road surface.
- Minimise environmental damage by using physical terrain features such as natural benches, ridge-tops and low gradient slopes.
- Make use of occasional short, steep gradients where necessary to avoid problem areas and to take advantage of desirable physical landscape features.
- Avoid mid-slope locations on long, steep or unstable slopes.
- Select drainage crossings that will minimise channel disturbance during construction and that will minimise cutting and filling.
- Avoid undercutting unstable, wet toe slopes when locating roads in or near valley bottoms.
- Avoid sensitive environments as far as possible. These include wetlands, thickets, forests, seeps, areas containing rare or endangered plants and the habitats of rare or sensitive animals. Take care to carefully evaluate areas that may appear to be ideal for road construction. An example of such a site is the quartz patches in the Succulent Karoo vegetation which, although very flat, are an important habitat for a diversity of rare succulents. Seasonal pools and pans, when dry, may also be tempting sites for road routing but they should be avoided, especially in arid areas, as they are very critical seasonal breeding wetland habitats for numerous animals.
- Consider each section of road in terms of visual impact. This includes not only the road itself but also the damage and mess that occurs during construction.
- Avoid ancient and cultural artefacts such as graves, rock paintings, petroglyphs, smelting sites, stone age industry sites and stone shelter walls. Also avoid more recent but historically significant buildings, stone wall stock pens, historical irrigation works and threshing floors.

The next step is to walk the route and to carefully consider the potential bio-physical impacts that the road, and the construction of the road, will have on the site. One needs to be flexible at this stage of the planning because on-site evaluation will reveal many aspects, or defects, that were not obvious when planning the route on a map or aerial photograph.

Once a final and suitable route is chosen (and approved where necessary), the route can be clearly marked out using wooden stakes driven into the ground on both sides of the proposed road.

Each individual section of the new route can now be planned in terms of the need for drainage of the road surface, the type of construction needed at each drainage crossing and the type of surfacing material required. An important aspect of this phase of the planning is the location of a suitable network of gravel borrow pits for road surface material.

3.3.1 Questions that should be asked before planning a new road in undisturbed wildlands

1. Would the local nature conservation authority approve of the road?
   It may be necessary or wise to get a professional opinion.

2. Who will need to use the road? Will it serve the interests of more than one user?
   A road serving the needs of many is a stronger motivation.

3. Are there no alternatives for access to the area?
   It is necessary to explore all the possibilities such as nearby existing roads.

4. Is the rainfall higher than 300 mm per annum?
   A higher rainfall will result in a greater incidence of soil erosion.

5. Does the rainfall come with thunderstorms and flash flooding?
   Accelerated soil erosion and road drainage in arid areas often occurs only during rare rainstorm events.

6. How much of the proposed road is on a slope of more than 1:4?
   Steeper roads are more susceptible to surface erosion and their construction results in more environmental damage.

7. If machinery were not available, would you still build the road?
   In other words, is the road really necessary or will it be 'nice to have'?

8. How much of the road is visible from a distance and would you still build it if it created a visible scar on the landscape?
   Aesthetic considerations are extremely important and your road should not spoil the natural beauty of the area for others.

9. Can you afford to spend half of the original construction cost per year on maintenance?
   The maintenance of rangeland roads is both critical and expensive.

10. Can you afford to rebuild sections of the road if they are regularly washed away during rainstorms?
    The capacity to repair roads must be a reality.

11. How soon after a disastrous rainfall event washes away the road can you get onto repairing it?
    Road damage results in environmental damage so attention to maintenance must not be delayed.

12. Do you think that your children and your grandchildren will one day bless you or berate you because of the road and its implications?
    Your road must not become a serious landscape management problem for those who follow in your footsteps.

3.3.2 The costs of a road compared to the long-term gains

The initial costs of building a road are minimal when compared to the long-term costs of road maintenance. Once a road is made, it constantly requires attention such as the trucking in of surface gravel, maintenance of pipes, fords and drainage and the occasional replacement of washed away infrastructure after heavy rains.

These long-term implications are usually not even considered during the initial planning of road building projects. Road management budgets should, therefore, consist of initial building costs and an annual estimate of maintenance costs.

The affordability of a road must be determined over the long term and the advantages of having the road must then be weighed up against the long-term cost implications.

The type of road needed is an important cost consideration. Roads built with heavy machinery require expensive rehabilitation and maintenance, while hand-cleared two-wheel tracks require little further attention. The nature of the terrain also has an impact on maintenance costs. The quality of the road surface and the level of maintenance required depends on what the road will be used for. Whatever the grade of road, the long-term cost implications must be carefully considered before any road building can take place.

The potential generation of income, either directly or indirectly, through the construction and use of a road can be used to help cover some of the long-term costs. Tariffs for road use can be set where there are multiple road users and entrance fees to public or private recreation areas need to be channelled into road maintenance.

The costs of a road should not be viewed only in terms of financial outlay for road construction and maintenance, but also in terms of the environmental costs.

The costs of the rehabilitation work that usually accompanies road construction projects must also be considered. Unavoidable storm damage to roads also frequently results in damage to the natural environment through which the road passes. This damage must also be repaired because it is part of the responsibility that the landowner or manager accepts by implication when constructing a road in undisturbed rangeland.

The cost of the maintenance of existing roads is equally important and must not be forgotten. These costs may also include repairing the environmental damage caused by insensitive road construction in the past. Unfortunately, the neglect of past landowners or users passes on to the new land user and the responsibility is also, rather unfairly, passed on. This emphasises the need for careful consideration and planning before any new road is made.

3.4   CONSTRUCTION METHODS

Road building is time consuming, labour intensive and extremely costly, and this is why careful planning is a necessity. The methods used should ensure the most permanent options possible for road surfaces, drainage control, stream crossings and soil erosion control as this will obviate the excessive and costly need for constant repair and maintenance.

One needs to aim for a relatively maintenance-free situation where only occasional attention to surfaces and drainage effectiveness is required.

Road building should follow a carefully thought out plan that makes allowance for and is sensitive to the negative environmental implications of the construction work. The only way to achieve this effectively is to be constantly at the site of construction or to check on it as regularly as possible. One cannot expect the road construction workers to be constantly aware of, or sensitive to, the environmental impacts of road building – the responsibility for environmental impact during construction lies with the manager or landowner.

It is necessary to deal effectively with drainage as the road building work progresses. This will ensure that heavy downpours during the construction period will not simply wash away the new roadway before it is complete.

The best policy to adopt when building a road is to avoid, as far as possible, construction methods that require major rehabilitation and stabilisation. A minimal impact approach will usually also ensure a low maintenance requirement. This implies that sufficient time and effort should be invested in determining the route of the road during the planning stage.

An often disregarded impact of road construction activities is the indirect human impact. Road construction workers may be tempted to collect firewood from the rangeland or trap smaller wildlife for the pot with wire snares. Fires that are often made at the work site to warm food or cold hands during inclement weather may also be a hazard in fire-driven ecosystems. Unseasonal wild fires can be devastating in many natural systems and the cumulative impact of wood harvesting and animal trapping along road construction routes is generally considered to be an unacceptable practice in natural rangelands. Road construction workers must be adequately informed prior to the commencement of the work as to what activities are not permitted in this regard.

The following section contains a few practical examples of tried and tested road building methods that will help to reduce the degree of maintenance of field roads and tracks.

3.4.1   A sensitive approach to road construction

Road construction has the potential to cause ecological disasters and we find examples of this wherever there are natural rangelands. Insufficient consideration for the welfare of the natural environment invariably leads to destructive practices which often result in ugly scars in the landscape, and these are most often the source sites for road building materials.

Whatever the material that is mined, extracted or collected from the rangeland, the question that needs to be asked is: What impact will the removal of the material have on the site and what can be done to mitigate this impact?

When stones are required for constructions, they are usually simply collected from any convenient stony area within the rangeland. This is a very destructive practice because each stone plays some small but significant part in the environment. It may be shading seedlings, or retaining moisture in the soil, or helping to slow the erosive force of run-off water or even sheltering some small animal. The removal of a truckload of stones represents a small-scale and localised ecological disaster which may be permanent. The important guiding principle is that whatever material is used, its removal must not have a negative impact on the environment, or that any resulting negative impact must be mitigated by a suitable rehabilitation action.

For example, when stones are required for construction, rather remove them from old agricultural stone walls, old building ruins or collect the stones that have been displaced during road building or the clearing of agricultural cultivation areas. The resultant environmental impact will be minimal as these are already disturbed or unnatural sites. Be very careful, however, not to remove stones from cultural heritage sites or any other site of historical significance. If in doubt, contact cultural heritage experts, the local museum or a university history department for assistance.

Aggregate, or gravel, for road surfacing should only be removed from a minimal network of specially identified borrow pits. The layout and management of borrow pits is more fully discussed in the section on road maintenance. Borrow pits should only be located in sites of low sensitivity and care must be taken to ensure that the required aggregate material is present at the site. Destructive experimental or exploratory excavation on a large scale must be avoided. Borrow pits must be completely and effectively rehabilitated when no longer used for the extraction of road construction materials. Details of borrow pit rehabilitation are given in the last part of this chapter.

It is critical that areas containing rare or endangered plants, sensitive habitats like wetlands, steep unstable slopes, archaeological sites and the habitats of sensitive rare animals should all be carefully avoided when planning both the road route and the extraction of road building materials.

Building up the road surface

Spreading the aggregate and cutting a camber on the surface

Compacting the road surface

Figure 3.3: Gravel road construction

3.4.2 Gravel road construction

Undoubtedly, the best way to build a hard-wearing, long-lasting gravel road is to lay down consecutive layers of road material starting with a sub-grade layer of rough material topped by finer layers of base and surface material.

The cost of this process depends on the distance to the nearest sources of road building material and the availability of machinery to load, transport and prepare the road surface. Road building is costly so the process of building up a good road surface, layer by layer, can perhaps be restricted to problem areas, high intensity use roads and roads where the building materials are available relatively close by.

Once the route of the road has been marked out, the first step is to clear the area to be surfaced of obstructions and heavy or woody plant material. Smaller stones need not be removed and will, in fact, help to build a stable foundation. Layers of aggregate are then deposited on the road site by whatever means is available. Figure 3.3 illustrates a fully mechanised operation. The aggregate is loosened and loaded onto a transport truck with a front-end loader and then transported to the road site. The truck has a hydraulic tipping loadbed which is ideal for spreading the aggregate over the road surface. If this type of mechanisation is not available, labour can be used to loosen and load the aggregate, but this is obviously more time consuming, if not more expensive. Work creation is sometimes an objective and the end result with hand-loading is the same. Once the aggregate has been spread at the desired thickness (minimum

of 150 mm) over the road surface, a light mechanised grader can be used to shape the material, spread it evenly and eventually cut the required camber on the road surface as illustrated in Figure 3.3. As an alternative to the mechanised grader, a light-wheeled grader blade drawn by a tractor can be used, and in the absence of any kind of grader, the road surface can be hand-shaped if enough hands are available.

The desired degree of surface compaction during the grading stage can be ensured by wetting the graded surface and then compacting it with a mechanised drum roller as illustrated in Figure 3.3. After preliminary compaction the surface can be graded again for final shaping and then again compacted with intermittent wetting if necessary. The degree of wetting and compaction will depend on the quality of the aggregate. A good quality aggregate (or gravel) has a good proportion of all sizes of material which fills all the spaces between the larger particles, forming a compact and stable road surface.

Although this type of mechanised road building will yield the best and quickest results, particularly for tourist class roads, a shortage of machinery or the funding to hire the machinery should not prevent the construction of good quality roads. The processes of material excavation, loading, spreading, surface shaping and compacting can all be done by hand if a tractor-trailer unit or truck is available to load and transport the aggregate. The practice of indiscriminately excavating road surface material all along the roadside in the absence of a transport vehicle must, however, be avoided.

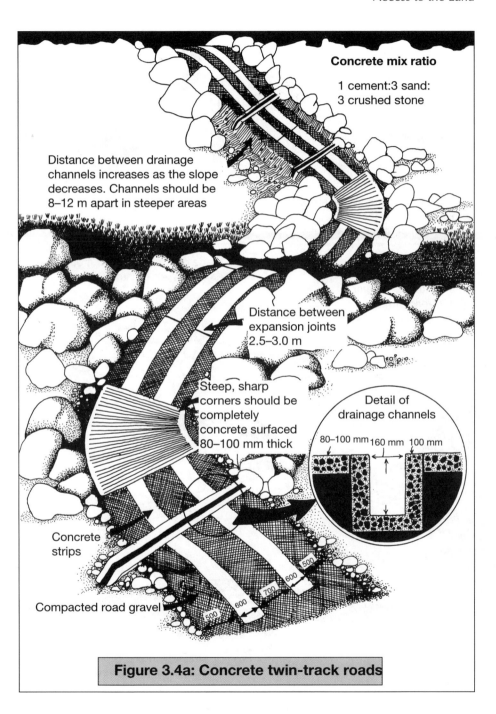

Concrete mix ratio

1 cement:3 sand:
3 crushed stone

Distance between drainage
channels increases as the slope
decreases. Channels should be
8–12 m apart in steeper areas

Distance between
expansion joints
2.5–3.0 m

Steep, sharp
corners should be
completely
concrete surfaced
80–100 mm thick

Detail of
drainage channels

80–100 mm 160 mm 100 mm

Concrete
strips

Compacted road gravel

Figure 3.4a: Concrete twin-track roads

3.4.3 Hard surfacing

The hard surfacing of all field roads with an all-weather concrete, asphalt or interlocking block surface is the ultimate option and if it was at all affordable and practical, most field roads would probably be hard surfaced. It is very expensive and is therefore usually only considered where hard surfacing can alleviate a vehicle traction problem or where road surfaces deteriorate quickly and repeatedly. Figure 3.4a illustrates a twin-track concrete strip method that was specifically designed for steep and rocky sections of mountain roads with loose stony surfaces. It can, however, be adapted for other problematic conditions.

Laying down concrete strips on steep sections ensures that the road will be accessible in all weather conditions and that the surface will not deteriorate as a result of vehicle tyres digging for traction into loose stone and gravel road surface material. Repeated temporary road repair is eliminated and the hard surfacing reduces the wear-and-tear on both tyres and vehicles. Erosion of the roadway material between and outside the concrete strips is prevented by casting run-off collection channels into the concrete and across the road. These channels function in the same way as the drainage humps by removing water from the road surface at regular intervals. Details of these drains are shown in Figure 3.4a.

Properly built, and correctly drained, these concrete twin tracks can significantly reduce expensive maintenance of unmanageable sections of road. The initial costs of hard surfacing may be high, but over time it may be the cheapest option in terms of maintenance costs. Figure 3.4b illustrates the basic concrete strip construction method.

Strip casting must take place from the top of the section to be surfaced to the bottom and each strip must be allowed to cure for at least seven days before driving over them. The concrete must be 100 mm thick and the strips should be roughly 600 mm wide and 700 mm apart. Tight corners should be completely concreted making one strip of 2 000 mm wide, as drivers tend to cut across and would dig ruts between the strips.

All concrete mixing by hand should be done in specially made mixing pans or in a motorised cement mixer. Any unavoidable spillage must be cleaned up immediately.

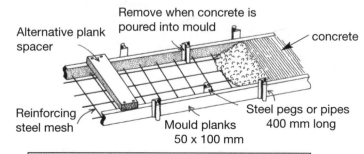

Remove when concrete is
poured into mould

Alternative plank
spacer

concrete

Reinforcing
steel mesh

Mould planks
50 x 100 mm

Steel pegs or pipes
400 mm long

Figure 3.4b: Mould for twin track strips

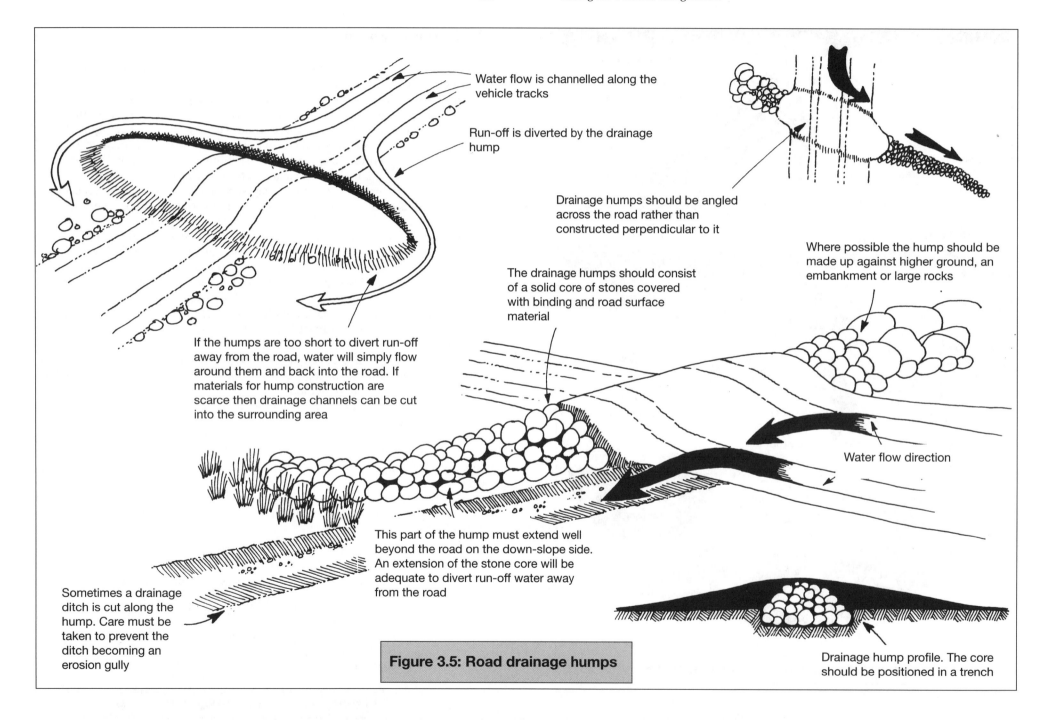

Water flow is channelled along the vehicle tracks

Run-off is diverted by the drainage hump

Drainage humps should be angled across the road rather than constructed perpendicular to it

Where possible the hump should be made up against higher ground, an embankment or large rocks

The drainage humps should consist of a solid core of stones covered with binding and road surface material

If the humps are too short to divert run-off away from the road, water will simply flow around them and back into the road. If materials for hump construction are scarce then drainage channels can be cut into the surrounding area

Water flow direction

This part of the hump must extend well beyond the road on the down-slope side. An extension of the stone core will be adequate to divert run-off water away from the road

Sometimes a drainage ditch is cut along the hump. Care must be taken to prevent the ditch becoming an erosion gully

Figure 3.5: Road drainage humps

Drainage hump profile. The core should be positioned in a trench

3.4.4 Water drainage off road surfaces

The objective with road drainage is to deflect run-off water off the road surface and into the natural vegetation alongside the road. This can be achieved effectively by constructing drainage deflection humps across the road surface as illustrated in Figures 3.5 and 3.6.

Effective drainage will prevent the continuous loss of road surface gravel, obviating the need for expensive resurfacing every time it rains. The drainage hump slows the water flow, directs it off the road surface and concentrates it at a stable overflow site.

The number of drainage humps required depends on the steepness of the slope, nature of the run-off, type of terrain, soil and vegetation cover through which the road passes as well as the number of natural drainages that cross the road.

Drainage humps are easy to build but certain essential requirements must be met for them to be effective. Figures 3.5 and 3.6 highlight the particular design requirements.

Drainage humps must be constructed with a solid core of either stones or coarse gravel covered with road surface material to form a gradual slope on both sides, and should extend well beyond the roadway on each side to prevent water from simply flowing around the hump and back into the road.

Drainage humps, particularly the core of rough material, are best built by hand because great care must be taken to ensure effective water deflection. The final road gravel topping can be put down with a front end loading machine or hand-shovelled off a tractor-trailer or truck.

The key to successful cross-road drainage is effective construction and continual maintenance to clear any blockages of water flow and repair storm damage as soon as it occurs.

Where run-off water is deflected off the roadway and into the surrounding landscape, particularly on slopes, the force of the water flow may eventually result in the formation of an erosion gully. It is critical that soil erosion be prevented at these sites of run-off water concentration. Figure 3.6 illustrates a method of slope protection at such a site and Figure 3.7 suggests an alternative way of dissipating the force of run-off water.

On slopes run-off water can be collected in a shallow channel cut along the up-slope side of the road. The road surface should be slightly angled towards the channel so that most of the run-off collects in it. This run-off is then deflected over the road and down the slope as illustrated in Figure 3.6. On steep sections of road it may be necessary to line the in-slope channel with a protective layer of stones which will help to slow down the water flow and prevent the erosion of the channel. This channel will have to be maintained to keep it free of plant material and silt that may accumulate and block water flow.

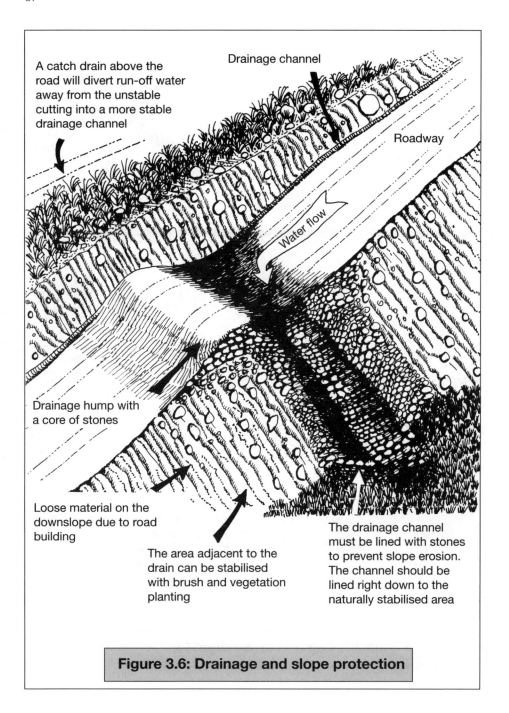

A catch drain above the road will divert run-off water away from the unstable cutting into a more stable drainage channel

Drainage channel

Roadway

Water flow

Drainage hump with a core of stones

Loose material on the downslope due to road building

The area adjacent to the drain can be stabilised with brush and vegetation planting

The drainage channel must be lined with stones to prevent slope erosion. The channel should be lined right down to the naturally stabilised area

Figure 3.6: Drainage and slope protection

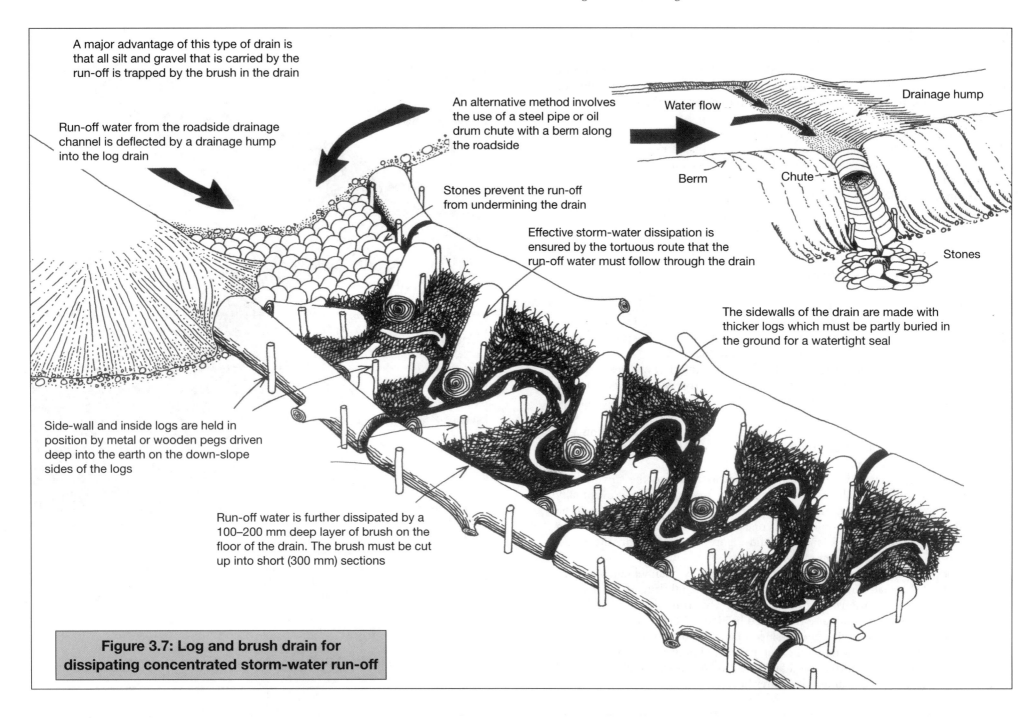

A major advantage of this type of drain is that all silt and gravel that is carried by the run-off is trapped by the brush in the drain

Run-off water from the roadside drainage channel is deflected by a drainage hump into the log drain

An alternative method involves the use of a steel pipe or oil drum chute with a berm along the roadside

Water flow

Drainage hump

Berm

Chute

Stones

Stones prevent the run-off from undermining the drain

Effective storm-water dissipation is ensured by the tortuous route that the run-off water must follow through the drain

The sidewalls of the drain are made with thicker logs which must be partly buried in the ground for a watertight seal

Side-wall and inside logs are held in position by metal or wooden pegs driven deep into the earth on the down-slope sides of the logs

Run-off water is further dissipated by a 100–200 mm deep layer of brush on the floor of the drain. The brush must be cut up into short (300 mm) sections

Figure 3.7: Log and brush drain for dissipating concentrated storm-water run-off

3.4.5 Dissipating accumulated run-off water

Once methods for road surface drainage have been implemented, the next challenge is to deal with the concentrated run-off water. Directing it off the road surface is achieved but then it must be prevented from creating a new soil erosion problem next to the road.

Figure 3.7 illustrates a simple log drain that dissipates the force of accumulated run-off water. By means of the angled logs and dense brush-packing in the drain, the force of the run-off water is checked, preventing the erosion of the soil surface. The logs and brush will also hold back road surface gravel, silt and organic material.

The size of the drain depends on the volume of water that needs to be dissipated. A wider and longer structure will be needed for greater volumes of run-off.

Rocks and stones can be used as an alternative to logs. The design remains basically the same and the brush-packing can either be retained or replaced. The stones will also effectively break the force of the run-off and trap water-carried debris. When stones are used, the outer walls should be completely enclosed with wire netting to prevent parts of the drain from washing away during flooding. The inside area can then be completely stone-packed or a series of mesh-enclosed gabion walls can be built across the drain between the side walls.

These drains will become excellent sites for grass seed germination, providing both moisture and shade under the brush-packing or between the stones. Eventually, the drain will be completely vegetated by a dense grass sward, which will help to dissipate the run-off water. Suitable grass seeds can be sown into the brush-packing or stone-packing for faster establishment of a vegetation cover.

By far the best way to protect a slope from soil erosion is to ensure that it has a dense, protective vegetation cover. Initially, however, some kind of mechanical surface protection will be necessary to stabilise the slope until the vegetation cover becomes well established.

In addition to the log drain it would be wise to implement further slope protection measures down-slope of the drainage locality. This can be done by using brush-packing, brush wattle or even a geotextile cover, all in conjunction with seeding. These methods are described in detail later in this chapter.

Diverting excess run-off into a natural drainage channel is the ultimate treatment for excess run-off water. Natural water channels are stable and protected by specially adapted plants like sedges and reeds, which help to prevent the accelerated erosion of the channel.

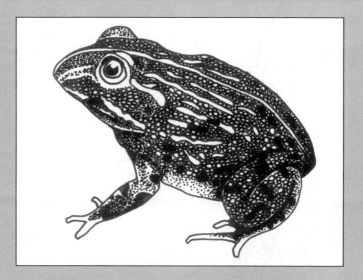

BOX 3.2
Wildlife in wheel rut and drainage hump puddles

Water sometimes collects behind drainage humps and in wheel ruts and repeated use of rangeland roads during wet periods results in the continuous deepening of these puddles. I was once very surprised to see a lumpy green object cartwheel up past my open window, together with the wet mud, while driving through a large muddy puddle after a thunderstorm. The generally arid area had experienced very good rains of late and there was water everywhere, particularly in the roads.

I stopped and went in search of my mysterious green object. It proved to be an immature giant bullfrog, a rare species only observed during very wet seasons in that arid region. The irate bullfrog headed back to the muddy puddle and to my horror, I saw that the road puddle was full of them – there were at least ten or fifteen. I had been happily splashing through these road puddles at speed, daily, while travelling to do my fieldwork, not knowing about the bullfrogs and probably killing many of them on the way.

It appears that even the deepening of a puddle behind a road hump can, in some way, impact on the wildlife of any area. I am certain that frogs can be found in road puddles almost anywhere, even if not rare species. This clearly illustrates the need for road maintenance and shows that even the filling in of mud holes in roadways is of importance if the unnecessary loss of wildlife is to be prevented. It is important to remember that the road impacts on the natural habitats of wildlife, and not the other way around.

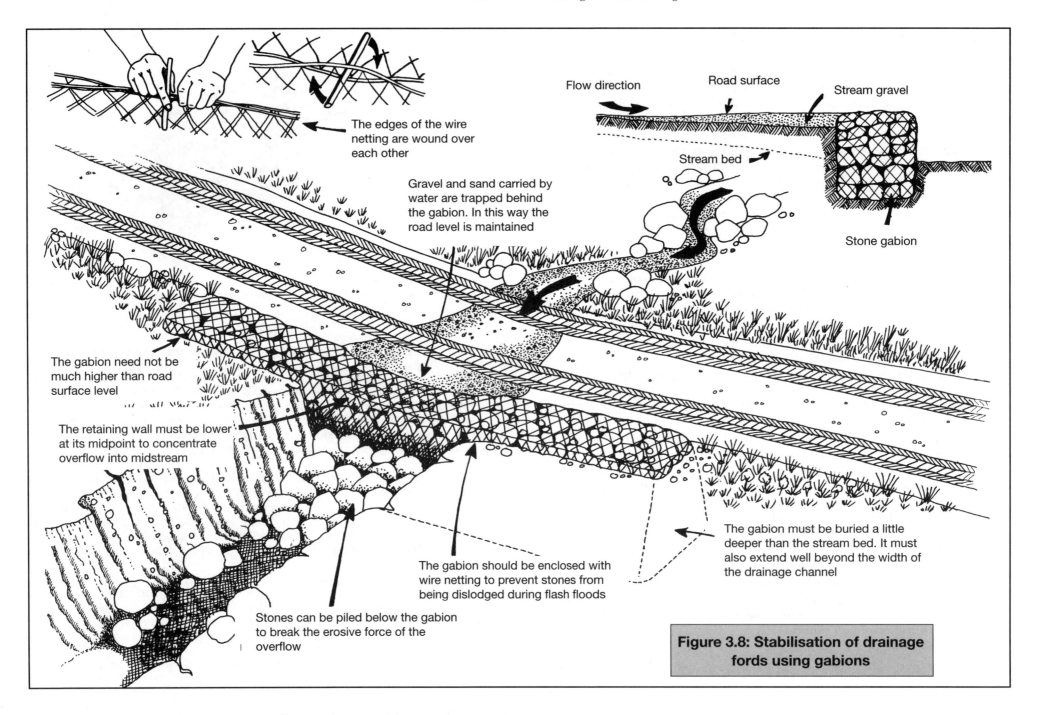

The edges of the wire netting are wound over each other

Gravel and sand carried by water are trapped behind the gabion. In this way the road level is maintained

Flow direction

Road surface

Stream gravel

Stream bed

Stone gabion

The gabion need not be much higher than road surface level

The retaining wall must be lower at its midpoint to concentrate overflow into midstream

The gabion must be buried a little deeper than the stream bed. It must also extend well beyond the width of the drainage channel

The gabion should be enclosed with wire netting to prevent stones from being dislodged during flash floods

Stones can be piled below the gabion to break the erosive force of the overflow

Figure 3.8: Stabilisation of drainage fords using gabions

3.4.6 Drainage crossings and retaining walls

Wherever a road crosses a natural drainage, run-off water will repeatedly wash away part of the road surface, leaving gullies of varying depth and width across the roadway. These gullies deteriorate with each period of rainfall, the ride becomes more uncomfortable and the vehicle takes more strain each time it has to negotiate these wash-aways.

Figure 3.8 illustrates a method that will prevent wash-aways and help to build a firm and permanent road surface but also permit the unimpeded flow of the drainage channel's water. The structure consists of a simple retaining wall that holds the road surface in place while permitting run-off water to flow over it (or through it). The structure is built like an erosion gabion, consisting of a stone retaining wall enclosed with wire netting. The gabion must extend well beyond the width of the road on both sides to prevent run-off water eating its way around it.

If wire netting is unavailable, the wall can be built in the same way but greater care must be taken to ensure that each individual stone is firmly lodged into position.

The gabion must be made a little lower at the centre of the drainage line to ensure that most of the run-off water is concentrated into midstream below the road. This can be done with a curved dip in the top surface of the gabion or with a stepped lower section built into the gabion top surface.

The upstream side of the wall should be lined with a fine geotextile or shadecloth to hold back fine silt and sand. Water-carried sand, silt and mud is held back by the structure and consolidates to form a firm and stable road surface over which run-off water can flow freely without eroding the surface.

Wire netting should be used to prevent stones from getting washed away during flash floods. First a foundation channel is dug across the drainage line. This foundation should be no less than 300 mm deep. The channel must then be lined with the wire netting before the stone packing proceeds. When the stone packing is completed the mesh is folded up over it like a blanket and fastened as illustrated.

Stones should be packed up against the overflow side of the structure to prevent the drainage flow from eroding the stream bed at the main point of impact. With larger structures the stream bed should be lined with stones for 1–2 m and these should also be enclosed with wire netting for maximum effectiveness.

Once the drainage crossing is fully stabilised, silt and sand will fill up between the stones and plants will take root, forming the final stage of drainage crossing stabilisation. Retaining walls can thus be completely vegetated and obscured by a plant cover, which will also make them more aesthetically acceptable. Suitable plant seeds can also be sown into the structure. Organic material will become trapped in between the stones, making the structure a fertile site for seed germination.

BOX 3.3

Road building and gully rehabilitation

Where roads pass through eroded or extensive drainage areas, treatment of the gullies and drainages upstream of the road with gabions or other soil erosion control methods will help to slow down the force of run-off water sufficiently to prevent the road from washing away each time there is a rainstorm. Establishment of vegetation in the gullies behind the erosion control structures will help to stabilise them permanently and prevent destructive run-off onto the road. The road itself can be stabilised with a retaining gabion wall for normal run-off. In this way the road is protected and an erosion gully system can be stabilised.

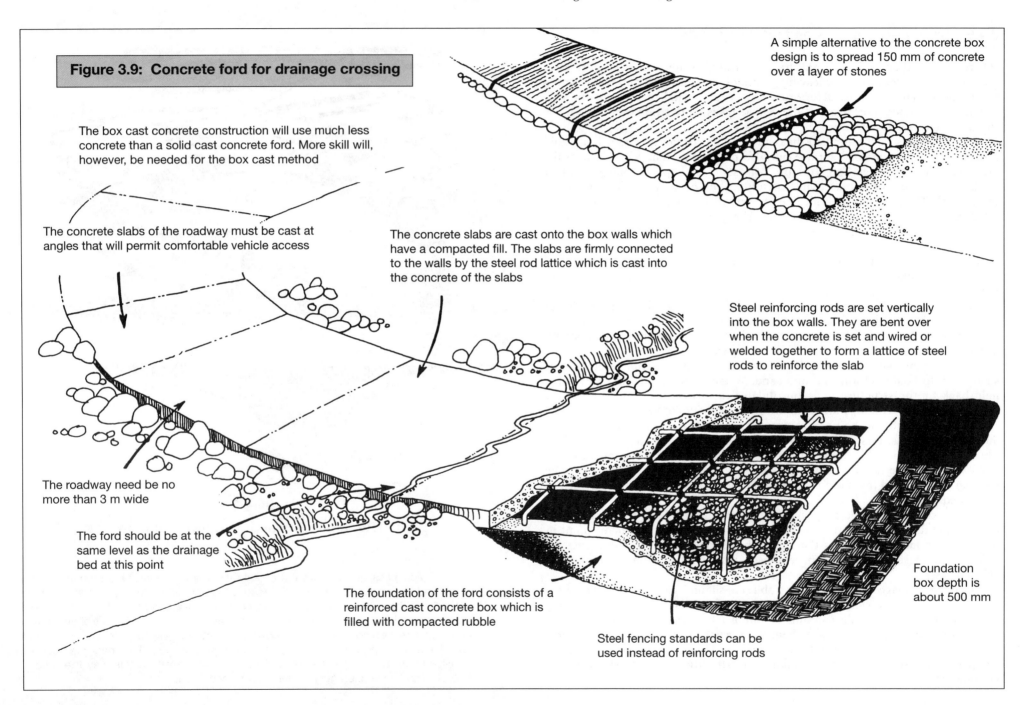

Figure 3.9: Concrete ford for drainage crossing

A simple alternative to the concrete box design is to spread 150 mm of concrete over a layer of stones

The box cast concrete construction will use much less concrete than a solid cast concrete ford. More skill will, however, be needed for the box cast method

The concrete slabs of the roadway must be cast at angles that will permit comfortable vehicle access

The concrete slabs are cast onto the box walls which have a compacted fill. The slabs are firmly connected to the walls by the steel rod lattice which is cast into the concrete of the slabs

Steel reinforcing rods are set vertically into the box walls. They are bent over when the concrete is set and wired or welded together to form a lattice of steel rods to reinforce the slab

The roadway need be no more than 3 m wide

The ford should be at the same level as the drainage bed at this point

The foundation of the ford consists of a reinforced cast concrete box which is filled with compacted rubble

Steel fencing standards can be used instead of reinforcing rods

Foundation box depth is about 500 mm

3.4.7 Concrete fords

A permanent solution to problematic stream crossings is to construct a low, concrete causeway or ford on the roadway. The ford surface must be made at stream bed level so that it does not impede the normal water flow of the drainage.

The ford surface is resistant to water erosion and will eliminate muddy conditions where the flow is constant or seasonally constant and even where the road is only occasionally inundated.

Like culverts, fords need to be expertly constructed to ensure that they are able to resist the destructive force of storm-water and undercutting. Figure 3.9 illustrates a reinforced box construction design that is cast in sections. An alternative to this approach is to use a solid concrete design but this will be considerably more expensive and is therefore only suited to situations with a solid rock foundation. The length of the ford depends on the stream width and the amount of storm-water or inundation that can be expected.

If properly constructed, concrete fords should not restrict the movement of fish along permanent streams. Fish are able to negotiate a limited concrete surface with even a minimal flow over it.

As with other drainage constructions, provision must be made for protection of the overflow point on the downstream side of the drift. This can be done by means of a single layer of stones, closely packed and enclosed in wire mesh to prevent them from being washed away during floods. This precaution need only be as wide as the stream bed and approximately 1.5 m long.

Although generally a low-maintenance structure, drifts need to be regularly checked for gravel, stone and plant debris build-up above the drift. This debris should be cleared away to ensure unimpeded water flow over the drift. Avoid the formation of pools next to the upstream side of the ford as they may lead to undercutting of the structure during periods of water flow.

The approach to the ford, as well as the exit, should be higher than the middle overflow area to ensure that the flow is concentrated in the middle part of the ford and directed into the stream bed.

The reinforced box construction is suitable for most situations, particularly where deep sand or mud covers the bedrock. The foundation sides should be cast as a single unit, while the surface slabs should be cast in sections, each separated by an expansion gap.

If the alternative of solid concrete slabs is used, then it is advisable to locate a number of steel pegs into the rock slab surface to help bind the concrete to the rock. This may, however, require drilling into the rock surface. A simple box construction, as with concrete road strips, can be used. The amount of concrete required can be marginally reduced by partly filling each section with a layer of stones.

BOX 3.4
Fords, causeways and fish migration

Many aquatic organisms undertake seasonal migrations up or down streams and rivers for breeding purposes. Natural population dispersal is also dependent on the freedom to move up or downstream. Populations of invertebrates, amphibians and fish may be negatively affected if these migrations are cut off in any way. The construction of low-water fords and bridges must therefore not cut off the movement of aquatic organisms.

Fish are often most severely affected when they are unable to negotiate barriers built across streams and are unable to move upstream to spawn at the onset of warm weather in spring. In extreme cases, it may be necessary to construct a fish ladder that will enable migrating fish to move over the barrier to spawn. Fords with culverts or pipes for stream-flow do not cut off fish movement, but concrete drifts or stone gabion walls without pipes may be too high or too wide for fish to negotiate them.

This is a frequent, although overlooked, problem with field roads and is even a bigger problem with large bridges and dam walls. It is important, nevertheless, to be aware of the requirements of fish migration when designing a stream crossing. A fish ladder consists of little more than a stepped series of ponds that will allow migrating fish to jump over the barrier in easy stages. It is relatively simple to construct, but will require some skill in masonry, brickwork or concrete construction.

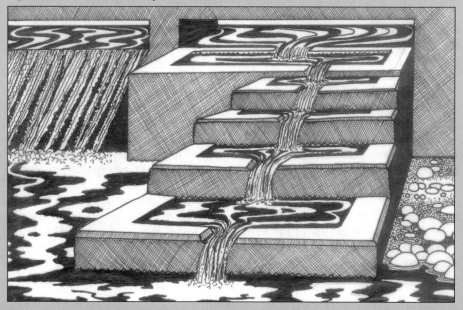

3.4.8 Pipes and culverts

Culverts are pipes that pass under a road to carry away storm-water flow, rather than permitting the run-off water to flow over the road. The pipes are usually located where natural watercourses cross the road. Pipes, however, are very expensive to install and should only be used where run-off is excessive and destructive, where run-off is continuous or where roads unavoidably pass through marshy conditions.

The pipe inflow wall must be built strongly enough to withstand a beating from storm-water as it usually brings stones and driftwood with it. The side wings must be wide enough on each side of the pipes to prevent water from eating around the structure and a horizontal apron must be installed to prevent water from undercutting the structure, as illustrated in Figure 3.10.

Culverts can be made out of pre-cast concrete or steel pipes, and using stone, brick or reinforced concrete to round off the construction.

Smaller culvert pipes can also be made out of sawn timber, stone or concrete slabs, short sections of wooden poles or even modified, old oil drums. When using these alternatives, adequate attention must be given to the strength of the 'pipe' in terms of load-bearing capacity. Common practice with forestry roads is to build a culvert out of sawn timber, or short, wooden poles, and then to cover the culvert with logs or poles to ensure load strength. The pole or log bed is then covered with road surface gravel. Timber or pole culvert constructions will, however, not have as long a lifespan as culverts made out of stone or concrete.

One of the biggest problems with pipes is that they can become blocked with branches, stones and plant debris, effectively forming a dam and eventually forcing water to flow over or around the road with the risk of roadway erosion. Pipes need to be kept clear of storm-water debris to function effectively.

A good way in which to prevent branches and debris from blocking a culvert is to build a simple branch trap slightly upstream of the pipe entrance. This trap can be made from steel fencing standards or reinforcing rod off-cuts. The general diameter of the metal should not be less than 20 mm. The trap is firmly welded together and must be securely embedded in the concrete apron at the pipe entrance. Water-carried branches will tangle up in the trap and only water and fine debris will pass into the pipe. The trap must, however, be regularly cleared of debris to function efficiently.

Provision must be made for emergency spilling of excess storm-water over the road. This can be achieved by constructing a raised drainage hump across the road on the downhill side of the culvert, but some distance from it. This hump will help to channel the overflow back into the drainage line. This overflow occurs when there is more run-off than the culvert can channel and is another good reason why a culvert system must be expertly constructed to prevent storm-water damage.

BOX 3.5

Culverts and animals

Many wild animals use culverts and pipes as temporary cover to hide from predators or to escape the hot midday sun. Inside a buried concrete or steel pipe it is shady, cool, sometimes moist and, in fact, a perfect temporary shelter.

Rock hyraxes use culverts and pipes to cross roads under cover, grey mongooses use them as latrines and monitor lizards live in them. Porcupines sometimes rest in pipes by day and even small birds are sometimes seen hopping along inside pipes.

Not only small animals make use of culverts. I have observed that the Cape mountain zebra and a number of antelope species will make use of large culverts (2 x 3 m) to pass under a fairly busy public road when moving from one side of a nature reserve to the other.

Branches and other organic material deposited in pipes by flood waters provide cover and are sometimes used by smaller animals like rodents, lizards, snakes and even toads as refuge cover.

The use of culverts and pipes by animals is of interest but care must be exercised to ensure that the waterway remains unobstructed in order to function efficiently when required.

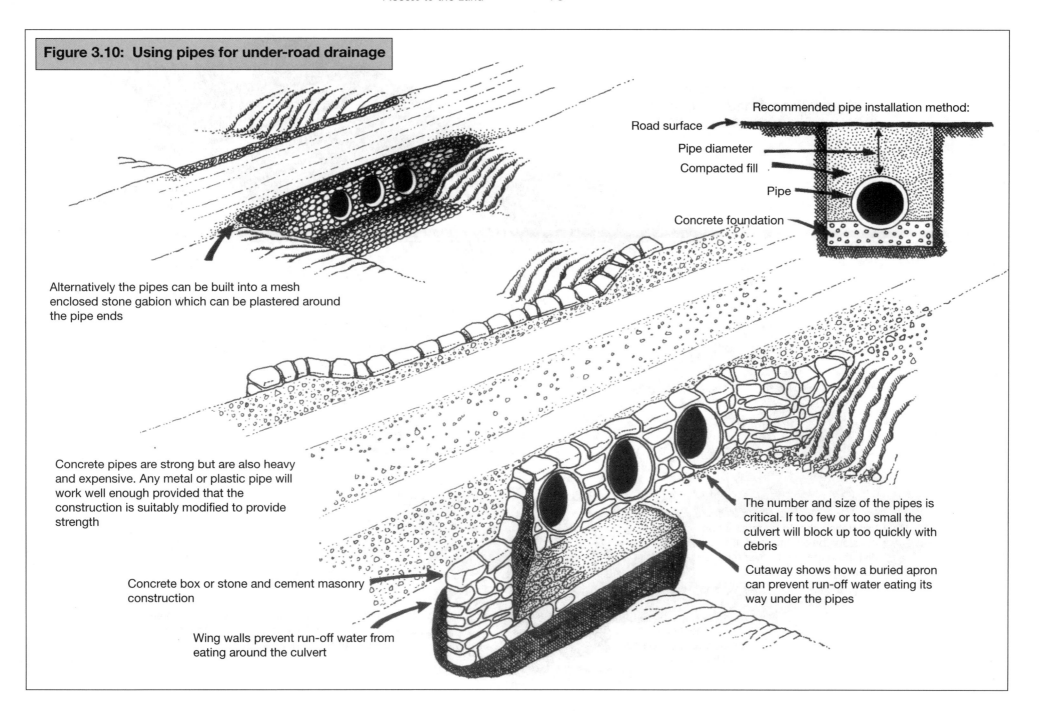

Figure 3.10: Using pipes for under-road drainage

Recommended pipe installation method:

Road surface

Pipe diameter

Compacted fill

Pipe

Concrete foundation

Alternatively the pipes can be built into a mesh enclosed stone gabion which can be plastered around the pipe ends

Concrete pipes are strong but are also heavy and expensive. Any metal or plastic pipe will work well enough provided that the construction is suitably modified to provide strength

The number and size of the pipes is critical. If too few or too small the culvert will block up too quickly with debris

Cutaway shows how a buried apron can prevent run-off water eating its way under the pipes

Concrete box or stone and cement masonry construction

Wing walls prevent run-off water from eating around the culvert

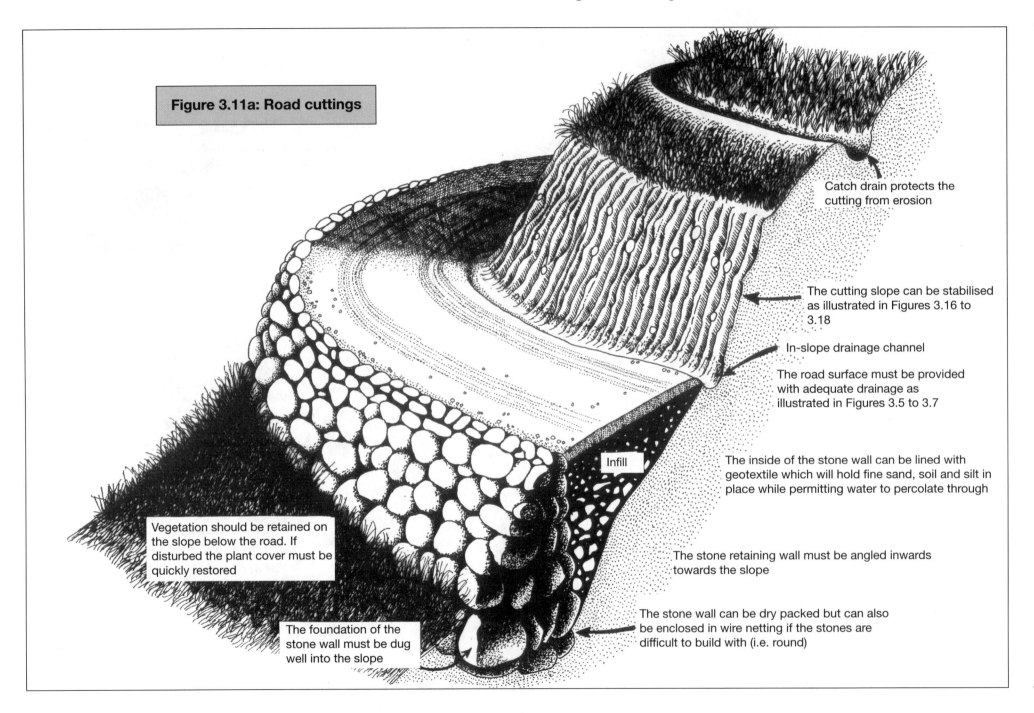

Figure 3.11a: Road cuttings

Catch drain protects the cutting from erosion

The cutting slope can be stabilised as illustrated in Figures 3.16 to 3.18

In-slope drainage channel

The road surface must be provided with adequate drainage as illustrated in Figures 3.5 to 3.7

Infill

The inside of the stone wall can be lined with geotextile which will hold fine sand, soil and silt in place while permitting water to percolate through

The stone retaining wall must be angled inwards towards the slope

Vegetation should be retained on the slope below the road. If disturbed the plant cover must be quickly restored

The stone wall can be dry packed but can also be enclosed in wire netting if the stones are difficult to build with (i.e. round)

The foundation of the stone wall must be dug well into the slope

At the water exit end of the pipes, provision must be made to protect the drainage line from the erosive force of the storm-water. This will be achieved partly by the apron of the culvert (see Figure 3.10), but this must be supplemented by a mesh-enclosed, flat packed section of stones, at least 1.5 m wide and the full width of the drainage channel.

3.4.9 Road cuttings

It is sometimes necessary to construct a road on a very steep slope. Generally, this type of construction should be avoided because of the intensity of the disturbance and also the higher costs involved. However, when it is the only option, great care must be taken to prevent the cutting from becoming a new source of accelerated soil erosion.

A cut-and-fill method is used, as illustrated in Figure 3.11a, but the road fill and surface may need a retaining structure to keep it in place. This is largely dependent on the sub-surface material on the slope. A cutting made in solid or near solid rock may be stable enough and not require a retaining structure, while cuttings made in conglomerate, loose shale, clay, earth or colluvium may need to be stabilised with a retaining wall as illustrated in Figure 3.11a and 3.11b.

The retaining wall should preferably be constructed of rock, must lean inwards towards the cutting and must have a wide deep foundation. The stone wall can be strengthened by encasing it in wire mesh, using either a gabion basket type of construction, or simply building the wall in layers, on the mesh and pulling it up and over the completed wall like wrapping a parcel. The cut material is used as roadway fill and any excess material should be removed and used elsewhere for road surfacing. Before the fill is worked into place, a sheet of geofabric should be fixed to the inside of the retaining wall. This will hold finer base material in place while still permitting water to filter through. The fill must be levelled and compacted from the bottom up to ensure that it does not subside when wet.

Cut-and-fill construction on steep slopes can be very messy, most often resulting in an unsightly spill of rocks and gravel along the slopes below the road. This visual impact can be eliminated with the construction procedure illustrated in Figure 3.11b. A retaining wall is first constructed along the roadway before the cutting is made – this will eliminate the down-slope movement of any rubble when the cutting is made.

Careful attention to drainage is critical. The road surface should be cambered in-slope and a shallow gutter made all along the foot of the cutting. As with all water channels, care must be taken to ensure that this gutter does not erode and become a gully. Adequate cross-road drainage is the key to successful drainage in cuttings. Provision must be made to direct run-off water off the road surface using drainage humps. A catch-water drain should be made above the cutting to direct run-off water away from the cutting slope. Care must be taken to ensure that this primary drain does not itself become an erosion channel.

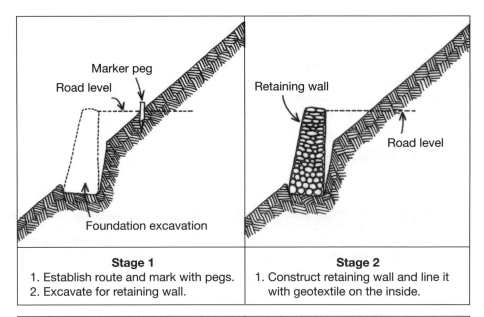

Stage 1
1. Establish route and mark with pegs.
2. Excavate for retaining wall.

Stage 2
1. Construct retaining wall and line it with geotextile on the inside.

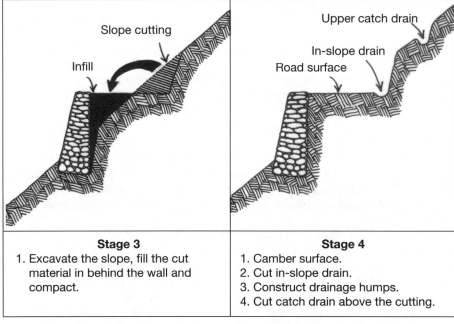

Stage 3
1. Excavate the slope, fill the cut material in behind the wall and compact.

Stage 4
1. Camber surface.
2. Cut in-slope drain.
3. Construct drainage humps.
4. Cut catch drain above the cutting.

Figure 3.11b: Procedure for the construction of cuttings

The cutting slope should be stabilised and rehabilitated where possible. When the cutting is made, the final cut slope should not be steeper than 60°, but preferably closer to 45° for ease of rehabilitation. Rehabilitation methods for steep slopes are described later in this chapter.

Roadway cutting scars are often the most visible part of a road in steep or hilly country. Aesthetic considerations should therefore play an important role in the design and rehabilitation of road cuttings.

3.5   MAINTENANCE

Maintenance is what roads are all about. From the day that a road is completed and is put into use, maintenance will be required. The builder of the road must accept the long-term responsibility of maintaining the road to avoid environmental damage. The effectiveness of the maintenance applied to any road system will determine the sustained longevity of the road system and the relative comfort with which the road can be used.

Maintenance is not cheap but failing to do the necessary repairs timeously can result in huge additional expenses when small problems develop into big ones – something that can happen at frightening speed.

Effective maintenance should be based on regular inspection, particularly after rainstorms, which are the major cause of damage to rangeland roads. A good practice is to keep a road maintenance register, particularly in areas where the roads are used by a number of drivers. Each road user can record details about maintenance requirements, indicating the type of problem, degree of urgency and locality of the problem area. These records can then be used to regularly plan maintenance input and budget for the necessary finances.

The costs of road maintenance need to be continuously reviewed and built into the financial and management planning of the area in which the road system is located. Underestimating the requirement for maintenance, and its cost, could have disastrous results if sustained road maintenance is neglected due to a lack of funds. This often happens, as can be seen by the generally poor quality of rangeland roads and the number of abandoned roads which become eroded scars on the landscape.

Because of the extensive nature of field roads and tracks, an appropriate approach must be developed for maintenance. Each area has its own particular problems and these should become 'hotspots' for attention. The following checklist highlights typical problem areas. One should attend to these 'hotspots' first and only then deal with the quality of the road surface.

Most often, roads are simply graded to improve the ride but little or no attention is given to the important problem areas. Grading the road can be a very destructive treatment option because with each treatment the roadway is cut a little deeper and eventually it becomes a wide gully, an ideal conduit for channelling destructive run-off water.

The type of maintenance required is largely determined by the substrate type, the climate and the topography. The skill with which the road was originally routed and built will also play an important role.

An important consideration with road maintenance is that it is not only directed towards the condition of the road and the ride when using it, but also towards reducing the impact of the road on the natural environment through which it winds its way.

3.5.1   Checklist of important maintenance inspection sites

1. Untreated/uncontrolled drainage crossings.

2. Steep sections of road without hard surfacing.

3. Sections of road without any drainage treatment.

4. Culverts and pipes – check for blockages.

5. Culverts and pipes – check for water eating around the structure.

6. Causeways and fords – check for undercutting.

7. Retaining walls – check for undercutting, water eating around the sides and road surface material loss through the wall.

8. Off-road drainage – check for soil erosion at run-off sites.

9. Cuttings – check for erosion of the slope below the cutting.

10. Wet areas – check for forced detours around muddy sections.

11. Sandy areas – check for forced detours due to loose sand sections.

12. Deterioration of surfaces – check for loss of fine material leaving only sharp stones and gravel.

13. Borrow pits – check run-off flow and potential for soil erosion.

14. Road surface erosion – establish the need for additional drainage humps.

15. Drainage humps – check for the formation of mud pools against the hump.

16. Drainage humps – check for effective deflection of run-off water.

17. Cuttings – check condition of the in-slope run-off gutters.

18. Cuttings – check condition of the catchments above cuttings.

19. Rehabilitation sites – monitor effectiveness of methods used.

3.5.2 Borrow pits

Borrow pits are the source of road surfacing material, usually obtained by mining for shale or gravel. The material is excavated and carted off to the area of road requiring surfacing.

Borrow pits are necessary, even if they are ugly, raw scars on the landscape and often an eyesore. If properly managed and carefully rehabilitated after use, they need not be permanently intrusive or remain an eyesore. The size, depth, spread and location of borrow pits is determined by the type of material that is available. The exploitation of the surfacing material must be sensitively managed and well planned. The big question is: How many borrow pits are required and how far apart should they be?

Figure 3.12, option 1, illustrates a road system with only two large borrow pits. This means that material has to be transported further to distant sites requiring surfacing. This necessitates more transporting with heavy loads of gravel which impacts the road surfaces. Bigger borrow pits are also more difficult to rehabilitate after use.

In Figure 3.12, option 2, the same road system is serviced by six small borrow pits, relatively evenly distributed throughout the road network. Transport of material is over short distances, the loads can be lighter and the smaller borrow pits are comparatively easy to rehabilitate.

The second option, consisting of numerous but small well-spaced borrow pits, appears to be the most practical. The layout that is best for a particular site, however, is also dependent on the vehicles and machinery available, the nature of the gravel, the quality of the roads and the degree of maintenance required.

The rehabilitation of borrow pits is dealt with in detail in section 3.6. One of the best options for borrow pit rehabilitation is their conversion into waterholes or small wetlands. With a little imagination, some landscaping and clever planting of suitable vegetation, redundant borrow pits can become important habitats for wildlife like fish, frogs, lizards, birds, rodents and invertebrates. Before the borrow pit is excavated, it will be useful to put all of the vegetation on the site on a pile and to push the topsoil into a separate pile for later use when rehabilitating the borrow pit.

When initially selecting sites for borrow pit excavation, make sure that the site selected is not sensitive in terms of rare plants or rare plant communities or specialised wildlife habitat. The insensitive placing of a single borrow pit can be responsible for the near extinction of a very rare butterfly species, an insect that is easily overlooked when looking for borrow pit sites. The impact of noise and dust disturbance on the surrounding environment must also be considered. Locating a borrow pit near an important migrant bird breeding locality, for example, will negatively impact on the breeding success of the migrant birds. It is therefore essential that the siting of borrow pits be carefully considered before any excavating is done.

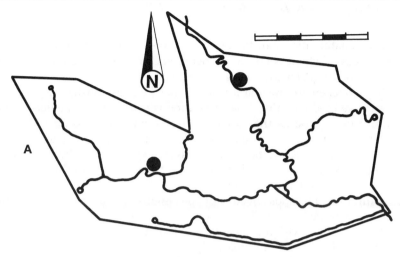

Option 1: Two large borrow pits
Transport distances for road surfacing materials are long, time consuming and therefore more costly.

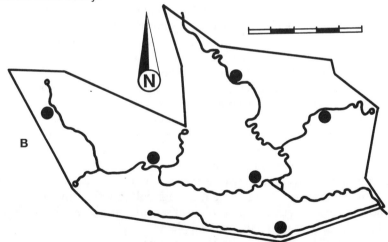

Option 2: Six small borrow pits
Transport distances are much shorter, the operation is much quicker and therefore more cost effective.

Figure 3.12: Spacing of borrow pits

3.6   ROAD DAMAGE REHABILITATION

The cost of rehabilitation can far exceed the cost of road building, which is a really good reason why it is absolutely necessary to route and build roads in the most environmentally sensitive manner possible.

In many areas environmental legislation has been established in an effort to ensure sensitive road planning. This legislation is usually implemented by means of an application process that involves the appointment of an independent consultant to carry out an environmental sensitivity analysis. To most landowners this will seem to be an unnecessary expense but when compared to the potential restoration costs that may result from ill-advised road building, consultancy fees are relatively cheap.

Rehabilitation methods need not be highly technical or particularly complicated. Simple, practical methods that stabilise disturbed surfaces and eventually cover them with a protective vegetation cover are all that is required. Very often, simple answers to apparently tricky rehabilitation problems can be found alongside the problem area site where conditions are still undisturbed. It only takes a little understanding, observation skills and some innovation to emulate nature and to help nature heal herself.

An extremely important aspect of the rehabilitation process is that of visual aesthetics. Road construction damage is unsightly and care must be taken not only to heal the scar in the long term but also to screen it off in the shorter term. Visual impact is particularly important in areas that are popular tourism venues or that are used for outdoor recreation and relaxation.

Successful rehabilitation is seldom a once-off exercise – it requires a trial-and-error approach to help determine the most cost-effective and suitable applications for any particular area. As with all other types of rehabilitation, the objective is to stabilise the soil surface and to establish a protective vegetation cover, similar to the original, as quickly as possible. The possibility of inadvertently introducing potentially invasive plant species into the rangeland via the rehabilitation programme must be avoided. It is inadvisable to rely on the advice given at nurseries or even by alleged agricultural and other experts. This advice, however well meant, is most often insensitive to the aesthetics, invasive potential and biology of the recommended plants.

It is best to allow nature to be your leading guide. Examine the natural vegetation surrounding the site in need of rehabilitation. Look at other disturbed sites in the area and try to emulate the natural healing process. Identify local plants that have potential and investigate the availability of seedlings or seed for these species.

Prescriptions given in the literature for a particular area as well as experience with similar rehabilitation projects close to the site will provide the best guidelines. The following methods will help where no previous experience exists.

3.6.1 Closing and rehabilitating unneeded field roads

Unneeded roads should be identified, withdrawn from use and rehabilitated. The objective for road rehabilitation is to establish a protective ground cover vegetation, similar to the original state, as quickly as possible. Figures 3.13 and 3.14 illustrate rehabilitation methods and the procedure is as follows:

- Ensure that a road or track will not be used by planting a row of short poles across the access at both ends. Simply placing large stones across the roadway is not sufficient because they can easily be moved aside.
- Divide the road into manageable sections of 50 or 100 m for treatment. Treat the sections with the greatest potential for soil erosion first.
- Retaining fences and brush-packing (see Figure 3.13): In steeper sections where erosion has occurred in the wheel ruts, construct a low fence across the road with a vertical section of mesh (300 mm) and a section of mesh lying flat on the ground (400 mm). Pack the entire structure with a dense layer of brush cut up into short (300 mm) sections and packed about 200 mm deep. The brush will slow the water run-off flow, retain moisture, trap silt, organic material and seeds, provide a protected environment for plant germination and hide an unsightly scar. Take care to ensure that all of the brush lies flat on the road surface and not above it.
- Stone cobbling and brush-packing (see Figure 3.14): This method is much the same as the previous one except that bands of stone are packed across the road to break the force of run-off water and trap water-translocated materials. As with the former method, brush is packed behind the stones to create a protective seedbed and, if available, mulch can be used to cover exposed road surfaces in between the bands of stone. Before the stones are placed, a strip of jute geotextile should be put down to prevent undercutting by run-off water. If geotextile is not available a layer of straw should be used as a bedding for the stones.
- The plants that are most suitable for establishment in the brush-packed sections are those that occur naturally in the general vicinity of the road. The best policy is to use fast-growing grasses, annuals and ground covers for initial establishment. Slower growing shrubs and small trees will help to 'hide' the original road route from view.

Note that the low wire mesh retaining fences are necessary to hold the brush-packing in place where water flow or wind would otherwise remove the brush and mulch. This is particularly necessary on steeper slopes and in windy regions.

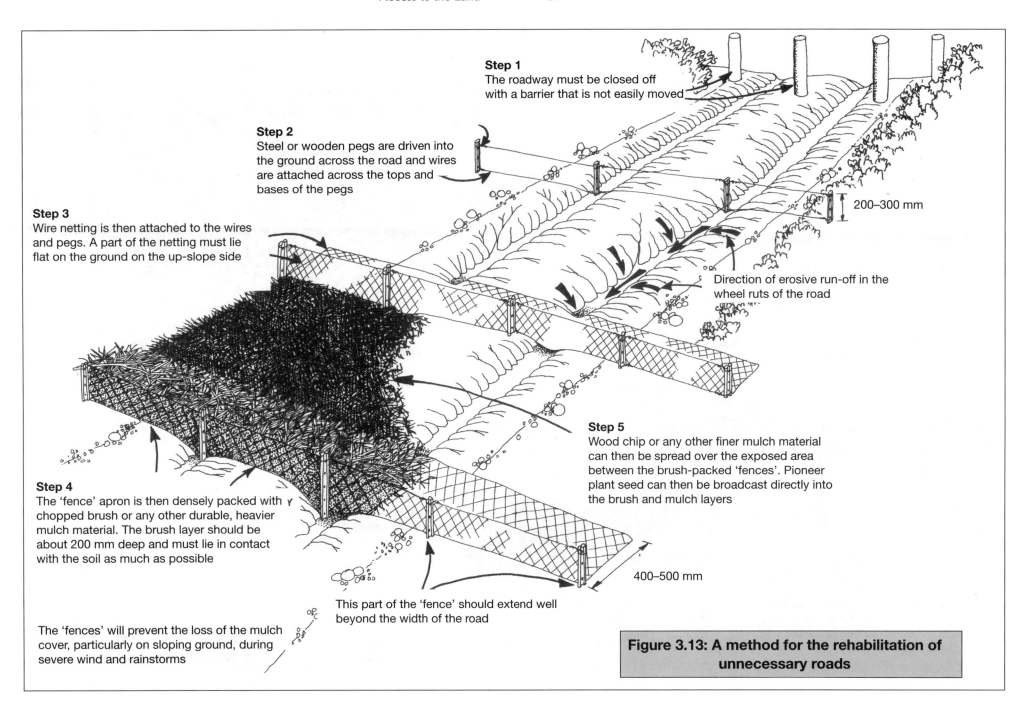

Step 1
The roadway must be closed off with a barrier that is not easily moved

Step 2
Steel or wooden pegs are driven into the ground across the road and wires are attached across the tops and bases of the pegs

200–300 mm

Step 3
Wire netting is then attached to the wires and pegs. A part of the netting must lie flat on the ground on the up-slope side

Direction of erosive run-off in the wheel ruts of the road

Step 5
Wood chip or any other finer mulch material can then be spread over the exposed area between the brush-packed 'fences'. Pioneer plant seed can then be broadcast directly into the brush and mulch layers

Step 4
The 'fence' apron is then densely packed with chopped brush or any other durable, heavier mulch material. The brush layer should be about 200 mm deep and must lie in contact with the soil as much as possible

This part of the 'fence' should extend well beyond the width of the road

400–500 mm

The 'fences' will prevent the loss of the mulch cover, particularly on sloping ground, during severe wind and rainstorms

Figure 3.13: A method for the rehabilitation of unnecessary roads

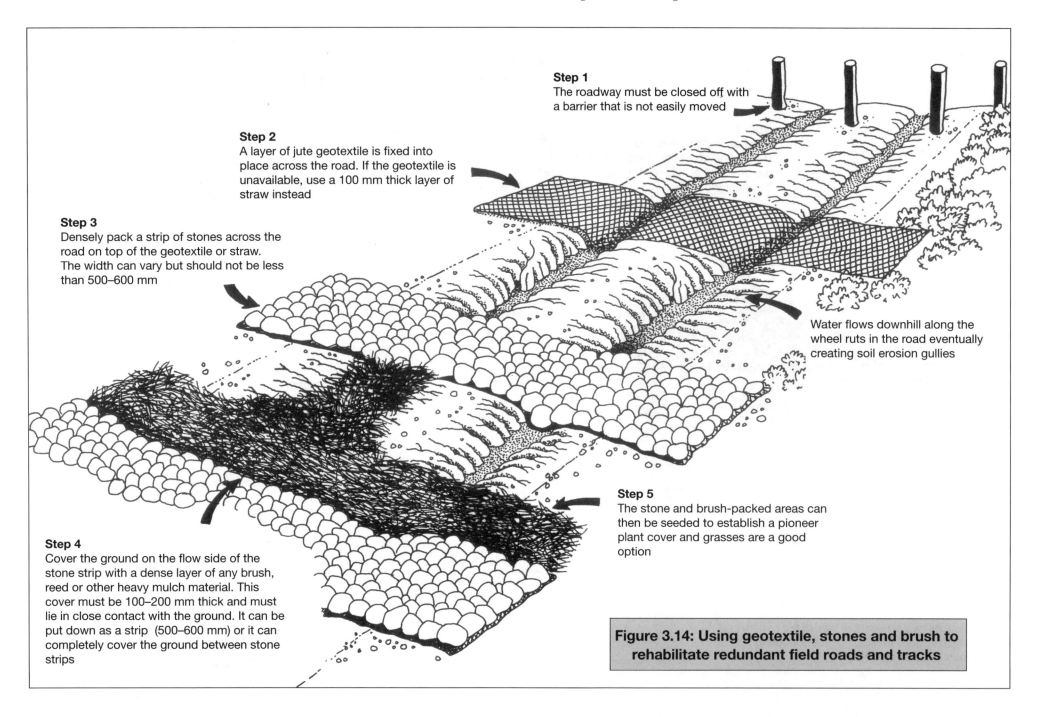

Step 1
The roadway must be closed off with a barrier that is not easily moved

Step 2
A layer of jute geotextile is fixed into place across the road. If the geotextile is unavailable, use a 100 mm thick layer of straw instead

Step 3
Densely pack a strip of stones across the road on top of the geotextile or straw. The width can vary but should not be less than 500–600 mm

Water flows downhill along the wheel ruts in the road eventually creating soil erosion gullies

Step 5
The stone and brush-packed areas can then be seeded to establish a pioneer plant cover and grasses are a good option

Step 4
Cover the ground on the flow side of the stone strip with a dense layer of any brush, reed or other heavy mulch material. This cover must be 100–200 mm thick and must lie in close contact with the ground. It can be put down as a strip (500–600 mm) or it can completely cover the ground between stone strips

Figure 3.14: Using geotextile, stones and brush to rehabilitate redundant field roads and tracks

3.6.2 The rehabilitation of road cutting slopes

The rehabilitation method described below is suitable where road cutting construction has resulted in a scree of loose sand, rubble and stones on the slope below the road. Cut-and-fill road building often results in these loose rubble slopes when not sensitively constructed as described in Figure 3.11b. They present a real challenge for rehabilitation because the slope is unstable and can easily wash away. The first step is therefore to stabilise the slope.

This can be done by constructing a retaining structure along the slope. Any material can be used but the use of low wire netting fences is suggested. The wire netting structure is robust enough to hold back gravel and stones. The low fence is made with steel or wooden pegs that are driven deep into the rubble on the down-slope side of the 'fence'. The 'fence' need be no more than 300–400 mm high. The wire netting is then fixed to a top-wire connecting the pegs and pinned flat onto the rubble surface on the up-slope side of the 'fence' as illustrated in Figure 3.15.

The 'fences' are then densely packed with a suitable brush or mulch material. This serves as a filter, helping to hold back sand, gravel and stones that are dislodged and move down the slope. Any leafy plant material can be used but lengthy brush material must be cut up into short bits so that the mulch lies flat on the surface and not above it.

Before the mulch is put down, the strips should be seeded with a suitable pioneer vegetation. The species used should be compatible with the surrounding vegetation. The best option, however, is initially to use fast-growing grasses that quickly establish a protective and soil binding cover.

The mulch on each structure should be packed the full width of the mesh (400–500 mm) and about 200 mm deep. The top strip below the road should be mulch-covered right up to the road edge.

These retaining 'fence' structures will hold the mulch in place on the slopes and the combination of wire netting and mulch will prevent the soil and gravel from sliding or washing down-slope. The mulch also creates a protected site for seed germination, with the establishment of a protective plant cover being the ultimate objective of this restoration method.

When using this method the number of mulched 'fences' needed on a particular slope will depend on the area that needs to be stabilised. In some cases only one or two may be sufficient, while in others many more may be required.

If there is a plentiful source of material nearby for mulching, the entire slope can be covered with mulch, but the retaining 'fences' across the slope will still be required to stabilise the loose soil and stone surface.

When the construction of a new road on a steep slope is planned, the usual scree of loose stone and gravel caused by road building should be avoided by means of the sensitive approach to building road cuttings that is illustrated in Figure 3.11b. Prevention is always better than cure.

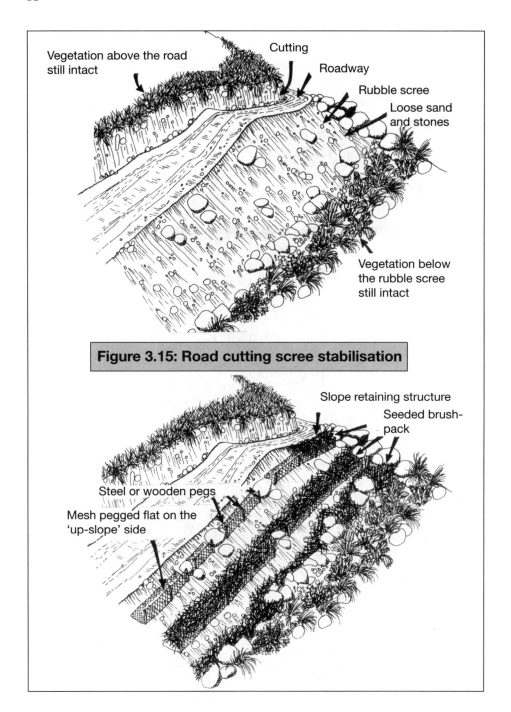

Figure 3.15: Road cutting scree stabilisation

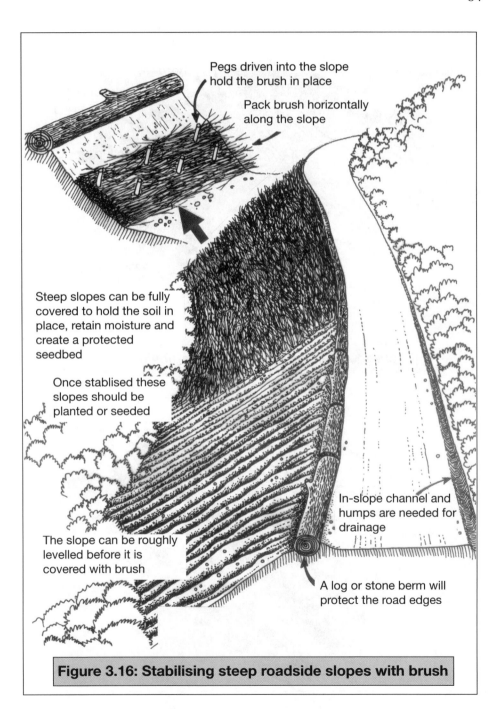

Pegs driven into the slope hold the brush in place

Pack brush horizontally along the slope

Steep slopes can be fully covered to hold the soil in place, retain moisture and create a protected seedbed

Once stablised these slopes should be planted or seeded

The slope can be roughly levelled before it is covered with brush

In-slope channel and humps are needed for drainage

A log or stone berm will protect the road edges

Figure 3.16: Stabilising steep roadside slopes with brush

3.6.3   The use of brush-packing and stakes to stabilise steep roadside slopes

Figure 3.16 illustrates the use of brush-packing as a complete brush cover or mattress, covering the entire destabilised and exposed soil surface. The brush is laid horizontally across the slope and care is taken to ensure that most of it lies flat on the soil surface and not above it.

Pegs are driven into the slope at intervals to help hold the brush mattress in place. This will prevent it from being washed down the slope by run-off water and will also hold it in position during windy periods.

A run-off gutter along the up-slope side of the road in conjunction with cross-road drainage humps will be required to protect the road surface. If excessive run-off is expected, then a stone or log drain, as illustrated in Figures 3.6 and 3.7, should be built at down-slope drainage points.

Brush should not be harvested from the slope immediately above and below the road because of the important role that the vegetation cover has in protecting the slope soil surfaces. Once treated, the brush-packed area can be seeded, or seed can first be broadcast before the brush is packed down.

In Figure 3.17 the use of brush wattles is illustrated as an alternative to a complete brush mattress cover. The wattles consist of bound bundles of branches that are pinned into grooves across the slope to form water and soil retention berms across the destabilised area. In wetter areas, live green branches of plants that root easily from cuttings can be used for the wattles. These then take root to establish a new protective cover. Another method for planting cuttings on moist slopes is to use truncheons of the plant that is to be established to pin the wattles to the slope.

In the more arid areas, these slopes will be too dry to establish plant cuttings. The best option will be to broadcast fast-growing pioneer plant seeds into the lines of wattles where the microclimate created by the brush will improve the success of germination. Seed can also be sown above and against the wattles where a light organic mulch of any kind will increase the germination success rate.

Figure 3.17 also illustrates the use of stones for slope stabilisation. The stones can either be packed in strips across the slope or they can be packed to form a complete protective cover where excess stones are available.

The stones can be packed onto a layer of straw or jute geotextile where the run-off is expected to be particularly heavy or swift. By cutting furrows across the slope before commencing with stone packing, sites for plant establishment can be made. These furrows will retain moisture, silt and humus under the stones, which will function much the same as brush-packing. The entire stone-packed area should be seeded.

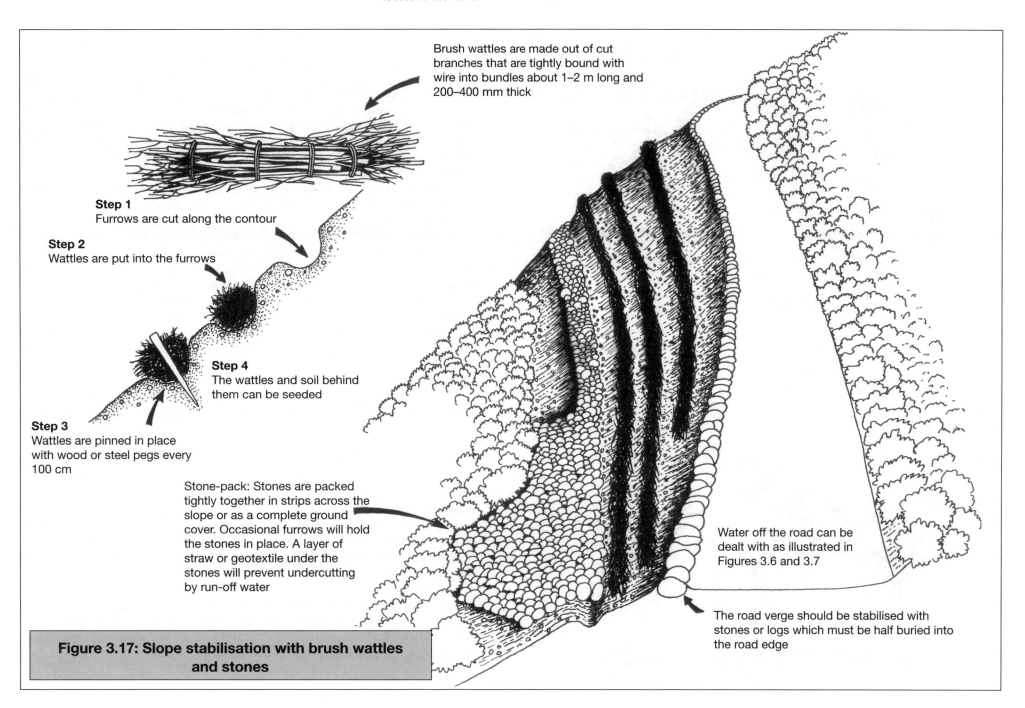

Brush wattles are made out of cut branches that are tightly bound with wire into bundles about 1–2 m long and 200–400 mm thick

Step 1
Furrows are cut along the contour

Step 2
Wattles are put into the furrows

Step 4
The wattles and soil behind them can be seeded

Step 3
Wattles are pinned in place with wood or steel pegs every 100 cm

Stone-pack: Stones are packed tightly together in strips across the slope or as a complete ground cover. Occasional furrows will hold the stones in place. A layer of straw or geotextile under the stones will prevent undercutting by run-off water

Water off the road can be dealt with as illustrated in Figures 3.6 and 3.7

The road verge should be stabilised with stones or logs which must be half buried into the road edge

Figure 3.17: Slope stabilisation with brush wattles and stones

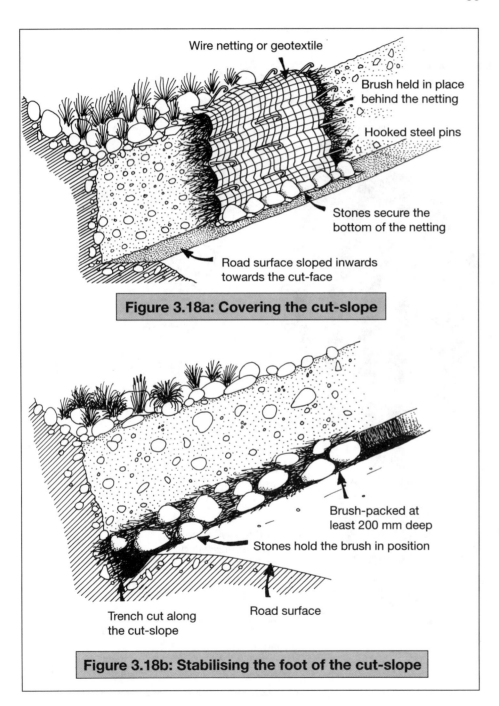

Wire netting or geotextile

Brush held in place
behind the netting

Hooked steel pins

Stones secure the
bottom of the netting

Road surface sloped inwards
towards the cut-face

Figure 3.18a: Covering the cut-slope

Brush-packed at
least 200 mm deep

Stones hold the brush in position

Trench cut along
the cut-slope

Road surface

Figure 3.18b: Stabilising the foot of the cut-slope

3.6.4   Vertical cut-slope rehabilitation

In Figure 3.18a the exposed surface excavated during road construction is completely covered with a layer of brush that protects the cut-slope from further erosion and also helps to build up a stable site for seed germination.

The brush must be held in position against the slope or else it will simply be removed by strong winds. The best way to achieve this is to secure a binding cover over the brush and to pin this cover to the slope. The cover can be made out of old fencing netting, jute geotextile or even shade netting. Alternatively, wire strands can be used to create a network that holds the brush in place. Figure 3.18a illustrates the use of fencing or coarse geotextile netting. In the illustration the netting is pinned to the cut-slope using specially made hooked steel pins. Alternatively, straight pins can be used, two at a time, to hold the mesh in place.

To brush-pack the slope, start at the bottom, putting a row of brush into place horizontally across the slope and fixing a section of mesh into place. Then put the next row of brush in place and fix in position, progressing upwards until the slope is covered. Care must be taken to make the brush cover as dense as possible. Straw can be combined with the brush to fill in the gaps.

The brush cover provides a protected site for seed germination, either for wind-blown seed or seeds sown into the brush-packed area. This method will also improve the negative visual impact of a roadside scar, softening the 'wound' with a natural organic cover.

In Figure 3.18b the cut-slope is not completely covered but cut vegetation is established along the bottom of it to help disguise the 'wound'. This method is better suited to areas where suitable brush is not as freely available for a complete cover of the cut-slope. Vegetation growing up against the cut-slope will help to improve soil surface conditions of the slope, shading it and lowering the temperature sufficiently to permit pioneer vegetation in arid areas.

A trench is made along the bottom of the slope, approximately 400 mm wide and 400 mm deep. The trench is then packed full of finely chopped brush, which is held in position with stones.

The trench can either be seeded with a suitable pioneer plant seed mixture before it is filled with brush or the seeds can be sown directly into the brush after it is put in place. In moist areas shrub or tree seedlings can be planted in the trench before the brush is applied.

The combination of brush and stones will retain moisture in the soil for seed germination and will also protect the seedlings from the elements and small herbivores. Soil erosion will be averted by the brush which will slow run-off water and also trap water-carried soil, gravel and silt and road surface material, further improving the quality of the seedbed in the trench.

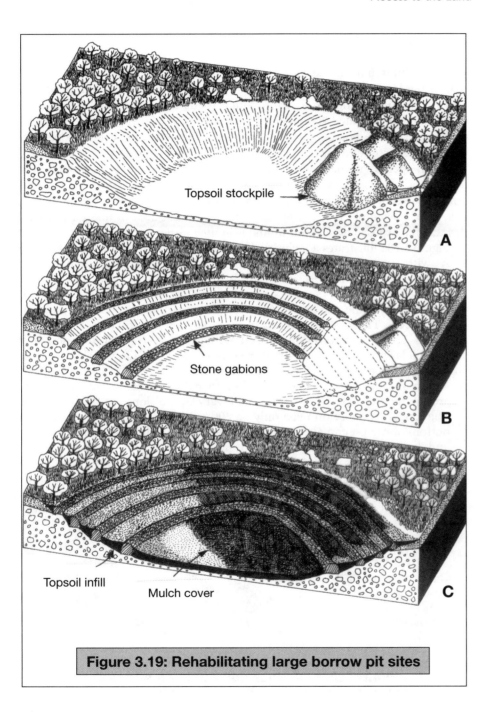

Figure 3.19: Rehabilitating large borrow pit sites

3.6.5   The rehabilitation of larger borrow pit sites

The rehabilitation of large borrow pit sites is illustrated in Figure 3.19. The three stages are as follows:

A The key to successful rehabilitation begins with the initial planning to establish a borrow pit. Before excavating the pit, all of the topsoil with its vegetation cover should be carefully stripped off the underlying gravel and stored in heaps at the edge of the borrow pit. The topsoil can be graded or bulldozed into heaps. The more plant material these heaps contain, the better, as they will be better aerated and will be able to absorb and retain moisture. The topsoil should not be permitted to dry out and become desiccated as this will kill off all the valuable soil organisms. If too wet or artificially wetted, however, seeds in the soil may germinate and rot or die. It may be wise to cover the topsoil heaps with sheets of plastic if prolonged wet weather is expected. Artificial wetting is not recommended. The storage heaps should not be too big because the large volume will exclude too much air, moisture and sunlight. Topsoil heaps should preferably not exceed 3–5 tons and it is best to shape the heap into a long, lower berm rather than a high cone.

B The first stage of rehabilitation is to cut the pit sides to the least steep angle possible – steep slopes and cut faces are simply too difficult to rehabilitate. The next step is to construct stone gabions on the gravel slopes. These gabions will hold back the topsoil that will finally be returned as a plant growth medium. Stone gabions can be replaced with log berms, wire netting and brush fences or geotextile barriers if stones are not freely available. The gabions are simply required to create a series of soil terraces on the otherwise hard and bare gravel surface.

C When the gabions, or whatever other type of retaining structure is used, are completed, the stockpiles of topsoil must be used to fill in behind the structure to create a series of soil terraces. The entire floor of the borrow pit should also be covered with topsoil. The depth of the topsoil is determined by the size of the stockpile and cannot be too deep. If the topsoil stockpile falls short of the requirement, suitable soil can be imported to help fill in the terraces.

The entire soil infill area must be covered with an organic plant mulch or fine brush-packing. Cut reeds, hay, wood chips or crop residue can be used, or leafy brush can be sensitively harvested directly from the surrounding rangeland. The terraces can then be seeded with grass and specially cultivated plants can be planted out.

3.6.6   The rehabilitation of small borrow pits

The rehabilitation of smaller borrow pits can follow much the same procedure as that of the larger pits. Natural rangeland often has a legacy of old, unrestored borrow pits, unplanned and strung along roads and tracks and contributing either to the accelerated soil erosion of the area or to the negative visual impact of the road. These borrow pits should be rehabilitated while keeping open only those that are required for ongoing repairs to the road network.

When opening up new borrow pits the topsoil should be stockpiled adjacent to the excavation area. A good practice is to divide the total borrow pit area up into three sections. Rehabilitation can then be done when the first excavation area is exhausted of gravel, while excavating the next area in line for gravel. In this way the exposed excavation wound is limited in size.

Figure 3.20a illustrates a technique for borrow pit rehabilitation as follows:

A   As with larger borrow pits, the slopes of the pit should be shaped to the smallest angle possible, without impacting on the undisturbed area beyond the pit. A series of soil-retaining structures can then be constructed along the bare slopes of the pit as illustrated in Figure 3.20a and 3.20b. These structures can be constructed with wire netting and brush or stone gabions enclosed with wire netting or wooden logs. Channels should be cut along the contour of the slope in which to position the soil structures and the soil behind them.

B   A humus-rich topsoil is then worked in behind these berms, creating a growth medium on the bare and often very sterile slopes of the borrow pit. The topsoil application need only be 200 mm deep and 500 mm wide. The bottom of the pit can also be soil-covered and then left to collect rainwater and develop an artificial wetland cover.

C   The entire borrow pit sides should then be completely covered with a fine brush layer or any other suitable organic mulch. The seeds of pioneer cover plants can either be sown onto the topsoil strips before the mulch is put down or they can be sown into the mulch cover when it is complete.

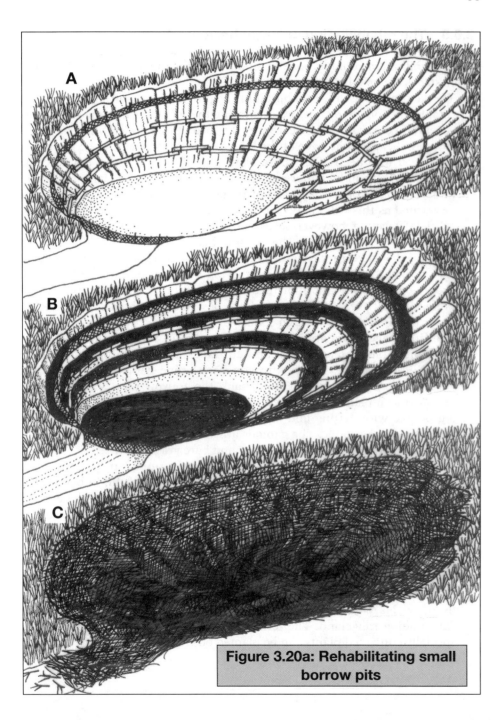

Figure 3.20a: Rehabilitating small borrow pits

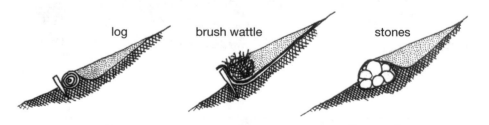

log   brush wattle   stones

Figure 3.20b: Various soil-retaining structures

3.7 RESPONSIBLE ROAD USE IN RANGELANDS

It is often the very people who are dependent on the use of roads in natural rangelands that cause the most damage to them. Inexperienced and insensitive driving in difficult terrain is one of the main problems. Drivers frequently attempt to negotiate difficult routes without converting their vehicles to four-wheel drive, only doing so when considerable damage has already been done by wheels spinning and slipping due to poor traction on loose, stony sections and digging into the road surface. Certain classes of road necessitate four-wheel drive and it should be engaged before negotiating difficult terrain and not after the vehicle is unable to continue any further and is already 'dug in'. It is a little appreciated fact that using an off-road vehicle in four-wheel drive will be a great deal less damaging to the vehicle and it provides a much more comfortable ride for the driver and the passengers on roads with bumpy surfaces.

Another frequent problem is indiscriminate driving off the formal road network and through areas of undisturbed natural vegetation. This is sometimes done to create a shortcut or to view some attraction like wildlife more closely. Vehicle tracks of this nature can cause permanent scars across the landscape, particularly in arid and semi-arid regions. Unplanned and unauthorised tracks of this type are seen by other travellers in the area who then also use them, thereby reinforcing and exacerbating their impact on the environment.

I have observed that unplanned tracks, the result of a brief wildlife capture operation, were still not rehabilitated and were still clearly visible fifteen years after they were made in an arid area. Clearly unplanned tracks should be avoided, and if completely unavoidable should be rehabilitated immediately after use. Few people appreciate that the low bushes that one can ride over with a vehicle are often much older than the lifespan of the vehicle and the damage to these plants is therefore long-lived.

Yet another typical problem is the development of new tracks alongside the original ones because these have become impassable. This happens when mud pools develop or where deep sand becomes too loose to support a vehicle in the original roadway. Drivers simply ride out a detour through natural vegetation, rather than fixing or arranging to have the problem area repaired. These detour tracks are extremely destructive and the result is an unsightly dual section of road.

It is clear that a sensitive road use policy is required for road and track use in natural rangelands. Each driver must be familiar with the policy and also be aware of the consequences of deviating from the policy in terms of environmental damage.

3.7.1 Some guidelines for responsible road use in rangelands

1. Respect the organisation or person that is responsible for the maintenance of the road and avoid destructive driving.

2. Respect other road users, local populace and other users of the rangeland.

3. Respect the rights of fauna and flora that may in some way be affected by the use of the road.

4. Never drive off the planned and approved road network.

5. Do not use rangeland roads when very wet unless absolutely necessary.

6. Use the appropriate gearing and change to four-wheel drive before negotiating difficult sections of road.

7. Respect private land and always request authority before entering private rangeland.

8. Always close gates that are found closed along the route.

9. Drive at an appropriate speed for the type of road. This should be no more than 60 km/hour on good roads and no more than 40 km/hour on unimproved tracks.

10. Help with the maintenance of the road by reporting critical road repair requirements to the relevant organisation or person.

11. Do not shy away from making temporary, emergency repairs – the time spent doing so will be appreciated by the other road users.

12. Never discard litter along the roadside in rangelands or elsewhere.

13. Never remove any item, for whatever purpose, that does not belong to you or which you do not have the necessary permission to remove.

14. Never turn around by driving through the natural vegetation on either side of the road. Rather look for a disturbed area, turning circle or a road junction in which to do a three-point turn. This is particularly important in the more sensitive vegetation types but the principle of causing minimum damage is appropriate in all kinds of habitats.

3.7.2 Driving off the road network is simply too costly

I recently witnessed an innocent but very destructive practice that, I am told, is commonplace on game reserves where visiting tourists are taken out on game drives in specially modified vehicles. The vehicle that I was in, together with nine other tourists, was purposely driven off the road and into natural shrubby rangeland to improve the game viewing and opportunities for photographing a white rhinoceros with a calf. The rhino, clearly well acquainted with this procedure, continued to lie in the shade of a tree and did not do anything amusing or spectacular. This prompted the tour guide to drive even closer, in a circle around the tree. This had been done before because there was almost a cleared track over the flattened shrubs around the tree.

The tour guide, when questioned, was unperturbed by the destruction of the vegetation and made it quite clear that good close-up game viewing for the tourists was his priority goal. The property on which this took place is approximately 450 ha in extent and there are three game vehicles, each of which transports tourists roughly twice a day.

During the balance of my game drive, now that I was sensitised to the problem, I noticed numerous other areas through which game drive vehicles had driven off the formal road network through relatively sensitive vegetation. The cumulative and destructive effect of these game drives, no less than six per day, merely strengthened my resolve that driving vehicles into natural, undisturbed vegetation should be avoided. Naturally there are a few exceptions – dense, short grassland comes to mind – but repeated driving off formal roads invariably leads to the creation of new roads.

3.7.3 Some thoughts on co-operative road management

The unnecessary duplication of rangeland roads can often be observed along boundary fence-lines. Each of the neighbours has his own road along the fence-line, a phenomenon that usually results in two sets of poorly maintained tracks alongside each other, separated only by the fence. Poor maintenance leads to soil erosion, with the potential for four erosion gullies, one in each of the wheel ruts.

I have also frequently come across tracks on both sides of an internal fence that separates sections of adjacent land or camps belonging to the same person. Again, the potential for soil erosion or storm damage is double what it needs to be.

Road maintenance is a difficult and costly necessity and there is simply no need to duplicate the responsibility for maintenance or the potential for storm damage on the road.

Neighbours can co-operate and by means of a simple system of ordinary flexible wire gates built into the boundary fence, each neighbour can manage a section of jointly used road. There need then be only one road which can alternate from one side of the fence to the other. Terrain and landscape features should determine on which side of the fence the road should lie. The use of the road and responsibility to maintain the road is then shared.

Similarly, there is no need to have a track on both sides of an internal camp fence. By means of gates, vehicles can gain access to a single road that lies only on one side of the fence. This approach will halve the cost of road building and road maintenance without affecting access.

As already outlined in this chapter, the construction of a road in natural rangeland needs to be carefully considered before any spade strikes the ground. It is often all too easy to simply ride out a new road route where the terrain permits but this is not a responsible approach and it will result in an unplanned network of largely unnecessary roads and tracks, each of which is a potential erosion gully.

CHAPTER FOUR

CLEARING THE LAND

Controlling alien plant invasions

4.1   Introduction

4.2   Objectives for control programmes

4.3   A strategy for control

4.4   Control methods

4.5   Rehabilitation

4.6   Monitoring

4.1   INTRODUCTION

Alien, invasive pest plants are plant species that have become naturalised outside of their normal geographic range. These plants occur in almost every corner of the globe and are known as environmental weeds because they grow, and flourish, where they do not belong. Alien plant infestations progressively invade the natural vegetation of their 'adopted' habitat, taking over from the indigenous plant species and often preventing their regeneration. Problems caused by invasive organisms are in the same league as droughts and floods, the loss of topsoil and rangeland deterioration. Invasive alien plants can completely alter the functioning of ecosystems and they also reduce the value of land for farming, nature conservation and eco-tourism. Invasions can significantly reduce the productivity of rangelands by out-competing indigenous vegetation.

Generally, these alien vegetation infestations form dense, monospecific stands which dominate, overtop or replace the natural vegetation of the area, thereby completely altering its nature and functioning. Most of the indigenous wildlife of any part of the earth is directly dependent on indigenous vegetation for survival using plants for food, cover, nesting sites and general refuge. Loss of indigenous vegetation and replacement by alien plants can therefore lead to local extinctions of a range of habitat-specific wildlife species, and the domino effects that these losses may cause can have a disastrous effect on ecosystem functioning.

Alien pest plants may be trees, shrubs, creepers, grasses, herbs or even water plants and are called 'invaders' to draw attention to their ability to spread aggressively and cause rapid and often irreversible changes in the landscape.

In the past, alien plant invaders were introduced deliberately or inadvertently, with infestations often originating from garden plants, agricultural crops, plantings for windbreaks, forestry or drift sand stabilisation.

Not only are invasive alien infestations found on all continents and in most countries, but they are also found in all types of habitats. They occur in deserts, semi-deserts, grassland, mountains, tropical and temperate forests, shrub-lands, savannas, wetlands and even Arctic and Antarctic regions.

Perhaps the most significant reason for the success of plant invaders is that they have become naturalised without the natural enemies that restrict them in their regions of origin. Few have been 'adopted' by indigenous insects and diseases. Plant invaders can therefore exploit their new environments, generally very similar in climate to their countries of origin, in a healthier state than the indigenous species. They grow and reproduce more vigorously than the indigenous species, which must contend with a host of natural enemies including fungi, viruses, bacteria, insects and other animals.

Figure 4.1 illustrates the invasion of high-altitude mountain habitats in arid areas by the prickly pear cactus (*Opuntia ficus indica*). The diminutive native

plants of these sites simply cannot compete with the uncontrolled invasion and are shaded out.

Alien plant invaders must not be confused with indigenous plants that become invasive. Local plants can become invasive as a result of habitat disturbances such as selective overgrazing and over-frequent fires. These local invaders, however, do not have the capacity to invade undisturbed vegetation, as is the case with invasive alien plants.

One of the reasons why many alien plants are such successful invaders is that they produce large amounts of long-lived seed. Many species have seeds that can remain dormant for as long as 50 years or more in the soil under the canopy of the parent plant. Because of the lack of specific seed predators, the seeds of many invasive alien plants are as much as 90% viable. This means that when the dominant parent plant is removed, the large and highly viable soil-stored seed reserve can quickly develop into a dense infestation, consisting of hundreds of plants on a site formerly occupied by a single mature tree.

The potential to invade new sites is unfortunately advanced by the seed dispersal activities of fruit- and seed-eating indigenous wildlife as described in Box 4.1. The seeds of many invasive alien plants are also dispersed by running water, eventually resulting in densely invaded river courses and wetlands.

Some invasive plants are wind dispersed and are known to be dispersed for up to 20 km from the selected site. Man is also an inadvertent disperser of invasive plants. Many invasions originated in building sand containing seeds, which was transported to construction sites in uninvaded areas. One can only wonder how many infestations were started with seeds that were transported on or in vehicular transport and the cargoes carried by them.

Similarly, the common but ill-advised practice of planting invasive alien trees for various purposes, for example, for shade (mesquite – *Prosopis glandulosa*) or for windbreaks (*Pinus halipensis* and *Populus canescens*) or using them for the rehabilitation of erosion gullies (*Agave americana*), has resulted in the widespread infestation of natural habitats.

The activities of man are often closely linked to the success of alien plant invasions. In many cases the invading plant is just a pioneering opportunist, which capitalises on prevailing conditions after man-induced disturbances. Typical examples are short, over-frequent burning regimes which favour fire-adapted alien plants, severe overgrazing resulting in the suppression of the indigenous vegetation and creating opportunities for invasive alien species and other landscape disturbances such as ill-advised cultivation and consequent soil erosion. In these cases plant invasions are usually the symptoms of unsustainable land-use options and the solutions to the alien plant problem must address the underlying landscape management problems and not only concentrate on the removal of the alien plants.

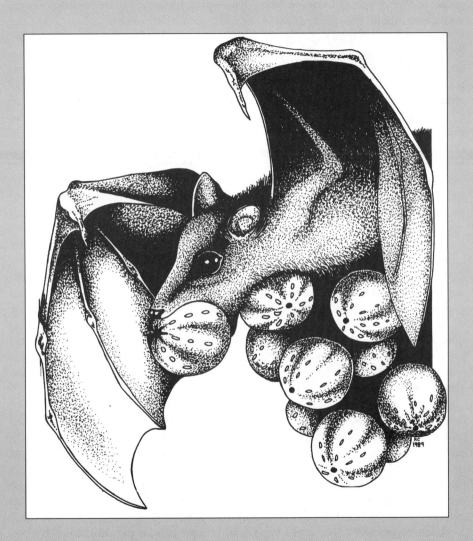

BOX 4.1

Wildlife as agents of dispersal for invasive alien plants

As with indigenous plants, invasive alien plants have mechanisms for dispersal. These mechanisms, together with the unchecked rate of seed production, result in the steady advance of the infestations into the indigenous vegetation.

Unfortunately, the indigenous wildlife of invaded areas plays a significant role in the dispersal of many alien plants. Seed dispersal by wildlife can occur in various ways but most frequently occurs when the animals feed on and ingest the fruits and seeds of the alien invaders and then transport them to new localities where they are released in the faeces of the animal. Many tropical invaders such as the loquat (*Eriobotrya japonica*), guava (*Psidium guajava*) and bramble (*Rubus* sp.) have succulent, fleshy fruits that attract a range of frugivores, particularly fruit bats, monkeys, wild pigs, birds and even antelope. Fruit bats, in particular, are highly effective dispersal agents, collecting ripe fruits in foraging areas and transporting them to feeding roosts where the seeds are discarded after feeding. Smaller fruits are ingested whole and the seeds excreted along the foraging flight lines of the bats.

Many larger herbivores like duiker, kudu, eland, giraffe and even elephant feed on tree fruits and seed pods. The seeds inside the pods are abraded but undamaged during the digestive process and are ready to germinate soon after they are ejected in the animals' dung, often at some distance from where they were consumed. Baboons and vervet monkeys are also highly efficient seed dispersers because they are particularly attracted to plant fruits, like those of the prickly pear, and their movements are not controlled by fences. In order to find sufficient good quality food, they range widely and while doing so efficiently introduce the seeds of invasive alien plants into new and uninfested localities.

Birds are also important dispersers of the seeds of invasive alien plants. Fruit-eating forest birds, such as the Rameron pigeon and the Knysna lourie, break open fruits and while feeding on them often drop the seeds onto the ground below where they are consumed by a variety of animals. The birds sometimes transport fruits to feeding localities where the seeds are discarded and many escape the attention of the forest floor feeders and then germinate to start new infestations.

Some invasive Acacia species (*Acacia cyclops*, *Acacia melanoylon*) have colourful, fleshy arils attached to the otherwise unpalatable seeds in the pods. Indigenous birds select these fleshy treats and either spread the seeds in their droppings or discard the unwanted seeds at the nearest convenient perch.

It is unfortunate that wildlife does not discriminate between the fruits of indigenous trees and those of alien trees. In the struggle for survival anything suitable is eaten and in our efforts to control invasive alien plants we need to be aware of the role that wild animals play in dispersing them.

Figure 4.1: Alien cactus infestations of inaccessible sites often occur as a result of the dispersal of the seed in the droppings of the animals that feed on the fruit

Rangelands that have become densely infested are very costly to reclaim and restore for agricultural, ecological or eco-tourism use. The costs of eradicating alien plant invasions often exceed the value of the land on which they occur. The greatest threat posed by alien plant invasions, however, is to the indigenous vegetation and all the wildlife that is dependent on it for survival.

The problem with alien vegetation invasion is that it is a relatively 'quiet' crisis. Many do not see it happening and even more people do not recognise it as an environmental crisis. Alien plants spread within the indigenous vegetation and an uninformed person sees nothing more than greenery, which is usually very attractive.

Educating landowners, land users and other persons responsible for land management concerning the alien vegetation threat is a critical first step in dealing with this problem. Not only must the land manager become informed, but also all other groups within the community. Many garden plant nurseries, for example, actively promote alien plants by selling potentially invasive plants to unsuspecting members of the public. Similarly, agricultural, forestry and municipal authorities continue to promote alien plants in a variety of potentially invasive applications.

An ignorance of the ecology of invasive plants is often also the reason why control operations are ineffective. Simply cutting down many of the invasive plants is often an inappropriate method of control, because many of them will simply resprout with an even more dense and vigorous foliage and seed production than before.

Unfortunately, this lack of appreciation for the ecology of alien invasive plants (and thus effective control strategies) often leads to the perception that the plants are uncontrollable and even invincible. This, in turn, frequently leads to apathy and indifference and the unchecked advance of the alien plants in natural vegetation and disturbed areas.

These are the perceptions that need to be changed through education and the determination of effective control methods that must be practically demonstrated and widely publicised. Invasive alien vegetation must not be permitted to degrade natural habitats unabated. Landowners and land managers have a great responsibility to play their part in helping to avert this crisis.

Effective control of alien vegetation infestations unfortunately carries a cost and this expense sometimes prevents even informed and concerned persons from getting involved in the fight against plant invasions.

Alien vegetation control need not imply huge capital expenditure. There is always a level of control that can be effectively implemented at low cost. Whatever the level of control, however, dealing with alien plants will require dedication and commitment to the task. The guidelines given in this chapter will hopefully encourage informed persons to make a difference.

4.1.1 Why bother to control alien plant invasions in natural rangelands?

We need to be concerned about alien plant invasions because of the economic implications of unchecked infestations. Alien plant invasions have, in some parts of the world, forced farmers off the land, leaving behind them a relatively unproductive wasteland with its numerous indirect and damaging impacts on the components of those ecosystems. The loss of productive farming areas, be it for cultivation, grazing, forestry or fisheries, represents a huge loss of economic activity and empowerment to the local communities. With a large proportion of the world's population in dire need of work and food, the loss of valuable, productive land to alien plant invasions should not be tolerated.

Closely related to the loss of land to alien plants, and sometimes the cause of it, is the impact that alien invasions have on water resources. Many invasions replace the native vegetation with more thirsty plants, at unnaturally high densities, which completely deplete the valuable water resource. This excessive use of the groundwater not only represents an economic loss in terms of water for domestic and agricultural use, but also the loss of biodiversity that follows when streams no longer flow and when wetlands dry out. The amount of water used up by large alien trees is generally underestimated and if spread over hundreds or thousands of hectares, it represents disastrous habitat change.

Alien vegetation invasions directly and indirectly impact on many other aspects of the natural environment, all of which carry an economic cost. Alien plants increase the fuel load in fire-driven ecosystems causing fires to burn with greater intensity, killing vegetation and organisms that would normally have survived natural fires. Alien vegetation frequently shades out all the native ground cover plants and together with groundwater depletion this results in an unprotected soil surface that is vulnerable to soil erosion.

The aesthetic implications of alien plant invasions may also impact on the economics of tourism. Visiting eco-tourists do not wish to see alien vegetation but pay to experience the natural conditions of their destination. Tourism is a growing industry world-wide and the trend is to empower indigenous peoples to provide a service to the tourists. Permitting natural habitats to become infested with alien plants will eventually jeopardise these economic empowerment spin-offs as well.

BOX 4.2

Alien vegetation and indigenous browsers

Although invasive alien plants are often utilised by indigenous browsing herbivores, the impact of the browsing is seldom sufficient to eradicate or control the infestations. Most browsers utilise succulent young shoots and growing tips, selecting them and then moving on to another plant to do the same before utilising older growth. Even in areas where the browsing pressure is high, only the reachable branch tips are utilised and the rest of the plant continues to flower and produce seed.

Even with a range of browser species all feeding at different heights, not enough of the plant is damaged to impair it permanently. Browsing can, however, have an impact on seedling growth. The small common duiker, for example, selects seedlings and saplings, continuously removing the new growth and preventing the plants from producing seed and growing any bigger. Eland, kudu and elephant damage trees by breaking off the branches that they feed on. Despite this, browser impact is generally not enough to control the spread of palatable alien plants because of the typically rapid rate of spread of these plants due to lack of the normal controls that restrict them at their place of origin.

It will not be practical to stock high numbers of browsers in an effort to eradicate alien plants because after the preferred browse has been removed, browsers tend to die before any permanent damage to the trees occurs. The implications of obtaining, introducing and containing high densities of large indigenous browsers makes this option too impractical and costly.

4.2 OBJECTIVES FOR CONTROL PROGRAMMES

To aim, in the short and medium term, for the complete eradication of alien plants is unrealistic. The objective should rather be to prevent the further spread of invasive alien plants into uninfested areas and to isolate the dense infestations within a landscape that is otherwise maintained free of alien plants. The complete eradication of alien plants would be an ideal objective but it is seldom a practical and achievable approach to the alien plant problem.

Establishing realistic goals for controlling alien plants in a particular area can be done by matching the goals to the available resources of funding, manpower and equipment. There is little sense in setting ambitious goals that will not be achieved due to a shortage of funding or other resources. The result of this error is often discouragement and loss of the will to carry on with the control programme because the ultimate goals appear to be unattainable.

The old saying 'prevention is better than cure' is directly applicable to the setting of realistic objectives. Dense, mature infestations cannot really get worse but they can get bigger and they can be a source of seed for further infestation. Dense infestations of mature trees are also expensive to eradicate and once they are removed, the affected site is in need of expensive rehabilitation. It therefore follows that, with limited funds for alien plant control, it would be a much more practical option to clear sparsely infected areas where a practical objective would be to completely eradicate the alien plants at comparatively lower cost. One thus isolates dense infestations and prevents them from increasing in size until their removal is practical or affordable.

Sparse infestations or occasional plants in natural vegetation are the real threat because they can mature, reproduce and increase in number, eventually becoming dense enough to have a negative impact on the natural vegetation. A practical objective for any area infested with alien plants is therefore to control or clear the plants starting with the least infested areas and working through the various degrees of infestation, starting with light and ending with dense.

BOX 4.3

Alien vegetation, fires and wildlife

In fire-driven ecosystems, tortoises instinctively manage to survive fires. They hide in amongst rocks, in fissures and even in holes in the ground such as rodent burrows. The fires pass harmlessly and quickly over these fire refuges, permitting the tortoises to return to their foraging soon after the fire has passed. Most other animals like lizards, snakes and small mammals manage to escape fire in much the same way.

Alien vegetation infestations, however, usually change the nature of the fuel load, increasing the amount of combustible plant material significantly and resulting in much hotter fires of high intensity. The hotter fires are able to crack rocks and even burn to a cinder plant bulbs that are 100 mm below the soil surface.

The increased fuel loads also result in fast-moving fires that can overtake fleeing animals that are normally able to escape fires in natural conditions. The result is that the animals, like the tortoises of fire-driven ecosystems, which have evolved ways in which to survive fires, are unable to live through and escape the extremely hot and fast-moving fires fuelled by high densities of invasive alien vegetation.

Those that do manage to escape, often become victims of an increased fire frequency, which is also a consequence of the alien vegetation infestations.

Alien vegetation can thus have a very destructive impact on the smaller natural wildlife of fire-driven ecosystems.

4.3 A STRATEGY FOR CONTROL

4.3.1 Planning

Many attempts to control invasive alien plants are not successful or yield disappointing and discouraging results. The reasons for this are varied but generally include the following:

1. **Poor planning:** Treatments are done occasionally when some spare time or workers are available. Control is thus a low priority and receives little attention.

2. **Impractical approach:** Starting clearing operations in densely infested areas rather than working from light to dense.

3. **Inflexible approach:** Not adapting control methods to local conditions. The response of the plants to treatment is not monitored with a view to adaptation and there is a lack of improvisation.

4. **Incorrect use of control methods:** Plants are treated but not killed, insufficient herbicide is used or ineffectively applied, control is attempted in the wrong season and many more similar practical problems.

5. **Control work is not followed up:** Treated areas are not diligently and timeously revisited to treat resprouting stems and new plants that germinate from seed. The great expense of initial control is wasted if follow-up control, which is considerably cheaper, is not done.

6. **Lack of guidance:** People who attempt to rid their land of alien plants receive little guidance from experts. Similarly, the workers who must carry out the control are seldom trained and receive little guidance.

7. **Lack of information about the costs of control:** Inexperience with alien plant control often results in poor financial planning, which stems from a lack of appreciation for the complexities of the fieldwork.

Any of the above, or any combination of them, can result in a landowner or manager becoming completely discouraged with the effectiveness of alien vegetation control. Control projects are often discontinued and the money invested in the project is lost due to the failure to control the alien plants.

Planning must ensure that these points are considered and that the most efficient use of the available funding is guaranteed and that the alien plants are effectively controlled.

There are a number of basic planning principles that can be used to guide alien plant control programmes and ultimately ensure success. Much has been learnt from the mistakes of the past, which now become the guidelines for future action.

- To succeed in controlling and eradicating problem plants, a well thought-out and practical plan of action is absolutely critical. A haphazard approach always fails.
- A landowner or land manager needs a long-term alien plant control programme for his property and this must include a budget of estimated costs of labour, equipment, transport and chemicals.
- Alien plant control can be expensive, labour-intensive and time-consuming. It is imperative that the planning and cost estimates are done correctly to ensure that limited funding is effectively used.
- Alien vegetation control must be viewed as a long-term programme and must also be fully incorporated into the other management practices on the property.
- The goals that the landowner or manager has for the property must be clear so that the alien plant control programme can be shaped around them and help to achieve them.
- The landowner or manager must be sufficiently motivated to sustain the control programme in the long term to ensure success. This is particularly applicable to the follow-up stages of control.
- It is almost impossible to totally eradicate invasive alien plants from a property – it is more practical rather to think in terms of effective control.
- The ultimate goal must be to reach a level of control where the annual input is low and the impact of the alien plants on the environment is low or negligible. This is known as the maintenance level of control.
- There are two levels of control, namely initial control and follow-up control. Initial control is usually the most costly, with costs reducing progressively through the follow-up controls until a minimal cost is reached at the maintenance level of control.
- To make any real progress with alien plant control, the follow-up operations must be seen as all-important. If the follow-up control phases are neglected, it is certain that the invasive situation will revert to the original condition, or sometimes worse.

4.3.2 Mapping

Irrespective of the species of invasive alien plants or the region that it is invading, the primary action for any control programme must be to assess the spread of the invasion and the density of the invasive plants. This information can then be transferred to a map which will become a very useful tool in the control operation.

A reconnaissance of the landscape must be done to determine the full extent of the alien invasion. It is extremely important that this fieldwork is carried out thoroughly because all planning for control work will be based on it. During this fieldwork stage, each patch of alien plants within the invaded area must be assessed in terms of density and maturity. The following classes can be used:

- Light: This means that only occasional plants are encountered.
- Intermediate: The occurrence of plants ranges from occasional to frequent.
- Dense: Plants occur in dense stands or are a dominant feature of the landscape.

Maturity of the infestations simply refers to the age of the plants. For example, in an area that is lightly invaded, are the plants young saplings or are they mature trees? Information about maturity is needed because the actual control methods to be used in any particular area are based on the density and maturity of the plants. Figure 4.2a illustrates a typical alien tree density mapping for a small nature reserve.

Much good quality field observation is required to draw up a useful map of alien vegetation infestations. An excellent way in which to collect or refine this information is to fly the invaded area in a helicopter. Photographs of the infestations can be taken for later use during mapping. Aerial reconnaissance is, however, very expensive and although very useful, is not essential for effective mapping.

A useful approach is to use elevated ground (high points) as a vantage point for mapping and then to walk through each area of infestation to determine what the average density and maturity of the invasive vegetation is.

Mapping can be done on a topographical map or aerial photograph and a scale of 1:10 000 to 1:20 000 is suitable for mapping alien vegetation invasions.

If maps of this scale are not available for your particular area, then use can be made of 1:50 000 topographical maps, but it will be necessary to photocopy the map and enlarge it by about 150%. If these options are equally unattainable, then the only alternative is to draw up your own map of the area of concern. When doing so remember to include landscape features like rivers, roads, rocky outcrops, dams and fences. These features will also help you to get the distances on your map as accurate as possible.

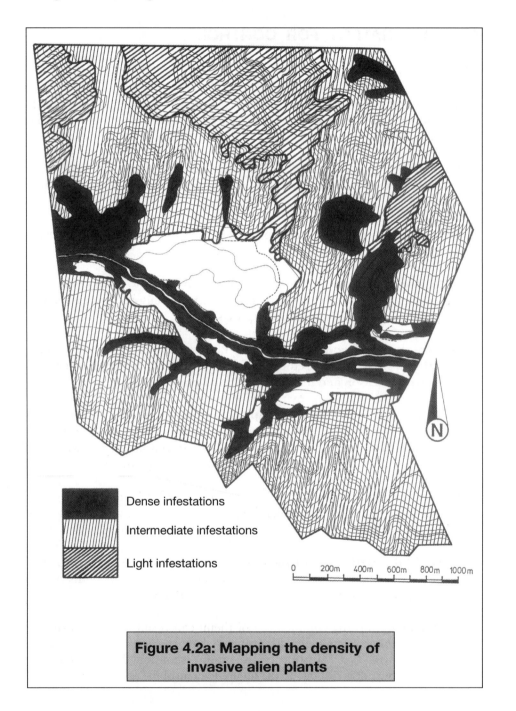

Dense infestations

Intermediate infestations

Light infestations

0   200m   400m   600m   800m   1000m

Figure 4.2a: Mapping the density of invasive alien plants

4.3.3 Prioritising control areas and the stages for effective control

Using the map of the alien vegetation infestations, the next step is to divide the area to be treated into control 'blocks'. This can be done by treating different types of vegetation as control blocks, or by dividing the entire control area into similarly sized control blocks, irrespective of the vegetation type. Figure 4.2b illustrates a typical layout of control blocks and makes use of roads and vegetation units as boundaries for the blocks. The aim here is to have a map of control blocks, each with a mapped rating of the density of the alien plant infestation for the most important invasive species. An important principle is that one must aim to reduce all species of invasive plants within each block rather than use a species-based approach.

Exactly where to start with a control operation will depend on the particular invasive characteristics and degree of invasion severity within the blocks. The starting point may even be determined by the amount of funding available at the time. A sensible approach would be to start clearing operations in blocks which contain the greatest amount of natural vegetation that is sensitive or vulnerable to alien vegetation infestation. This would include vegetation types that contain high numbers of endemic plants or animals or the vegetation of very specialised habitats such as wetlands, dune fields and limestone areas.

However they are selected, the control blocks must be prioritised using these same criteria so that the landowner or manager has a clear picture that dictates exactly where to start and where to go next.

Within each control block, and for each invasive plant species within the block, the following stages for selective control should be used as a guideline:

Stage 1: Clear sparsely infested areas first (apply follow-up within 3–6 months).

Stage 2: Clear small isolated infestations next (apply follow-up within 3–6 months).

Stage 3: Stop edges of dense infestations from spreading (apply follow-up within 3–6 months).

Stage 4: Reduce area of dense infestations working from the edges inwards (apply follow-up within 3–6 months).

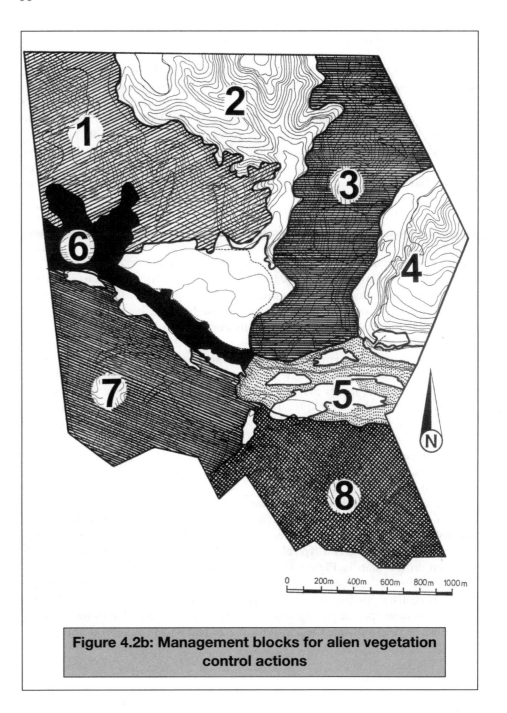

Figure 4.2b: Management blocks for alien vegetation control actions

4.3.4 Control programme schedules

So far our practical approach to alien vegetation control consists of a map that shows the spread and density of the plants. The map also shows how the area has been divided up into control blocks. We also have a guideline for control that indicates where to start within a particular control block (stages for effective control). What we do not yet have, however, is any indication of the timing involved and a prioritisation of the control blocks. Prioritisation of the control blocks is based on the 'urgency' of the control needed in a particular block. This must be based on the density of the infestations in the block and the sensitivity of the block to infestation.

For a control programme to be truly effective, those responsible for the clearing should have clearly defined objectives that are coupled with prioritisation and timing. Predicting exactly how long it will take for a control team to clear a particular block is no easy task and requires experience and skill.

A simple, practical approach is to make an experimental start with the programme, measure the progress once teams are operating efficiently and then extrapolate this progress for the entire area or block to be cleared, using the information already collected about density and spread of the infestations.

Naturally, this programme must be integrated with other management requirements of the farm or area. The amount of time available for alien vegetation control must thus be estimated and then incorporated into the schedule. If control teams are specially dedicated to the control of aliens, the schedule is somewhat simplified. It can also be expected that a schedule for a small area of 10–500 ha will be much less complex than that for an area of 1 000–10 000 ha. The schedule must simply be designed to cater for the particular needs of the area to be treated. Both the control programme and the work schedule should be adaptable. Trying to follow a rigid, fixed programme strictly is seldom possible because there are always unforeseen hold-ups, breakdowns and even bad weather that can force one to make changes to the schedule. These temporary hitches should not be seen as disasters. As long as control work can continue, a difference is being made and the objective is closer.

The following table is a typical, very simple, control programme schedule. It is based on the map in Figure 4.2b and illustrates what the manager hopes to achieve within a fixed period of time. The timing is given in 12-month periods, which is realistic for the terrain and type of infestation on the reserve. Control teams thus have specific timing objectives and it is even possible to make use of incentives to help motivate the control teams to reach their targets on time.

Alien vegetation control schedule

Priority ranking of blocks	Control block number	Infestation rating	Vegetation type	Follow-up action	Time frame
1	8	Intermediate	Fynbos shrub-land	Every three months after initial control	Year 1
2	7	Intermediate	Fynbos shrub-land	Every three months after initial control	Year 1
3	4	Intermediate	Fynbos shrub-land	Every three months after initial control	Year 2
4	5	Intermediate and dense patches	Fynbos shrub-land	Every three months after initial control	Year 2
5	1	Intermediate light	Fynbos shrub-land Forest	Every three months after initial control	Year 2
6	2	Light	Forest	Every six months after initial control	Year 3
7	5	Dense	Riverine thicket	Every three months after initial control	Year 4
8	6	Dense	Riverine thicket	Every three months after initial control	Year 5

4.4   CONTROL METHODS

The control of invasive alien plants can be mechanical, chemical or by means of natural biocontrol. Biocontrol will be discussed in section 4.4.10. It often happens that all three control methods are used simultaneously, each contributing in its own way to ensure the eventual death of the alien plants.

The choice of a control method depends on a range of factors including the type and ecology of the plant, the density of the infestation, the nature of the terrain, the climate, the season and also the availability of resources like labour, funds, transport and training.

If the best method is not known, a recognised, effective method for a similar species should be tested for broader field application.

Whatever method is used, an important aim must be to kill the plant the first time around – ineffective methods or inefficiently applied methods simply necessitate revisiting the site to retreat the plants at double the cost of transport, labour and chemicals.

The cheapest control method that effectively kills the alien plants should be used. The use of chemical treatments, for example, is expensive and often the same result can be achieved using a little more time and skill and no chemicals at all.

Workers who do the alien control fieldwork should be fully trained, irrespective of the methods used. With adequate training, the application of control methods will be more effective, chemicals will be used more sparingly and efficiently and funds will therefore be spent more effectively.

The ecology of the alien plant concerned must be clearly understood for the control methods to be successful. Some plants readily coppice from the stems when cut down. Others sucker from the roots when the main stem is cut. Many plants have invasive soil-stored seed reserves which germinate when the parent plant is removed. Many plants, notably cacti, can grow from a small piece that may be left behind after initial control. These are all survival strategies that must be carefully considered when planning a control programme.

Once fieldwork begins, it is essential that the success and general efficiency of the control methods are carefully monitored. It may be necessary to adapt the control method slightly to accommodate local conditions and this should be done before too much time is spent on a particular control block using an ineffective method.

Similarly, the general progress of the control programme should be carefully monitored. This has more to do with the motivation of the workers than the methods used but is nevertheless important for the eventual success of the programme.

To be completely successful, one should always remember that alien invasive plants most often reach habitats by means of seeds which can move over long distances or survive for many years in the soil. So whatever control method is used for mature alien plants, one must not forget the potential for reinfestation from seed, which can be soil-stored, wind-transported, water-transported or animal-dispersed. Reducing the potential to reinfest from seed should therefore be an important part of every control method.

The following sections of this chapter describe some of the methods commonly used for controlling a variety of invasive alien plants, but the decision of which method to use for a particular alien plant infestation must be based on, or include, some of the following:

- The method used must be based on the ecology of the plant, the density of the infestation, the terrain, the climate and available resources.
- Use methods that are known, tested and successful.
- The use of unknown methods should first be tested before wider application.
- Train all staff who are to apply the control methods.
- Use the cheapest method that effectively kills the plants.
- Make sure that the plants are killed first time around.
- Ensure that the method can deal with the plants' survival strategies.
- Monitor the success of the control method application.
- Monitor the motivation of the staff applying the control method.
- Use only chemicals registered for the plant species or plant type.
- Try to use 'species-specific' chemicals and use sparingly.
- Ensure that the available funding can sustain the chosen method.
- Try to restrict reinfestation from seed with the method used.
- Always incorporate follow-up control methods in the planning phase.

4.4.1 Felling trees

The first option in the control of invasive trees is physically to cut them down. As an alternative to cutting them down, trees can also be killed standing, as will be described.

A Chainsaw operation: The most widely used method for tree-felling is to cut them down with a petrol-driven chainsaw. Using this machine is quick and efficient but the operator must be well trained to use it and the machine must be carefully maintained. The chainsaw is a sophisticated piece of equipment and if correctly operated it can significantly reduce the costs of labour when felling trees. Chainsaws are available in a range of power sizes, weights and cutting bar lengths. The size of chainsaw best suited to alien tree felling is a robust mid-range machine that can be used both for felling and pruning branches.

Although modern chainsaws have many safety features, they are relatively dangerous machines with an exposed cutting bar and rotating chain that can slice off a human hand or foot with very little effort. In addition to the intensive training required to operate the machine, the operator should wear special protective clothing. These garments are made of materials specially designed to 'clog up' and stop the chainsaw's cutting action. The operator should also wear protective headgear which must incorporate a face mask and ear protectors.

The chainsaw is an extremely noisy machine so ear protection is essential and the face mask helps to prevent eye injuries that may be caused by flying bits of wood and bark. The chainsaw is not simply a machine that anybody can pick up and use – it is powerful and dangerous and sufficient training is essential.

The actual method of cutting is a specialist and technical procedure. Thick trees are felled using a range of cuts which are designed to make the tree fall in a predetermined direction – this also being an important safety factor. Figure 4.3 illustrates chainsaw operation and the type of felling notches used.

Felling big alien trees must be done in the most sensitive manner possible. If trees to be removed occur within indigenous forest or thicket, for example, felling must be done in such a way that the minimum damage to the indigenous vegetation occurs.

Smaller trees are more easily cut down with little damage to the surroundings and can be cut up into short sections with the chainsaw for removal for firewood or restoration work.

The chainsaw is thus an excellent labour-saving machine that is ideal for the removal of mature trees but operator training, strict safety measures and careful chainsaw maintenance are critical.

B Handsaw operation: A simple two-man bush or bow saw can be effectively used for cutting mid-sized to small trees. As with all tools, the operator must know how to use it and how to care for it – a certain amount of training is necessary but nothing as intense or detailed as is required for chainsaw operation.

Generally, the bow saw is operated by two people, each delivering a cutting pull stroke alternatively, as illustrated in Figure 4.3 (B). As with the chainsaw, wedges are cut out of the tree trunk on opposite sides. The wedge cuts must be directed in a way that ensures a predetermined direction of fall. The removal of each tree must be planned in terms of the direction of fall to ensure the minimum damage to the surroundings and maximum operator safety.

Once the tree is felled, the saw is used to cut the trunk up into the required lengths for removal after all the lateral branches have been removed. Bow saw operation must not be hampered by loose branches of previously cut trees or lower branches of the tree to be cut. All loose material in the path of an efficient saw operation must be cleared away before beginning with a new cut. This principle is also applicable to the use of the chainsaw.

A hundred years ago, before the mechanical chainsaw was invented, all tree felling was done with a two-man saw and massive tree trunks were then cut into straight planks using the same saw with a vertical cutting action in a saw pit. By comparison, felling invasive alien trees is a simple operation.

C Slasher operation: The slasher is the ideal tool for cutting down the thin trees of many dense alien tree infestations. Stems of up to 80 mm thick can be cut as illustrated in Figure 4.3 (C). As with the bow saw, even a simple tool like the slasher requires limited but essential basic training. There isn't much difference between a sword-wielding Samurai warrior and a conservation worker wielding a long slasher blade through the air – the effect would be much the same if somebody's head, back or arm were to get in the way.

Safety is therefore very important with slasher operation. The operator must first clear away any hanging branches that can interfere with cutting strokes. He must also ensure a safe working distance from other operators – a distance of at least 3 m is recommended.

The slasher will cut cleanly if correctly used and kept sharp. Using a blunt slasher will cut less efficiently and cause greater strain on the operator's arms and back as it will require many more cuts to fell the trees. A variety of slasher lengths are available and the one most suited to a particular task will depend on the type of plants to be cleared and the skill of the operators.

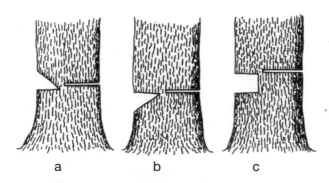

a   b   c

Cutting a felling notch (undercut) with a chainsaw

a   Conventional undercut is made using converging sawcuts or a combination of sawcut and axe. Most often used on smaller trees.

b   Both cuts are made with a saw. The waste is put on the stump; otherwise it is the same as the conventional undercut method.

c   Two parallel cuts are made with a saw and the waste is chipped out with an axe or adze. Most often used for felling trees larger than 760 mm diameter.

A   Chainsaw operation. This is the most suitable method for felling larger trees

B   Handsaw operation. This method can be used for felling young and medium thickness trees

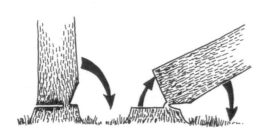

C   Slasher/hookbill operation. A method suitable for felling young trees and saplings

Figure 4.3: Felling invasive trees

4.4.2 Ring-barking, debarking and frilling trees

Alien trees can also be killed without felling the tree. These methods involve either the removal of the life-giving bark and cambium of the tree or the injury and herbicide treatment of the wounded areas, as illustrated in Figure 4.4. These methods may prove to be a more economical option for certain tree species or size and density of trees. The main advantages over felling trees are that the tree is left standing to die, there is no cut material to be removed and it can be done without chainsaws and the training required to operate them.

A Stripping: This method is ideal for saplings and small trees. All the bark is removed from waist height down to ground level. The tree dies because it can no longer transport nutrients and sap up to the leaves and it is left to rot after death. No herbicide is used. This method is simple and very quick to apply and many hundreds of trees can be killed in a day by only a handful of workers. However, great care must be taken to ensure that all the bark is removed right down to the sapwood, all around the stem.

B Frilling and old engine oil: This method is effective on small to medium thickness trees, which can be left standing after death. A section of the bark, approximately 600–800 mm long, is severely damaged around the tree with a light axe or slasher. Cuts are made with an angled strike into the sapwood. The damaged area is then liberally treated with dirty old engine oil by applying it with a brush. The angled cuts hold the engine oil in place long enough for it to enter and clog the sapwood. This method is relatively easy to apply and is quick and relatively cheap. Care must be taken to ensure that enough oil can be absorbed by the sapwood.

C Cutting and stripping: With this method the young tree is first cut down, leaving a stump of 300–500 mm standing. All the bark is then removed from the stump on the same day. Care must be taken to remove all the bark right around the stump, right down to the ground. This method is ideal for young trees and saplings that occur at high density and for tree species that coppice from the stump when the tree is cut down. The method is also relatively quick to apply with young trees.

D Frilling and herbicide: This method can be used for medium to large trees, which can be killed and left standing. As with frilling and old engine oil, the bark and sapwood must be severely damaged with downward cuts right into the wood of the tree. A section of at least 800–1 000 mm should be damaged around the tree, or the damaged area can be from waist height down to ground level. The damaged area is then drenched with a suitable herbicide that is most efficiently applied by spraying it on. If a knapsack sprayer is not available, the herbicide can be applied with a brush. As with other frilling and debarking methods, care must be taken to ensure that the tree is treated right around the trunk. It is best to use a herbicide that is specifically prescribed for large woody tree species.

E Ring-barking: This method is also good for medium to large trees but it is not suitable for trees that coppice from the roots when the stem is cut. All of the bark and sapwood is removed right around the tree in a ring that is 500–700 mm wide, cut at about waist height. An axe or heavy slasher can be used to strip the bark and no herbicide is applied. This method is quick to apply and is cost-efficient for tree species that can be left standing to die and that do not resprout from the base of the stem or roots. If used on a tree that does coppice, follow-up control must ensure that the new growth is killed with a foliar herbicide before the new stems are longer than 1 m.

F Ring-barking for trees that coppice: The method is basically the same as the previous one, except that all the bark and sapwood is removed right down to below the ground. This means that some surface digging is required to expose the sub-soil stem. No more than 150–200 mm of the sub-surface stem need be exposed, but it is important that all of the bark and sapwood be removed from the stem and root bases. This method is suitable where herbicide is unavailable and for tree species that resprout from the lower stem when ring-barked as previously described.

Figure 4.4: Ring-barking, frilling and debarking to kill alien trees

A   Stripping: All the bark is removed from waist height down to ground level. No herbicide is applied and the tree is left standing to die.

B   Frilling and old oil treatment: Angled cuts are made with an axe into the sapwood and the injured areas are treated with old engine oil. The tree is left standing to die.

C   Cutting and stripping: Trees are cut down and the stumps are then stripped of bark down to below ground level with a cane knife or light axe.

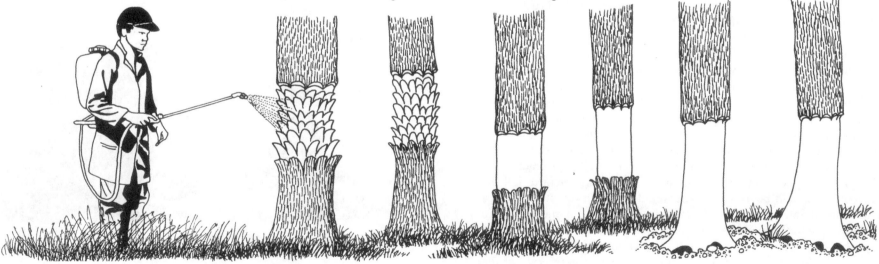

D   Frilling: Cuts are made with an axe at an angle into the wood. Herbicide is then applied with a knapsack sprayer or brush.

E   Ring-barking: Removal of all the bark and cambium around the tree trunk with an axe or cane knife. No herbicide is applied.

F   Ring-barking for coppicing species: All the bark and cambium is removed right down to below the ground with a cane knife, axe or slasher. No herbicide is used.

4.4.3 Controlling dense, bushy invasions

Alien vegetation invasions consisting of lower growing bushy plants with thinner trailing stems require a different approach. These plants have numerous light stems that form a dense mat over the ground, often thorny and impossible to walk through.

One must clear away the dense mass of foliage and stems to get at the main core or trunk of the stem mass. This can be done by hand with a long-handled slasher, by hacking at the canopy repeatedly until gaining access into the bushy mass, as illustrated in Figure 4.5. All of the stem and foliage mass must be cut away until only the thick, woody core remains.

The woody core can then be treated as illustrated in Figure 4.4 (D), by either damaging the stems and then spraying with herbicide or by stripping off the bark to ground level and applying herbicide to the stems. The mass of foliage and branches can be cut up and used on site as a soil surface protecting mulch or it can be disposed of by burning it in heaps.

An alternative to slashing by hand is to cut the dense branch material away with a petrol-driven mechanical brush-cutter with a toothed disc blade. The brush-cutter is much faster, but runs on petrol and oil and must be well maintained if it is to work effectively. The person who operates the brush-cutter must also be specially trained. Safety aspects are extremely important when using an open mechanical blade and the operator should wear protective clothing. As with hand-slashing, all of the foliage and branches are cut away to gain access to the core stem which is treated in the same way.

This operation is relatively labour intensive and time consuming due to the difficulty in dealing with the dense mat of springy plant material. Once the plant has been treated, it is essential that a follow-up control action be done at the start of the next growing season when the root stock of coppicing species produces new shoots. The regrowth must be sprayed with a contact foliar herbicide. The only alternative to spraying is to dig up the roots, which is not always practical.

Generally, the cutting and spraying of the main stem is sufficient to kill the plant, but exceptions should be expected. The initial cutting away of the foliage and branches should take place in the growing season when the roots are pushing nutrients up into the foliage and stems for growth and flowering. Cutting them down at this stage will help to deplete the reserves of the plant. Spraying to kill the new growth after initial clearing will further deplete the reserves of the plant and further restrict growth and seed production. The key to success with this type of invasive plant infestation is repeated attention until the plants are finally killed.

The bush can be cut down by hand using a slasher

Alternatively a power brush-cutter can be used

Figure 4.5: Removing dense, mat-forming infestations by hand

4.4.4   The use of a rotary tractor-drawn brush-cutter

A tractor-drawn brush-cutter can be successfully used to clear away any dense, alien vegetation infestations consisting of stems no thicker than 30–40 mm. It works particularly well on dense new growth and regrowth after initial clearing. The principle for control is that with continued cutting, the plants eventually do not have the reserves to resprout, and then die. Repeated cutting should be done during the growing season and the plants should be cut off as close to the ground as possible.

The real advantage of using the tractor-drawn brush-cutter is that all the above ground plant material is cut off and shredded into a rough mulch, which is an excellent protective ground cover and also facilitates the germination of rehabilitation seeding. The mulch cover preserves moisture in the topsoil, protects seedlings from the sun and also reduces the ground temperature in hot and more arid regions.

The tractor-drawn brush-cutter has a rotary flail or blade operation which is powered by a tractor power take-off (PTO). The brush-cutter is a robust implement and works in exactly the same manner as a standard garden lawnmower. The combination of tractor and skid-like construction of the brush-cutter enables brush-cutting to be done in fairly uneven terrain (see Figure 4.6). Brush-cutting in areas with large stones will, however, be problematic.

The brush-cutter can be used on fairly advanced woody infestations and can cut woody stems up to 40 mm thick, depending on the alien species involved. It can also be used to cut down bushy creeper-type invasions, which generally have lighter stems but are difficult to clear away because of the fine, almost spongy mass of stems that are difficult to cut individually.

The brush-cutter is operated by simply pulling it over the plants – it pushes the plants flat and chops the flattened material up, resulting in a rough mulch. Denser material or plants with thicker stems must be treated at slower operation speed. An alternative way to operate the brush-cutter when dealing with dense, bushy invasives is to lift the brush-cutter above the plants, reverse into the bush and drop the brush-cutter into it. The method used must be suitably modified for each particular application. It may, for example, be necessary to go over a cleared patch a second time and from a different approach angle to ensure that all the material is properly cut and reduced to a useful mulch.

A variation of the brush-cutter operation principle is the use of a specially modified rotary chipper machine that is front-mounted onto a tractor or onto earth-moving type equipment. The operation is much the same as that of the brush-cutter except that the work is done ahead of the machine. An advantage of the chipper operation is that thicker stems can be cut. As with the brush-cutter, the alien plants are pulverised and transformed into a useful, rough mulch cover. The stems can then be treated with herbicide or repeatedly cut with the front-mounted chipper.

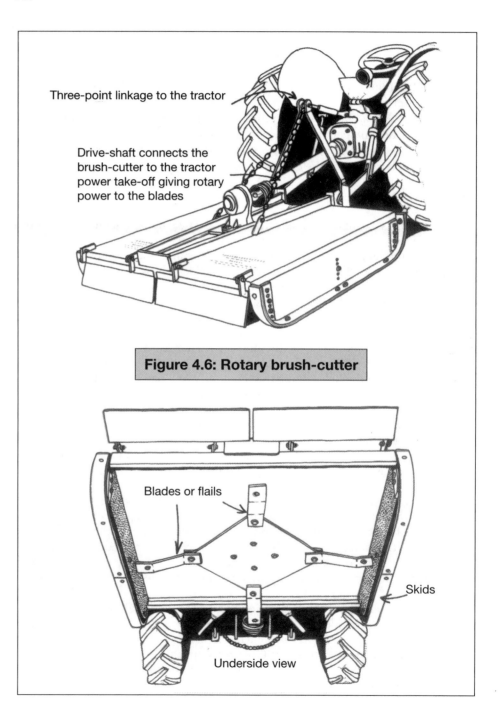

Three-point linkage to the tractor

Drive-shaft connects the brush-cutter to the tractor power take-off giving rotary power to the blades

Figure 4.6: Rotary brush-cutter

Blades or flails

Skids

Underside view

The advantages of this type of mechanised clearing are:

- Speed: Mechanised initial clearing is considerably faster than hand cutting.
- Mulching: The success of mechanised initial clearing is immediately observable.
- Personnel: Only a single implement operator is required. This can be very advantageous where labour is unavailable or not cost-effective.
- Follow-up: The cleared site is free of heaped-up, cut, brush material, which facilitates the ease of follow-up work.

4.4.5   Tree plugs

The tree plug is an innovative, effective and selective method of chemical control for young and mature invasive trees. The plug itself is a small plastic cylinder that has a moveable inner sleeve (Figure 4.7). It contains a lethal dose of 0.4 g of dry glyphosate granules. The plastic capsule inside is broken when the moveable inner sleeve is hammered through it and the weed killer is then released to be taken up into the capillaries of the tree.

The tree is first cut down as close to the ground as possible with a chainsaw or handsaw. Holes are then drilled into the trunk using a special cutter on a low speed drill or a hand auger of the correct thickness. A specially constructed hammer is also available for knocking holes into the wood. The tree plugs are then inserted into the holes and hammered in. When hammered, the weed killer is released when the plastic capsule breaks inside the hole.

The number of plugs needed to kill the tree depends on the size of the tree. A tree with a diameter of about 50 mm will only require one plug, while a tree with a diameter of about 250 mm will need about five plugs to kill it. The plugs should be inserted as close to the roots as possible because the glyphosate is a systemic herbicide that is taken up and transported throughout the stump and the roots, with the roots being the priority.

The advantage of these plugs over conventional liquid herbicide is that they are easier to transport and apply and can be administered in any weather conditions. They are also more environmentally friendly because all the weed killer is inside the tree and none can spill over and affect any of the natural vegetation. The tree plug method also requires minimal follow-up. This is not the case with liquid herbicide application, which often requires repeated follow-up spraying to be effective.

The tree plug is therefore ideal for use in sensitive habitats like wetlands where general herbicide spraying is not desirable. It can also be applied in remote and broken terrain without having to carry cans of liquid herbicide and spraying equipment. It is thus suitable for application in steep mountainous areas, areas of dense vegetation, sensitive habitats and where personnel and financial resources are limited.

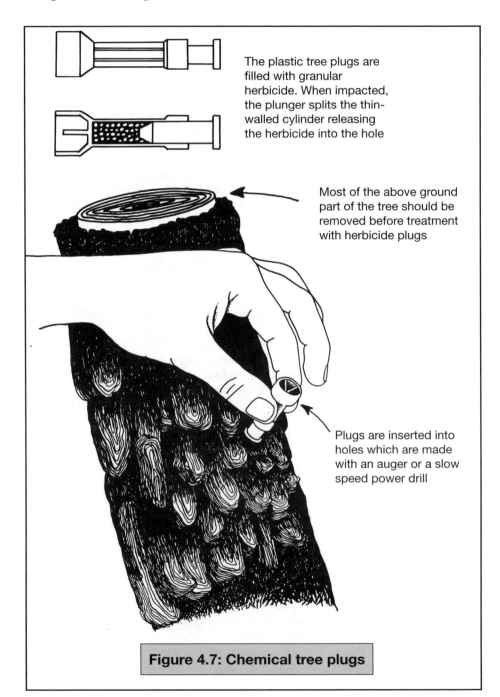

The plastic tree plugs are filled with granular herbicide. When impacted, the plunger splits the thin-walled cylinder releasing the herbicide into the hole

Most of the above ground part of the tree should be removed before treatment with herbicide plugs

Plugs are inserted into holes which are made with an auger or a slow speed power drill

Figure 4.7: Chemical tree plugs

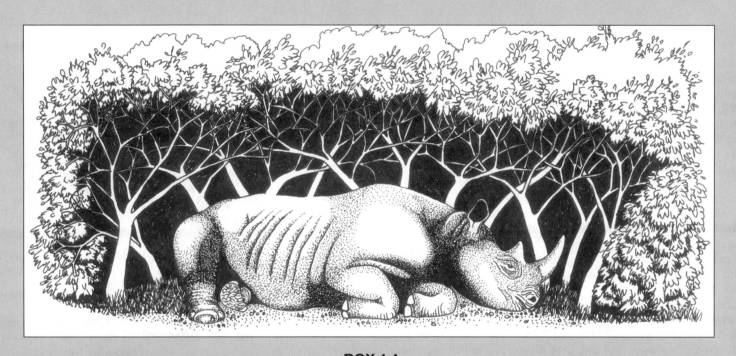

BOX 4.4

Retaining selected, alien shade trees for larger wildlife

A case can be made for retaining some stands of alien trees where they fulfil a particular habitat requirement for wildlife. Often areas that become densely infested with alien plants are almost devoid of all indigenous vegetation and the invasive trees provide the only shade in the area. I have come across many such situations on small game farms where, although variously infested with alien plants, the area is otherwise suitable for certain wildlife species.

Shade is an important habitat requirement for many wildlife species and the shade seeker does not discriminate between alien and indigenous vegetation when looking for a resting site with a shady canopy. In fact, alien vegetation infested areas are often devoid of ground cover under the canopy of the trees, which is also to the liking of many wildlife species when resting. Both white and black rhinoceros, for example, enjoy wallowing in the cool sand under a shady tree canopy, as do warthog, kudu, eland and many other species.

Isolated pockets of invasive trees appear to be favoured over continuous dense infestations by some species, such as white rhinoceros, while dense infestations are to the liking of thicket-loving animals like black rhinoceros, nyala, bushbuck, eland and impala. These thicket or woodland species also tend to eat the seedlings of invasive trees, which helps to keep the rate of invasion under control. However useful alien trees may be for shade, one must always consider the consequences of retaining these trees. They will continue to produce seeds for dispersal and reinfestation which is opposed to the objective of alien plant eradication. Patches of alien trees can be retained for shade but should eventually be replaced by indigenous plant alternatives. The best way to do this in an area that is in need of shade is to establish thickets of local indigenous species inside fenced exclosures as a long-term measure for shade provision. The patches of alien trees can then be removed when the patches of established vegetation are ready to be used.

If the shade trees are alien, but non-invasive, they can be retained with no risk of spreading and their continued presence will be a consideration of aesthetics rather than invasive potential. The best policy is to aim for the total removal of all aliens in the long term. Every effort should be made to replace even the useful alien plants eventually, particularly if they have the potential to become a source of seed for renewed infestation.

4.4.6   The control of larger cactus plants with herbicide

Alien cacti can become highly invasive, and in some arid regions can become so dense that not even stock or wildlife can move through the infested areas. Cacti are also difficult to eradicate because they are usually thorny and bits that break off can take root and reinfest already cleared areas. A further complication is that some of the cacti that infest subtropical areas are relatively small and grow within dense thicket vegetation, which makes the plants very difficult to locate.

The larger cacti, like the prickly pear, can be easily and effectively eradicated with systemic herbicide. Systemic herbicides are taken up and transported throughout the plant in its vascular system, killing all the plant parts simultaneously.

The herbicide is applied by jabbing holes into the plant and then administering the herbicide into the holes, as illustrated in Figure 4.8. A simple 10 mm steel rod with a sharpened point is used to puncture the plant at various points throughout the main plant stems. The herbicide can then be applied into each hole with a plastic disposable syringe or any other suitable method. About 2 cm³ of the herbicide is put into each hole. The holes should be angled downwards into the stem so that the applied herbicide stays in the hole, thereby ensuring effective absorption by the plant.

Each and every plant must be treated in this way. The method is generally very effective, but if at first the plants do not die, then a second application will be necessary.

The method is very easy to use and very little training of workers or staff is necessary. A good practice is to keep a spiking tool, syringe and some of the herbicide in each vehicle that moves through the infected area and to stop and treat all plants that are seen from the road network. Sporadic treatments like this will contribute to the overall success of the control operation, but a strategic approach to control as described in section 4.3 will always be necessary.

The plants that are effectively treated die standing, and eventually rot and break down until nothing remains of them. The alternative to the use of chemicals is the complete removal of the cactus plants. This is a labour-intensive operation and the plants also have to be transported to a 'safe' site if reinfestation is to be prevented. If transporting the plants is not possible, they can be stacked on a stone surface, sheets of plastic or corrugated iron to prevent re-rooting. The chemical control described is definitely a more practical and cost-effective approach.

Biocontrol methods, or agents, are also available. These are insects – a moth and a scale insect – that feed only on the prickly pear and do not have the potential to damage agricultural crops or indigenous plants. The moth larva mines into the leaves, feeding on them and eventually killing the plant, and the scale insect forms dense colonies on the leaf surface, feeding on it and eventually killing the leaf. More information about biocontrol is provided later in this chapter.

Spiking the stems

Figure 4.8: The control of larger cactus plants with herbicide

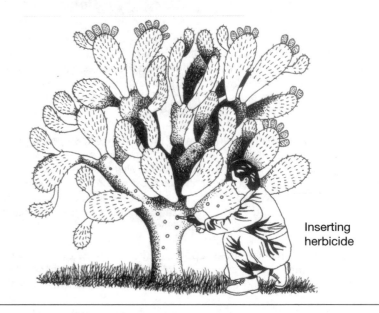

Inserting herbicide

4.4.7   The control of dense stands of cactus with herbicide

Many cacti grow in very dense clumps, typically with long straight, vertical stems tightly packed together. It would be very difficult and impractical to try to treat the stems individually as described in Figure 4.8 – they are simply too close together and too numerous to treat effectively.

The principle for treatment is basically the same as described in Figure 4.8, except that the herbicide is sprayed over the exterior of the plants rather than inserted into holes in the stems. Effective absorption of the herbicide by the plant is ensured by first damaging the plants with a heavy stick or spade. Cutting the plants with a sharp blade (slasher, cane knife or machete) is not recommended because numerous bits that could take root may be cut off the parent plants. By damaging the surface of the stems, wounds are made through which the herbicide can penetrate. When damaging the plants, remember that any section of stem that breaks off, intact, and falls to the ground, can take root and start a new plant. These bits must be carefully sprayed with herbicide to prevent reinfestation.

Spraying should be done during the active growing season when nutrients and water are being transported to all parts of the plant. This activity is essential for the systemic herbicide to be effective because it kills the plant from within via the vascular system.

Care must be taken to spray all the plants to ensure the lowest survival rate. In very dense stands, treatment strips should be marked off with a length of rope or any other suitable tape or string. The strip can then be treated completely before moving the rope to mark the next strip to be treated. This procedure will ensure that the entire infestation is adequately treated and spraying is not duplicated.

The effectiveness of herbicide spray coverage can be further improved by adding a colourful dye to the herbicide. It then becomes possible to see clearly what the degree of herbicide coverage actually is, as well as where treatment has already been applied.

Dense stands of these cacti are difficult to eradicate because the stems are so close together. Follow-up control is therefore essential in every treated area. The success of the control action should be evaluated two to four months after the initial control effort and follow-up control should be applied immediately to prevent the expansion of any new growth.

The effectiveness of the herbicide can sometimes be negated by heavy mist or rainfall, which can wash the herbicide off the plants. It is therefore very important to initiate cactus control programmes during hot dry periods with little chance of unexpected rain. Herbicides are usually expensive and every effort must be made to ensure that the effort put into eradication is not wasted.

As with the larger cacti, complete removal by hand is simply impractical. The plants are spiny and must be removed to safe disposal sites or stacked to die on solid artificial or rock surfaces. This is a labour-intensive approach, is difficult to implement and there is also the chance that bits of the plants being transported will be dropped, unseen, in new and uninfested sites.

Spraying damaged cactus plants

A pump action knapsack sprayer is required for the effective treatment of dense infestations of cactus plants

Figure 4.9: The control of dense stands of cactus with herbicide

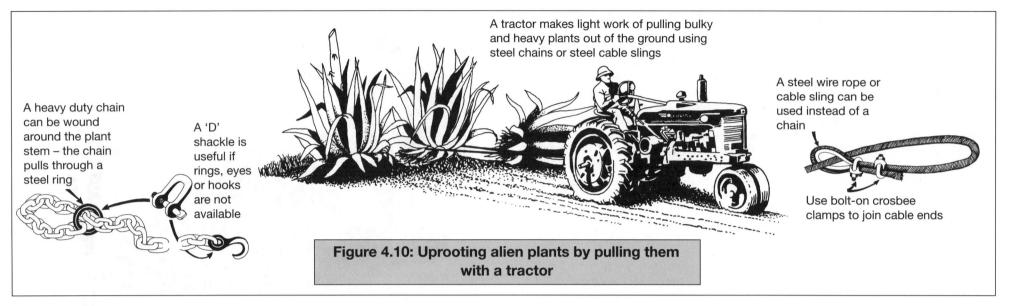

A heavy duty chain can be wound around the plant stem – the chain pulls through a steel ring

A 'D' shackle is useful if rings, eyes or hooks are not available

A tractor makes light work of pulling bulky and heavy plants out of the ground using steel chains or steel cable slings

A steel wire rope or cable sling can be used instead of a chain

Use bolt-on crosbee clamps to join cable ends

Figure 4.10: Uprooting alien plants by pulling them with a tractor

4.4.8   Pulling alien plants with a tractor

Some succulent alien plants have a large above-ground body but very small root systems. Typical of these plants are the Central American agaves which invade arid habitats world-wide. In some semi-arid regions, agaves are planted in gully erosion systems to help combat accelerated soil erosion, while in some subtropical areas, sisal is extensively planted as an agricultural crop. Agave is also used as an emergency stock feed during droughts in arid and semi-arid regions.

A source for the invasion of natural rangelands thus exists and although relatively slow-growing, once they are established, agave species form very dense infestations. Because they are large fleshy plants, it is difficult to cut them down. The leaves are thick and heavy and require strenuous effort to cut them off. Many of the agaves have spiny leaf margins and sharp, dagger-like leaf tips which also makes manual cutting very difficult.

The best way to remove these plants is simply to pull them out of the ground. They are shallow-rooted and offer little resistance, but nevertheless require a heavy vehicle or machine to pull them over. A tractor, or any other heavy farm or construction machine, can be used.

A heavy chain or steel cable is coiled around the base of the plant. There is no need to knot or secure the chain or cable to the plant – it must simply be looped around the base. When hooked onto the tractor, the cable or chain is drawn tight and pulled until the plant is uprooted as illustrated in Figure 4.10.

Once pulled out, the plants must be stacked, roots uppermost, to dry out and die. If the roots are left in contact with the ground, they will re-root and the plant will survive. When all the plants that need to be removed are uprooted, the site must be examined for tiny seedlings which grow tightly up against the parent plants and are often left behind unobserved when the large plants are removed.

If a large area of unprotected soil results after the plants are removed, the large leaves of the plant can be cut off, cut up into shorter sections and packed over the ground to form a protective ground cover into which grass seed can be sown.

Although the agave species are not considered to be vigorous invaders, they are nevertheless alien outside of the Central American area and should not be tolerated in any natural rangelands. The presence of these large, succulent alien plants detracts from the natural aesthetic appeal of any area of natural rangeland.

Pulling alien plants with a tractor can also be used to control a variety of other invasives that are not too deeply rooted. An example is the dense thickets of lantana (*Lantana camara*) which are easily uprooted. In Australia, dense stands of the invasive boneseed (*Chrysanthemoides monilifera*), which is a South African plant, are effectively eradicated by tractor-pulling. Most invasive shrubs can be effectively removed by tractor-pulling, but some digging will be required to expose the upper roots around which the cable or chain must be fastened.

4.4.9 The tree puller

The tree puller, or wrench, is a very simple, yet effective hand tool for the removal of saplings and young alien trees. It is ideal for clearing light, new infestations and for removing new plants during follow-up operations.

The tool simply clamps around the tree to be pulled and the clamping pressure is the result of leverage of the footplate against the ground when the long lever is pulled downwards. The sapling is then pulled out of the ground, roots and all, by applying continuous downward pressure on the handle, as illustrated in Figure 4.11.

Trees with a maximum diameter of 25–30 mm can be pulled out of the ground with a heavy-duty puller, but even bigger trees of up to 60 mm in diameter can be lifted in soft soils. Lighter models of puller are available for smaller applications.

The real advantage of this tool is that the entire plant, with its roots, is removed so that no coppicing is possible. The tool requires no maintenance, nor does it need fuel or oil to function. It is therefore ideal for use in remote and rugged terrain. It is also relatively easy to use, which obviates the need for any special training.

Commercial tree pullers come in a variety of sizes. A heavy-duty puller weighs approximately 8 kg, while a light model weighs about 5 kg.

Where soil is very soft or sandy, an additional steel or thick wooden footplate can be used to prevent the puller simply sinking into the ground when leverage is applied.

The tree puller is commercially available in most regions but if not, it can be made up by any competent welder or tool maker. The basic design is very simple and Figure 4.11 illustrates two alternative designs that are commercially available in South Africa and the United States of America.

Use of the puller is vastly superior to cutting saplings or grubbing them out with a bush-pick or hoe. A real advantage of this method is that the complete root system is removed and follow-up maintenance is not required. The use of the puller is therefore cost-effective and the result is permanent.

With downward pressure on the handle the clamped sapling is easily levered out of the ground

Footplate

Jaws

Footplate

Figure 4.11: Tree pullers

Both puller types have jaws which clamp firmly on the tree stem when the handle is pulled downwards. The footplate provides a fulcrum for leverage.

4.4.10 Biological control

Alien plants become naturalised and invasive because they flourish in the absence of their natural enemies in their new host region. The biological control of invasive plants involves the deliberate use of these natural plant enemies, which are specially collected from the area of origin of the invasive plant. By introducing these natural plant enemies, without their own natural controls, it is sometimes possible to decrease and even completely eradicate invasive alien plants.

Great care, however, must be taken to ensure that the selected biocontrol agent is completely host-specific and that it will not attack closely related indigenous plants of the host region and thereby itself become a new invasive, problem organism. Potential biocontrol agents must therefore be carefully screened in quarantine while conducting exhaustive trials that will ultimately ensure that the agent is completely host-specific and therefore 'safe' to use. The Plant Protection Research Institute (PPRI) of South Africa is the agency tasked with this long-term and extremely important research. Individuals visiting foreign countries should not be tempted to return home with a bottle filled with potential solutions for alien plant invasions. The well-intentioned release of untested organisms is extremely risky and could cause disastrous crop or natural vegetation damage if done without the preliminary testing for plant host specificity.

When a suitable biocontrol agent is declared 'safe' it can be released onto the invasive plants to multiply and prey on its host species. The procedure of screening a potential biocontrol agent is unfortunately a time-consuming and lengthy process and therefore also rather expensive.

Once cleared as safe for introduction, successful biocontrol agents can become the most cost-effective method of alien vegetation control and in some cases may result in the complete eradication of the problem plant. This ideal situation, however, takes considerable time to develop and biocontrol should not completely replace mechanical and chemical control methods, but should rather be introduced simultaneously to assist with the overall control strategy. Biocontrol is thus not a miracle 'quick-fix' option.

The advantages of biocontrol are numerous:
- There is no pollution as no chemicals are used.
- The biocontrol agents are only released if completely host-specific, so there is no danger of introducing a new alien problem organism.
- Biocontrol agents are self-dispersing.
- Once successfully introduced, biocontrol is permanent – there is no need to regularly re-apply as is the case with chemical application, which has to be continuously followed up.

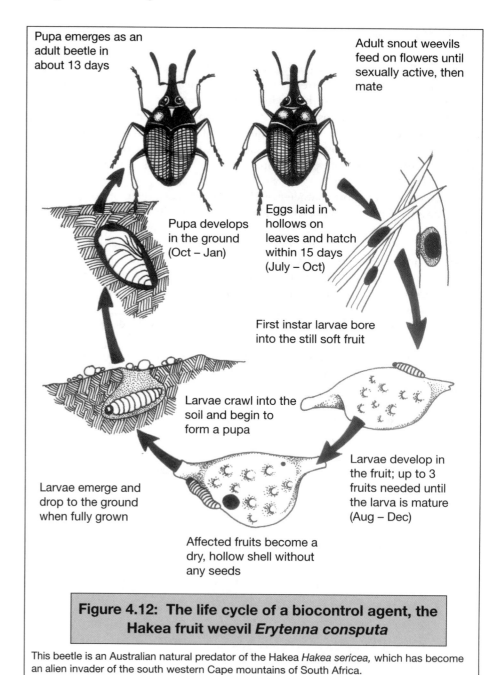

Pupa emerges as an adult beetle in about 13 days

Adult snout weevils feed on flowers until sexually active, then mate

Pupa develops in the ground (Oct – Jan)

Eggs laid in hollows on leaves and hatch within 15 days (July – Oct)

First instar larvae bore into the still soft fruit

Larvae crawl into the soil and begin to form a pupa

Larvae develop in the fruit; up to 3 fruits needed until the larva is mature (Aug – Dec)

Larvae emerge and drop to the ground when fully grown

Affected fruits become a dry, hollow shell without any seeds

Figure 4.12: The life cycle of a biocontrol agent, the Hakea fruit weevil *Erytenna consputa*

This beetle is an Australian natural predator of the Hakea *Hakea sericea*, which has become an alien invader of the south western Cape mountains of South Africa.

It is important to appreciate that the objective with biocontrol is not to eradicate the invasive alien plant but to reduce its competitiveness with the indigenous plant species, which reduces the density of the infestation and its overall impact on the environment.

The main disadvantages of biocontrol are that the level of control that the biocontrol agent will achieve is not known beforehand and there is a delay before biocontrol agents achieve their full impact. There is, however, a very positive benefit to cost ratio – the benefits of biocontrol normally outweigh the drawbacks and it still represents a comparatively cheap and safe option for the control of alien plant invasions.

Biocontrol agents for alien trees come in a variety of forms and operate in many different ways. It is often the best strategy to release a variety of control agents for one particular alien plant species. Most agents are insects, mites or fungi. Insects (often beetles, moths and flies) are usually flower head or flower bud feeders, seed feeders, leaf miners or stem borers. It is most often the larvae of the insects that do the damage. Flower, fruit or seed feeding insects will not destroy the plant but will reduce the reproductive potential of the plant. To really damage an alien plant, flower and seed feeders, stem borers, leaf miners and fungal agents should be simultaneously introduced for maximum effect.

Some insect agents (certain wasps and midges) attack the growing tips of the host plant and manipulate the host to divert valuable resources into gall production rather than the production of flowers, seeds, stems and leaves. A gall is a globular, woody swelling, sometimes used by the insect agent as a site for egg laying or as a food source for larvae. Some fungi also cause growing tips to gall. However formed, the result is the same – the reproduction of the host plant is severely disrupted.

Some insect biocontrol agents can complete their life cycle in as little as ten days from egg to new adult, while others may take as long as ten months to complete their cycle. Figure 4.12 illustrates the life cycle of a typical biocontrol agent.

From a practical point of view it is only possible to release a biocontrol agent that has been shown to be strictly host-specific and that is approved by local nature conservation, agricultural and environmental agencies. If no known biocontrol agent is available, then the control of alien vegetation must be limited to mechanical and chemical methods.

The PPRI of the Agricultural Research Council of South Africa can be contacted regarding the acquisition of approved biocontrol agents for release on alien plants.

For information and advice on biological control contact:

ARC–PPRI, Rietondale

Private Bag X134, Pretoria, 0001

Tel: 012–329 3269 Fax: 012–329 3278

E-mail: weeds@plant2.agric.za or riethdb@plant2.agric.za

BOX 4.5
Alien plant invasions and wildlife habitat

Most alien plant invaders form dense thickets, sometimes in areas where continuous thicket habitat is not a natural state for the region. In many areas these thickets provide an increased amount of cover and food for a variety of wildlife, particularly birds and smaller, terrestrial wildlife.

An example of a species that has benefited from the spread of woody alien tree invasions is the caracal, a shy and secretive cat. Caracal numbers have increased together with invasions of Australian *Acacia* species in the fynbos of South Africa. These invasions provide an increased source of food for seed-eating rodents, which has resulted in a dramatic increase in the populations of the striped field mouse, an important source of prey for the caracal.

A decrease in the numbers of small fynbos antelopes has been popularly attributed to the predation pressure of the increased densities of caracal. While this increased predation may play some role, it is more likely that declining numbers of these antelopes is a direct result of habitat alteration from a short, shrubby and very diverse vegetation to a dense, monospecific woodland with a higher fuel load and more frequent fires.

These invasive thickets benefit a range of bird species which use them for roosting, and to a limited extent, feeding, but they also disadvantage birds that favour open habitat such as larks and chats, as well as specialist feeders such as sunbirds and sugarbirds.

ARC–PPRI, Cedara
Private Bag X6006, Hilton, 3245
Tel: 033–355 9420/19/18 Fax: 033–355 9423
E-mail: ntto@natal1.agric.za

ARC–PPRI, Stellenbosch
Private Bag X5017, Stellenbosch, 7600
Tel: 021–887 4690 Fax: 021–883 3285
E-mail: vredtg@plant3.agric.za or vredcl@plant3.agric.za

ARC–PPRI, Addo
Private Bag X3, Addo, 6105
Tel: 042–233 0342 Fax: 042–233 1232
E-mail: carl@addo.agric.za

Zoology Department, University of Cape Town
Rondebosch, 7701
Tel: 021–650 3400 Fax: 021–650 3301
E-mail: hoff@botzoo.uct.ac.za

4.4.11   The use of fire to eradicate alien plants

Fire can be effectively used to control some alien plant infestations but, as with most of the other described control methods, the ecology of the alien plant must be clearly understood for effective control planning. Plants are affected by fire in a variety of ways and many mature trees are not affected by fire at all. The effect of fire on a particular problem plant must be known before any attempt is made to control the infestation with fire. Fire can be a very useful tool, but it can also have no effect or even a negative effect if improperly used.

The most critical requirement when using fire is the follow-up control after the fire. The seeds of alien plants that are adapted to fire-driven ecosystems are generally stimulated to germinate in the post-fire environment, and in the absence of competition from other plants, they do so in their thousands. Many alien plants have huge soil-stored seed reserves which necessitates a major input into follow-up control after the fire.

Another important consideration with the use of fire is that the alien plant invasions usually increase the fuel load considerably, which results in unusually intense fires that may have a harmful impact on the natural vegetation, the wildlife and the soils of the site. In areas where the natural vegetation is almost completely replaced by alien plants, fires can result in unnaturally extended periods of soil surface exposure in the post-fire period with an increased risk of soil erosion occurring, as illustrated in Figure 4.13.

Figure 4.13: The use of fire in the control of alien vegetation

Hand-pulling

Spraying with herbicide

Figure 4.14: Follow-up control

The use of fire also has many practical implications. If alien trees are burnt standing, the post-fire environment is often difficult to work in, because of the high density of charred tree stems. This complicates follow-up work, which usually entails hand-pulling the seedlings or spraying the seedlings with herbicide.

The use of fire is always risky because of the danger that the fire may escape into adjacent non-target areas causing damage to property or agricultural losses. The degree of risk depends on the type of natural vegetation of the area and also the prevalent land use. The use of fire to control alien vegetation must therefore be well considered before it is implemented. Much experience is needed to set fires and even more importantly, to deal with runaway fires. The aspects of weather conditions, fuel load, fuel moisture and expected fire behaviour must be well understood before fire can be used to control alien plant invasions.

As with most other control methods, staff involved in fire management need to be specially trained and experienced. The training is particularly critical because of the inherent danger with fire. Sudden changes in wind direction may trap unwary workers, and if insufficiently trained, they may be caught by the flames or be asphyxiated by the smoke.

4.4.12 Follow-up control

Follow-up control should be systematically done according to the control programme schedule and within the system of control blocks that were used for the initial control operation. Follow-up control must not be treated as a haphazard tailing-off of the control operation but rather as a critical component of it. The initial and follow-up phases are equally important and one cannot be done effectively without the other.

Follow-up control should be done before the regrowth or seedlings have the time to develop substantial root systems or dense voluminous foliage, which may require more expensive herbicide treatments. The timing will depend on the type of plant and the climate, but a practical time for follow-up control treatment is when plants are 100–500 mm in height.

Hand-pulling: Follow-up clearing (and initial clearing of seedlings) is most effectively done by hand-pulling (Figure 4.14). This method is labour intensive but is still cost effective when compared to the cost of herbicide spraying. Pulling should be done when plants are still smaller than 500 mm in height and the best results can be achieved when the ground is wet after rain. When the seedlings are difficult to see in other vegetation, the block should be divided up into strips with tape or line to facilitate systematic searching and pulling to ensure that most of the plants are located and destroyed. Very little skill is required for hand-pulling but workers must be guided by the use of control blocks and the systematic coverage of the control block in strips. Unskilled, temporarily employed workers are ideal for this task and vast numbers of alien plant seedlings can be cleared in a day.

Spraying with herbicide: Plants that resprout from cut stems as well as bigger saplings can be treated by spraying with a foliar contact herbicide (Figure 4.14). The disadvantage of using chemicals is that they are expensive and the spray application can be wasteful. Workers need to be trained in the safe use and application of herbicides for cost-effective and satisfactory results. Herbicide is effectively applied with a knapsack sprayer as illustrated in Figure 4.14. There is a great variety of herbicides available for alien plant control. These include foliar-absorbing, bark-absorbing and root-absorbing types. Care must be taken to preferably use selective herbicides that are known to be effective for the plants that must be killed. This approach will save both time and money. Extreme care must be taken to limit the impact of non-selective herbicide treatments on non-target, locally indigenous plants.

4.5   REHABILITATION

Clearing away dense infestations of alien plants may leave the soil surface exposed and vulnerable to soil erosion. It can happen that dense, alien tree thickets desiccate the soil over time, making it even more vulnerable to water and wind erosion when unprotected. Timeous action is therefore required to prevent the inclusion of the costs of rehabilitating accelerated soil erosion into the alien plant control programme.

Rehabilitation must not be viewed as an add-on, 'nice to have' phase, but rather as a critically important part of the control programme because it makes little sense to replace an invasive weed problem with a soil erosion problem. The rehabilitation requirements should be estimated when the planning is done because the potential restoration requirements may help to determine the selection of the control methods used.

Rehabilitation after clearing will generally consist of two stages – a soil surface stabilisation stage and a plant cover establishment stage. The timing of the restoration is extremely important. The forces of nature will not wait until management is ready to do restoration work – the restoration process can therefore proceed even while workers are still cutting down the alien trees. In areas where soil surfaces will become exposed, the restoration process should proceed together with the initial clearing operation.

Nature makes this possible because much of the plant material that is cut down can be used to stabilise the exposed soil surfaces. The branches and foliage of trees and shrubs make an ideal soil surface protecting mulch if cut up into short bits and densely packed over the soil. Alternatively, brush can be reduced to a finer mulch with a wood chipping machine if available. Figure 4.15 illustrates this method.

Exposed soil surfaces can be stabilised in a variety of ways as was shown in Chapters Two and Three. The best approach for a particular site may require an innovative combination of methods, particularly on slopes and in drainage areas. Whatever method is used, the aim must be to hold the soil surface in place to provide a seedbed for a new and protective vegetation cover.

Once stabilised, the cleared site should be seeded with a suitable, fast-growing pioneer vegetation. The establishment of grasses is generally most effective. Once the area is stabilised with a vegetation cover, consideration can be given to the re-establishment of elements of the original indigenous vegetation cover.

An alternative to this planting approach is to prepare a seedbed immediately after clearing by lightly raking the soil surface. The soil surface need only be loosened to a depth of about 20 mm and this can be done by hand using an ordinary garden rake.

The seed can then be broadcast over the raked area by hand at a rate of between 3–6 kg/ha. It is not necessary to bury the seed because it will be suitably pressed into the soil when the brush-packing commences. The overall success of grass seed germination is considerably reduced when seeds are planted too deeply. No more than a 1–3 mm soil cover is needed.

Once seeded, the area can be covered with a layer of chopped brush. The foliage of the alien plants that are cut down can be used, but care must be taken to avoid the use of material containing seeds. This means that the initial clearing operation should ideally be done before the alien plants set seed. This precaution will ensure that the soil-stored seed bank of the invasive plant will at least be reduced by one season of seed production.

The brush should be cut into lengths of no more than 300–400 mm and must be packed across the drainage direction of the site for maximum soil surface protection. Care must be taken to ensure that most of the cut brush lies in close contact with the soil surface.

This mulch layer must not completely 'seal' the soil surface from the sun. The brush should be packed to a depth of 100–200 mm, the actual depth depending on the type of material that is available. It is important that light and water can still penetrate the brush or mulch cover to ensure seed germination and seedling growth.

An important part of the rehabilitation of former alien plant infested areas is the continuous follow-up control that will be needed to eradicate the new plants that germinate from the usually considerable soil-stored seed bank. Dedicated and organised follow-up will eventually exhaust the seed bank and rehabilitation will then be almost complete.

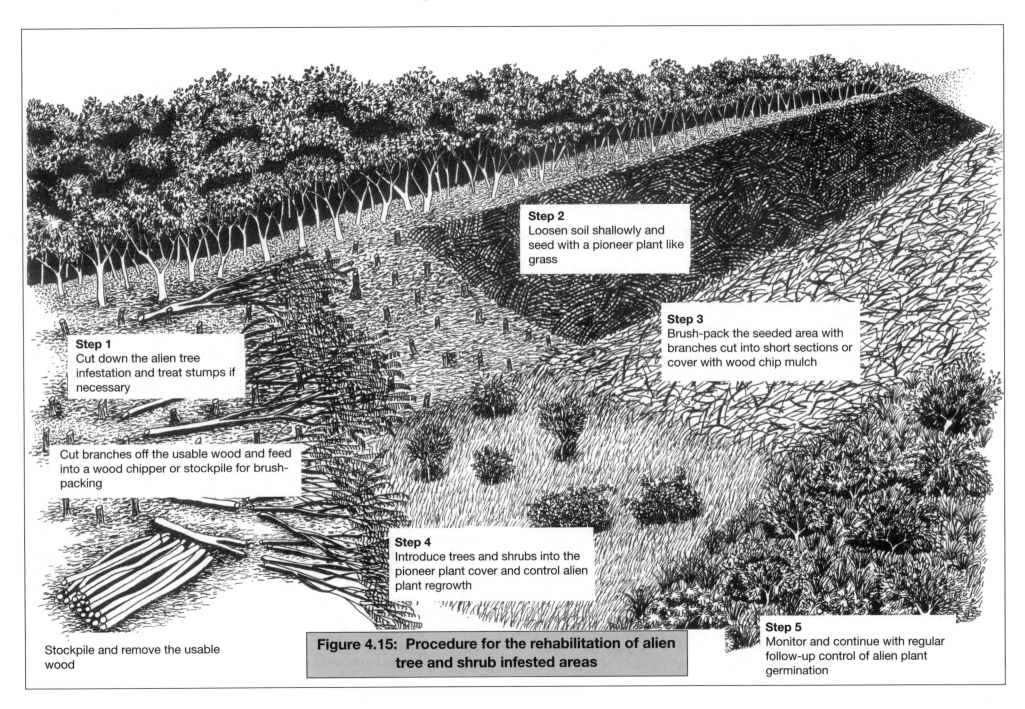

Step 1
Cut down the alien tree infestation and treat stumps if necessary

Cut branches off the usable wood and feed into a wood chipper or stockpile for brush-packing

Stockpile and remove the usable wood

Step 2
Loosen soil shallowly and seed with a pioneer plant like grass

Step 3
Brush-pack the seeded area with branches cut into short sections or cover with wood chip mulch

Step 4
Introduce trees and shrubs into the pioneer plant cover and control alien plant regrowth

Step 5
Monitor and continue with regular follow-up control of alien plant germination

Figure 4.15: Procedure for the rehabilitation of alien tree and shrub infested areas

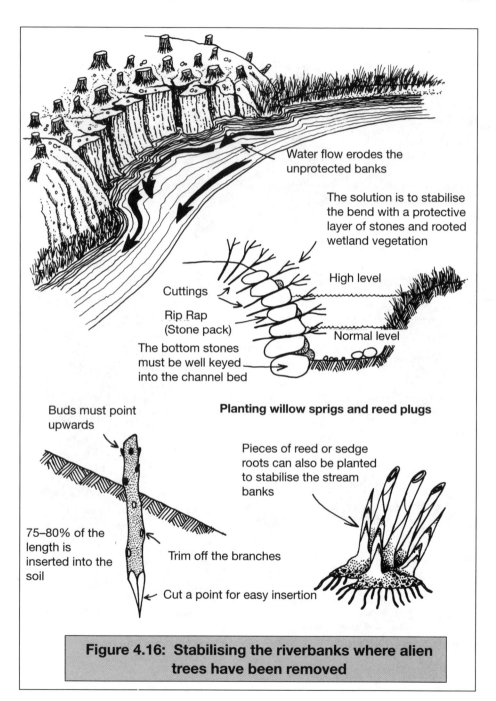

Water flow erodes the unprotected banks

The solution is to stabilise the bend with a protective layer of stones and rooted wetland vegetation

Cuttings

High level

Rip Rap (Stone pack)

Normal level

The bottom stones must be well keyed into the channel bed

Planting willow sprigs and reed plugs

Buds must point upwards

Pieces of reed or sedge roots can also be planted to stabilise the stream banks

75–80% of the length is inserted into the soil

Trim off the branches

Cut a point for easy insertion

Figure 4.16: Stabilising the riverbanks where alien trees have been removed

4.5.1 The rehabilitation of riverbanks

It often happens that the dense infestations of alien vegetation that occur along streams and rivers do not bind the soil of the riverbanks as well as the former, specially evolved indigenous vegetation did. The alien plants occur opportunistically in the wetter riverine habitat, but their root systems do not overlap in response to the particular local soil, moisture and climatic conditions and as a result are not resilient enough to survive these conditions.

The result is that these alien infestations are invariably uprooted and washed away during severe storms and flooding, which exposes the riverbanks to water erosion. Without the natural riparian vegetation to slow down the run-off, the force of the flow increases and so does the damage to the unprotected riverbanks, which crumble as they are undermined by the erosive flow of water. It is hardly necessary to discuss the far-reaching environmental impacts of riverbank erosion on both the terrestrial and the aquatic habitats along rivers, and also on the lowland regions into which these rivers flow.

Alien vegetation eradication strategies should be sensitive to the vulnerability of destabilised riverbanks and a special effort must be made to stabilise the banks after clearing and before permanent damage occurs.

Once cleared of alien plants, relatively stable and less steep banks can be protected by using the cut alien plants as a protective ground cover. Felled small trees and larger branches can be packed across the sloping bank, perpendicular to the direction of flow, with the thicker material closest to the permanent water. The trees or logs must be fixed to stakes driven into the bank to hold them in place. The area of riverbank covered in this way should then be densely planted with a suitable mix of locally indigenous riparian plant species. A mixture of small trees, reeds, sedges and grasses will generally give the best results.

The greatest challenge is to rehabilitate riverbanks that were damaged in the past and that have highly unstable, vertical edges that cave in with each flood. The banks firstly need to be shaped to a gentler gradient of about 45°. This slope must then be lined with stones, from the stream bed to the top edge as illustrated in Figure 4.16. Geotextile can be incorporated as a layer under the stones if it is considered necessary.

The key to success with this method is the vegetation that must be established quickly into this protective stone lining. The stones simply serve to hold the bank in place while the interlocking roots of the plants grow and spread through the soil of the bank and so stabilise it. It is important that the indigenous reed (*Phragmites australis*) be used for revegetation, because the alien Spanish reed (*Arundo donax*) is highly invasive in wetland habitats, depleting the water and diverting channels with its dense, impenetrable thickets. Similarly, the indigenous willow (*Salix capensis*) should be used rather than the alien weeping willow (*Salix babylonica*), which has already invaded many South African rivers.

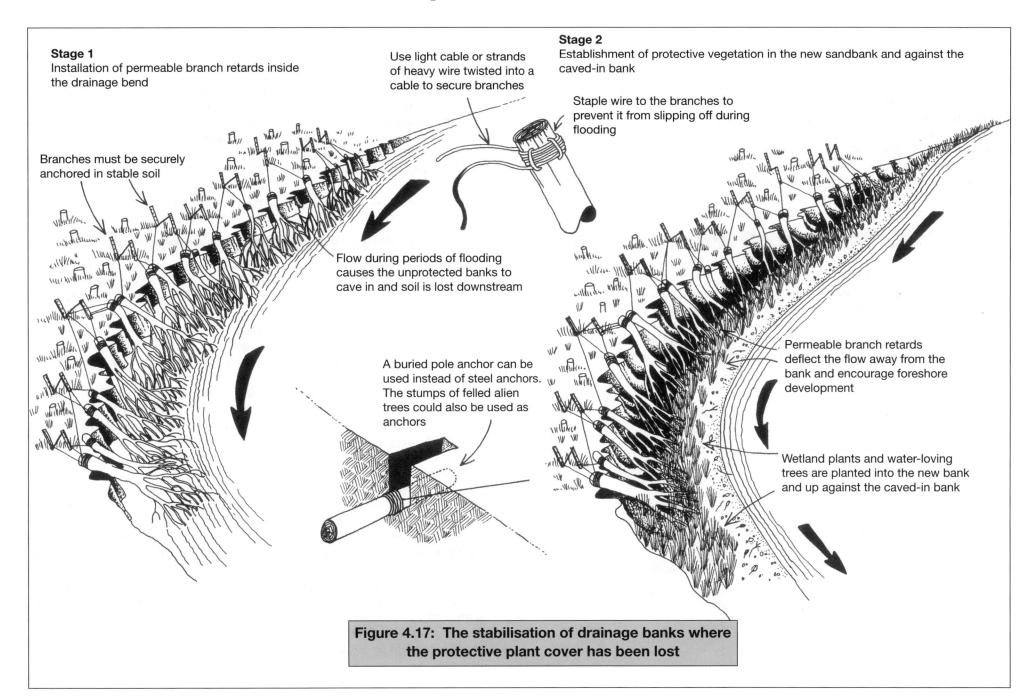

Stage 1
Installation of permeable branch retards inside the drainage bend

Use light cable or strands of heavy wire twisted into a cable to secure branches

Stage 2
Establishment of protective vegetation in the new sandbank and against the caved-in bank

Staple wire to the branches to prevent it from slipping off during flooding

Branches must be securely anchored in stable soil

Flow during periods of flooding causes the unprotected banks to cave in and soil is lost downstream

A buried pole anchor can be used instead of steel anchors. The stumps of felled alien trees could also be used as anchors

Permeable branch retards deflect the flow away from the bank and encourage foreshore development

Wetland plants and water-loving trees are planted into the new bank and up against the caved-in bank

Figure 4.17: The stabilisation of drainage banks where the protective plant cover has been lost

Naturally, the choice of plant is critical. Here we must be guided by whatever grows naturally along undisturbed sections of the same river. The ideal plants to use must be fully adapted to the site, must be particularly useful in controlling soil erosion and should also be of value for wildlife in terms of cover and forage.

Truncheons, or cuttings, of the plants can be set into the bank as the stone lining is built up from the bottom upwards. The cuttings of woody species should be densely planted, with at least four per square metre (see Figure 4.16).

In some situations, caving-in riverbanks can be treated by reducing the force of water flow against the riverbank in river bends. Here the alien trees that are cut down can be positioned tightly adjacent to each other, with the foliage lying downstream, and the trunks firmly anchored to the bank. The branches reduce the erosive impact of the water and also become a site for silt deposition. The entire length of impacted riverbank should be treated with densely packed, felled trees, rather than short sections positioned only at the problem spots (see Figure 4.17).

It is clear that the planning of alien vegetation control programmes in areas with riverine habitats must incorporate riverbank stabilisation. It is also critical that the stabilisation work is done immediately after sections of riverbank are cleared and that the restoration work is not left until after the entire area has been cleared of alien plants. It may also be necessary to jointly incorporate a variety of the soil stabilisation methods that were outlined in Chapter Two.

4.6   MONITORING

It is important to monitor the progress and success, or lack of success, of alien vegetation control programmes. A great deal of time, effort and finance is committed to these operations so it is absolutely critical that the result is carefully measured in some way. Monitoring can help to identify aspects of the control programme that may need to be modified and improved to achieve the successful control of invasive alien plants.

Monitoring can be done by using either fixed-point photography or a marked plot questionnaire.

The method and procedure for fixed-point photography was described in Chapter Two (see Figures 2.17 and 2.18). The application of the method for alien clearing programmes is identical except that an alien control programme record sheet is used in conjunction with the photographs (see Figure 4.19).

If the fixed-point photography method is not used, monitoring sites can be marked and the same record sheet (Figure 4.19) can be used to record condition at the site. A number of monitoring points, spread throughout the rehabilitation area, can be permanently marked with a steel or wooden peg driven into the ground. To help locate the pegs, it is a good idea to paint them before installing them. White or yellow paint should be used for the best visibility and the pegs should stand approximately 1 m above ground to make them observable from a distance (see Figure 4.18).

The locality of each peg can be recorded with global positioning co-ordinates if a GPS is available – otherwise simply number each peg with a permanently attached tag and indicate its locality on a map of the area. The best method for marking the pegs is to use a small aluminium or galvanised steel plate with the site number stamped on it. Stamping or engraving the identification number and date of the monitoring site on a plate is the most permanent way in which to mark the peg. Paint or stick-on lettering simply does not last. The plate is then firmly screwed or wired to the peg. However marked, the peg must not be lost, and if found, must be easily identified.

In areas where large animals are likely to damage the pegs, heavier materials like thick wooden poles or steel sections buried deeply into the ground will be required.

The monitoring form (Figure 4.19) is used at each peg to record the rehabilitation methods used, species planted, plants that are successfully germinating, plant cover, soil erosion and reinfestation rate. The monitoring interval should be three to six months but this will depend on rainfall and the rate of vegetation recovery in the area.

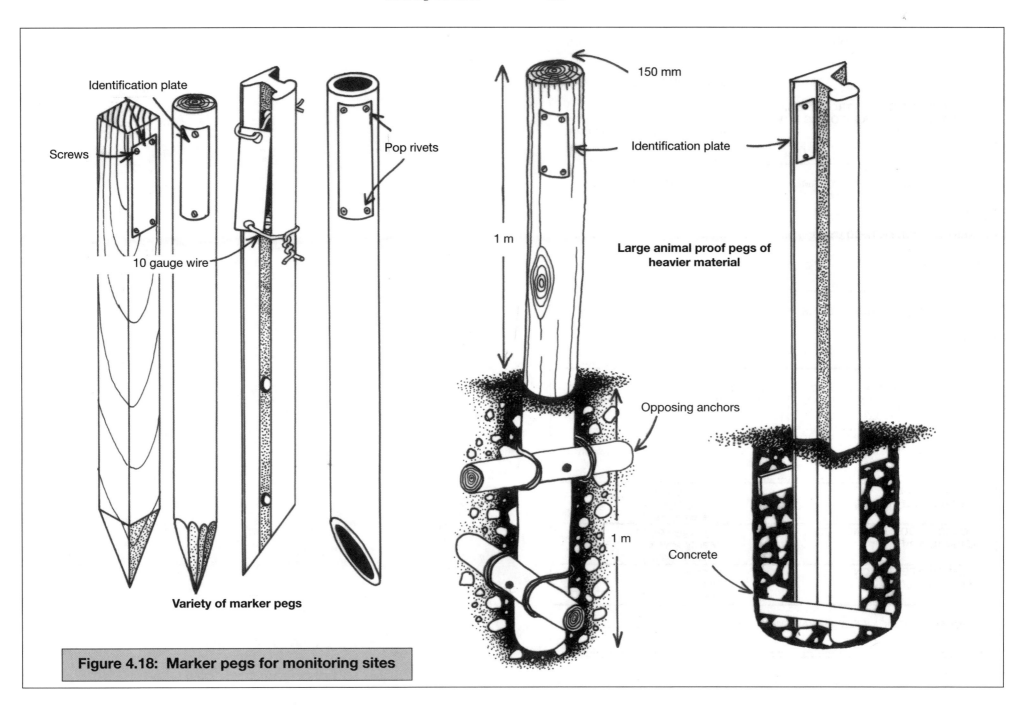

Variety of marker pegs

Identification plate

Screws

10 gauge wire

Pop rivets

150 mm

Identification plate

1 m

Large animal proof pegs of heavier material

Opposing anchors

1 m

Concrete

Figure 4.18: Marker pegs for monitoring sites

Figure 4.19: Alien vegetation control programme record sheet

ALIEN VEGETATION CONTROL PROGRAMME RESTORATION MONITORING SITE	MONITORING SITE NUMBER: ....
	DATE OF RESTORATION WORK: ....
FARM / RESERVE / PROPERTY NAME:	DATE OF SITE EVALUATION:

1. RESTORATION METHOD USED: ....
....
....

2. PLANT SPECIES ORIGINALLY ESTABLISHED: ....
....
....

3. PLANT SPECIES IN A 10 m RADIUS PLOT (Indicate dominance as follows):

VERY FEW	OCCASIONAL	COMMON	DOMINANT
....	....	....	....
....	....	....	....

4. SOIL SURFACE IS (Estimate % of plot):	Densely covered	
	Partly covered	
	Bare/Exposed	
5. COVER ON SOIL EROSION IS (Estimate % of plot):	Densely covered	
	Partly covered	
	Bare/Exposed	
6. ALIEN REINFESTATION IS (Estimate % of plot):	Dense	
	Intermediate	
	Sparse	

7. RECOMMENDATIONS FOR MANAGEMENT INPUT: ....
....

8. NAME: ....

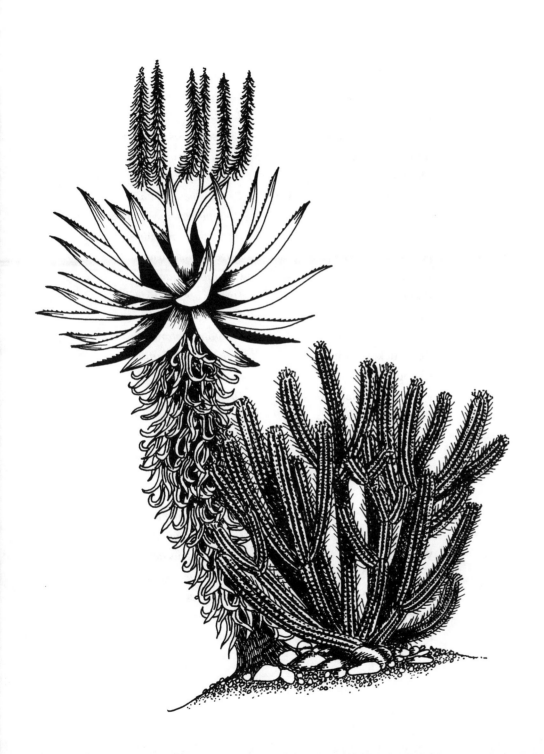

APPENDIX,
BIBLIOGRAPHY
and INDEX

APPENDIX: LIST OF SCIENTIFIC NAMES OF THE ANIMAL SPECIES MENTIONED IN THE TEXT

Because they are well known to me, I have written about South African animals in this book. The impact that these animal examples have on their environment, and the environment on them, remains similar irrespective of where the reader may be. The function that my African aardvark has (i.e. a kind of natural excavator and earth mover) is duplicated to a similar extent in South and Central America by the giant armadillo (*Priodontes maximum*) and the giant anteater (*Myrmecophaga tridactyla*). Each of the animal species listed below thus has an ecological equivalent or at least a comparable species in the other rangelands that are spread over the earth.

Aardvark	*Orycteropus afer*
Baboon	*Papio ursinus*
Badger, honey	*Mellivora capensis*
Bat, Egyptian fruit	*Rousettus aegyptiacus*
Buffalo	*Syncerus caffer*
Bullfrog	*Pixicephalus adspersus*
Bushbuck	*Tragelaphus scriptus*
Bushpig	*Potamochoerus porcus*
Caracal	*Felis caracal*
Duiker, common	*Sylivicapra grimmia*
Dung beetle, flightless	*Circellium bacchus*
Eland	*Taurotragus oryx*
Elephant	*Loxodonta africana*
Fox, bat-eared	*Otocyon megalotis*
Gemsbok	*Oryx gazella*
Gerbil	*Gerbillurus paeba*
Giraffe	*Giraffa camelopardalis*
Grysbok	*Raphicerus melanotis*
Hare, Cape	*Lepus capensis*
Hare, scrub	*Lepus saxatilus*
Hippopotamus	*Hippopotamus amphibius*
Hyrax, rock	*Procavia capensis*
Impala	*Aepyceros melampus*
Klipspringer	*Oreotragus oreotragus*
Kudu	*Tragelaphus strepsiceros*
Lizard, monitor	*Varanus albigularis*
Lourie, Knysna	*Tauraco corythaix*
Mole, Cape golden	*Chrysochloris asiatica*
Mole rat, Cape	*Georychus capensis*
Mongoose, grey	*Galerella pulverulenta*
Mongoose, yellow	*Cynictis penicillata*
Monkey, vervet	*Cercopithecus pygerythrus*
Mouse, striped field	*Rhabdomys pumilio*
Nyala	*Tragelaphus angasi*
Pigeon, Rameron	*Columba arquatrix*
Porcupine	*Hystrix africaeaustralis*
Rabbit, riverine	*Bunolagus monticularis*
Rat, whistling	*Parotomys brantsii*
Reedbuck, mountain	*Redunca fulvorufula*
Rhebok, grey	*Pelea capreolus*
Rhinoceros, black	*Diceros bicornis*
Rhinoceros, white	*Ceratotherium simum*
Rock rabbit, Hewitt's red	*Pronolagus saundersiae*
Snake, blind	*Rhinotyphlops lalandei*
Squirrel, ground	*Xerus inauris*
Steenbok	*Raphicerus campestris*
Suricate	*Suricata suricatta*
Tortoise, angulate	*Chersina angulata*
Warthog	*Phacochoerus aethiopicus*
Wildebeest, black	*Connochaetes gnou*
Wildebeest, blue	*Connochaetes taurinus*
Zebra, Cape mountain	*Equus zebra zebra*
Zebra, plains	*Equus burchelli*

BIBLIOGRAPHY

Ayres, Q.C. 1936. *Soil erosion and its control*. McGraw-Hill Book Company, New York.

Bennet, H.H. 1955. *Elements of soil conservation*. McGraw-Hill, London.

Henderson, L. 2001. *Alien weeds and invasive plants*. Plant Protection Research Institute Handbook No 12. Agricultural Research Council, Pretoria.

Hindson, J. 1991. *Earth roads, their construction and maintenance*. Intermediate Technology Publications, London.

Jacks, G.V. and Whyte, R.O. 1949. *The rape of the earth: a world survey of soil erosion*. Faber & Faber, London.

Leopold, A. [1949] 1987. *A Sand County almanac and sketches here and there*. Oxford University Press, New York.

Leopold, A. 1993. *Game management*. Charles Scribner's Sons, New York.

Middleton, N. and Thomas, D. (eds) 1993. *World atlas of desertification*. United Nations Environment Programme. Edward Arnold, London.

Milton, S.J. and Dean, W.J. 1996. *Karoo veld: ecology and management*. Agricultural Research Council, Range and Forage Institute.

Morgan, R.P.C. 1986. *Soil erosion and conservation*. Longman Scientific and Technical, UK.

Nilsen, R. (ed.) 1991. *Helping nature heal: an introduction to environmental restoration*. Whole Earth Catalog. Ten Speed Press, Berkeley.

Olckers, T. and Hill, M.P. 1999. *Biological control of weeds in South Africa (1990–1998)*. African Entomology Memoir No 1. Entomological Society of Southern Africa, Johannesburg.

Packard, S. and Mutel, C.F. (eds) 1997. *The tall grass restoration handbook for prairies, savannas and woodlands*. Island Press, Washington.

Reij, C., Scoones, I. and Toulmin, C. (eds) 1997. *Sustaining the soil: indigenous soil and water conservation in Africa*. Earthscan Publications, London.

Savory, A. 1990. *Holistic resource management*. Workbook, Island Press, Washington.

Savory, A. with Butterfield, J. 1999. *Holistic management: a new framework for decision-making*. Island Press, Washington.

Stallings, J.H. 1957. *Soil conservation*. Prentice-Hall Field Crop Production Series. Prentice-Hall, Englewood Cliffs, N.J.

Stirton, C.H. (ed.) 1978. *Plant invaders: beautiful but dangerous*. Department of Nature and Environmental Conservation, Cape Town.

Tainton, N. (ed.) 1999. *Veld management in South Africa*. University of Natal Press, Pietermaritzburg.

Tongway, D. 1994. *Rangeland soil condition assessment manual*. Division of Wildlife and Ecology, CSIRO Australia, Canberra.

Tongway, D. and Hindley, N. 1995. *Manual for soil condition assessment of tropical grasslands*. Division of Wildlife and Ecology, CSIRO Australia, Canberra.

Van Schalkwyk, C.J. and Mathee, J.F. la G. (eds) 1984. *A primer on soil conservation*. Bulletin No 399. Division of Agricultural Engineering, Department of Agriculture, Pretoria.

Vietmeyer, N.D. (ed.) 1993. *Vetiver grass: a thin green line against erosion*. Board on Science and Technology for International Development. National Academy Press, Washington.

Zaremba, W. 1976. *Logging roads*. Logging reference manual. Bulletin 52, Vol 3. Department of Forestry, Pretoria.

INDEX

aardvark 31, 126
Acacia sp. 93, 115
agaves, eradication 112
aggregate *see* gravel
alien plants 39, 44, 80, 91–124
    awareness 94
    control 94–118
    control schedule 100
    dispersal 93, 109
    impact on wildlife 96
    monitoring 100, 122–124
    post-removal rehabilitation 118–119
    riverbanks 120–121
    seed stored in soil 116
    shade trees 109
    uprooting 112
animals
    impact of roads 58
    impact on soil 31, 35, 39
    see also individual animals
antelopes 39, 58, 74, 93, 115
archaeology 63
artefacts 61

baboons 31, 93
badgers 31
bad-lands
    damming 43
    reconstruction 40–43
bats, fruit 93, 126
biological control 114–115
birds 35, 39, 58, 74, 79, 93, 115
    perches 39
boreholes, perennial 4
borrow pits 61, 63, 79
    rehabilitation 79, 87–88
brambles 93
browsers 95
brush 36, 38, 44, 118
    check dams 20, 22–23, 25, 26–27, 29,
        33
    cutting 106–107

drains 68
    harvesting 37, 84
    wattles 84–85
brush-packing 37, 39, 40–43, 68–69,
    80–88, 118–119
    slope stabilising 84–86
buffalo 31
bullfrogs 69, 126
bullrushes 42–43
burning 10, 16 *see also* fire
bushbuck 109, 126
bushy invaders 106–108

cactus infestations 92, 94, 100
    control 110–111
caracal 115, 126
chainsaws 102–103, 108
chemicals, alien control 101, 108 *see
    also* herbicides; tree, plugs
chippers 37
concrete
    fords 72–73
    roads 65, 72
conservation 12
cuttings, road 76–78

dams, earth 29, 43
    small 32, 40–41
debarking 104–106
deforestation 10
drainage
    bad-lands 40
    contour 42
    crossings 71–73
    cuttings on roads 76
    natural 41, 42, 69
    pipes 75
    roads 60, 61, 63, 65–77, 84
duiker 93, 95, 126
dung beetles 31, 39, 126

ecosystems 5
eland 13, 31, 52, 93, 95, 109, 126

elephants 31, 93, 95, 126
endangered plants 61
environment
    analysis 61, 63, 80
    awareness 89, 94–95
erosion
    roads 56–57
    sheet 11, 16, 19, 26–27, 29
    slopes 67
    soil *see* soil erosion
exclosures 52–53

felling 'invaders' 102–103
fences 36–37, 42
    electric, solar-powered 52
    road closure 80–82
    slope retention 83
fertile areas 35
fertilisers 5
fire 63, 92, 95, 117
    animal reaction 96
    breaks and erosion 116
    intensity 116
    'invader' eradication 116
    'invader' impact 96, 116
fish
    ladder 73
    migration 58, 73
floods 41, 62, 71
footprints 31
forests *see* deforestation
frilling trees 104–105
frogs 58

gabions 20, 29, 42, 69–71, 75, 77,
    87–88
    construction 21, 24
game reserves 90
geotextiles 21–22, 26–30, 37–39, 42, 69
    properties 29
    retaining walls on roads 71, 77
    riverbank rehabilitation 120
    road rehabilitation 80–82
    slope rehabilitation 28, 38–39, 86
giraffe 93, 126

glyphosphate herbicide 108
grasses 33, 39, 40, 42, 44–45, 80,
    82–83, 87, 118–119
    roots 44
gravel 87–88
    pits 61, 63, 79 *see also* borrow pits
    quality 64
grazing 2, 35, 37, 92
    monitoring 49
    rotation 4
    see also overgrazing
guavas 93
gullies 11, 12, 16, 19, 20, 26–27, 29, 30,
    39, 92
    networks 24, 41–42
    profile measurement 50
    roads 71, 78, 90
gutters 77, 84

Hakea fruit weevil 114
hares 39, 126
hay 37
herbicides 97, 104–108, 110–111
    spraying 104–106, 111, 117–118
herbivores, exclusion 52
heritage sites 61, 63
hippopotamus 31, 126
hollows, erosion control 31–33, 37, 40
hoof prints 31
hummocking 11
humus 10, 19
hyraxes, rock 58, 74, 126

impala 109, 126
indigenous plants 42, 109, 118
insects 58, 92
    biocontrol 110, 114–115
'invaders' 92, 106 *see also* alien plants
invertebrates 20, 31, 35, 39

kudu 93, 95, 109, 126

labour 5, 17
land
  ethic 3–4
  management 4
  use, sustainable 2, 4
  value 12
landscape
  rehabilitation *see* rehabilitation,
    landscape
  restoration *see* restoration,
    landscape
lantana removal 112
lizards 39
logs 38–39
  drains 68–69, 84
  pit rehabilitation 88
  riverbank rehabilitation 120
loquats 93

magnesium 18
manure, animal 33, 39
mapping
  alien invader control 98–99, 122–124
  rangelands 14, 16, 49–50
  road routes 61
mechanisation 5, 17
mice, field 115, 126 *see also* rodents
mima mounds 35
moles 31, 58, 126
mongooses 31, 58, 74, 126
monitoring methods 47–51, 100,
  122–124
monkeys 93, 126
mulch 26, 27, 29, 33, 35, 37–40, 44, 45,
  87, 107, 118–119

nature conservation 62
nyala 109, 126

overgrazing 10, 13

pedestalling 11
photography
  alien invaders 98, 122
  erosion monitoring 17, 47–49, 52
pigs, wild 93, 126

pipe drainage, roads 75–77
Plant Protection Research Institute
  (PPRI) 114–115
plants, endangered 61, 63, 79
porcupines 31, 58, 74, 126
puddling plough 32–33

rabbits 39, 126
rainfall 8–10, 12, 17, 18, 33, 62, 71
reconstruction, radical 40–43
reeds, *Phragmites australis* 42–43, 120
rehabilitation, landscape 4–6, 14
  after alien control 118–122
  riverbanks *see* riverbanks,
    rehabilitation
  roads *see* roads, rehabilitation
  slopes *see* slopes, rehabilitation
  reptiles 39
restoration, landscape 5–6, 118 *see
  also* rehabilitation, landscape
revegetation 5 *see also* seeding
rhinoceros 31, 58, 109, 126
rills 11, 16, 19, 20, 24
riverbanks
  rehabilitation 4, 120–122
  stabilisation 122
roads
  animal crossings 58
  building 29, 55–90
  closures 80–82
  concrete 65
  construction methods 63–78
    gravel roads 64
  cuttings 76–78, 83
  gully rehabilitation 71
  maintenance 62, 78–88, 90
    checklist 78
  planning 61–62
  rehabilitation 80–85, 89
  specifications 60
  standards 59
  strip 65
  use 89–90
rodents 39, 115

seeding 29, 41, 43–45, 69, 83, 118–119
seeds 26–27
  alien 92, 101–109
  germination 18–19, 27, 29, 31, 33,
    36, 39, 44, 71, 80, 83, 84, 86, 118
  monitoring 49
shade
  cloth 71
  net 30
  trees 109
shredders 37
shrubs, indigenous, planting 45–47,
  80, 86
silt traps 24, 28, 29, 33, 36, 45, 71
slashers 106
slopes
  protection 67, 69
  rehabilitation 83–86
  road cuttings 76–78
snakes 39, 58, 126
sodium 18
soil
  condition guide 50–52
  fertility 34–35
  formation 10
  forms 11
  particle size 8
  temperature 37
soil erosion 4, 7–53
  after 'invader' control 118
  control methods 14, 15, 17
  prevention 118
squirrels, ground 31, 126
stones 20, 27, 37, 39–43, 69–71, 73, 80,
  82
  pit rehabilitation 87–88
  riverbank rehabilitation 120
  road building 63
  slope stabilising 84–86

termites 31, 35
terracettes 11, 19
topsoil 39, 79, 87–88
tortoises 39, 96, 126
tourism 90, 95
tree(s) 42, 80, 86

cuttings to repair banks 122
felling 102–103
frilling 104
invasive aliens 92, 95
plugs 108
pullers 113
ring barking 104–105
water consumption 95
tyres 26–27

vegetation cover 9–10, 18–20, 33, 39,
  41, 42, 45, 69, 80, 83, 87, 118
  monitoring 49
vetiver grass 44–45

walls, retaining, roads 76–77
warthogs 109, 126
water
  infiltration 10, 18–20, 39, 41, 44
  resources, *and* alien plants 95
wetlands 24, 41, 43, 45, 59, 61, 63, 79,
  108, 120
  vegetation 40
wildlife 12, 39, 69, 89, 92–94, 108, 115,
  122 *see also* individual animals
  alien plant dispersal 93
willow, *Salix capensis* 120
wind erosion 8, 11, 33, 36, 37
wire netting
  dam construction 23, 28, 37, 43
  drain construction 69–71, 73
  pit rehabilitation 87–88
  retaining walls 76–77, 83, 86
  road closure 81

zaï 33 *see also* hollows, erosion control
zebra 74, 126